SEE ME

SEE ME
Prison Theater Workshops and Love

Jan Cohen-Cruz

with Finn K. and Ausettua AmorAmenkum, Alexander Anderson, John Bergman, Kevin Bott, Reginold Daniels, George Ferguson, Rand Hazou, Saul Hewish, Kathy Randels, Jess Thorpe, and Gloria "Mama Glo" Williams

NEW VILLAGE PRESS • NEW YORK

Copyright © 2024 New Village Press

All rights reserved. Except for brief text portions quoted for purposes of review, no part of this book may be reprinted, reproduced, or utilized in any medium now known or hereafter invented without prior permission in writing from the publisher.

Published in the United States by New Village Press
bookorders@newvillagepress.net
www.newvillagepress.org
New Village Press is a public-benefit, nonprofit publisher
Distributed by NYU Press

Paperback ISBN 978-1-61332-247-5
Hardcover ISBN 978-1-61332-248-2
eBook Trade ISBN 978-1-61332-249-9-1
eBook Institutional ISBN 978-1-61332-250-5

On file with the Library of Congress

Cover Illustration: Russell Craig, *I Am Groot*, 2022. Acrylic on textiles and leather purse fragments. By permission of the artist.

CONTENTS

List of Figures — ix

Foreword by Simon Ruding — xi

Preface — xv

Introduction — 1

PART I: INTERGALACTIC TRAVELERS
BY FINN K. AND JAN COHEN-CRUZ

The story of a relationship born of a prison theater workshop, told from two perspectives.

1. Beginnings — 9

   How Finn and I came to be part of the Trenton State Prison drama workshop—he as an incarcerated participant, joining the workshop to overcome what he describes as his false selves, and I as cofacilitator and member of a street theater troupe.

2. Backstories — 14

   Finn and I delve into our soberingly different backgrounds—his, a violent family and childhood; mine, loving and full of opportunities but nonetheless stiflingly middle-class—which led us both to leave home at fifteen and join the workshop in our early twenties.

3. The Workshop — 23

   The fascinating and diverse core participants who got to know one another as human beings, devising scenes from personal experience. The difference between how I imagined people in a maximum-security prison and who they actually were. The tension between collectivity and a self-serving ethos.

4. Intensification · 29

Trust and affection build from making theater together. The temporary closure of the prison to outsiders turned Finn and me to letter writing, deepened our relationship, and made the workshop, when it returned, more precious. The street theater director purchased a house so core participants leaving prison could live with us and continue the work.

5. Performances · 42

The workshop developed productions that we shared with the prison population, ranging from a collection of scenes and poetry to Kafka's *The Trial*, adapted to participants' experiences.

6. The Year of Living Way Too Dangerously · 58

Incompatible ways of balancing personal needs, a series of bad decisions in response to impossible circumstances, and the prison administration's concern over the unity of inmates of different backgrounds in the group led to the workshop's demise.

Coda. Afterlives · 74

A reflection on how the workshop influenced Finn's life and mine over the fifty years that followed, including our abiding commitment to collectivity and our enduring friendship.

PART II: EXPANDING UNIVERSES

Five dialogues about different kinds of relationships born of prison theater workshops.

7. Life and Love in the LCIW Drama Club · 81
by Ausettua AmorAmenkum, Kathy Randels, and Gloria "Mama Glo" Williams

How each of the authors came to the Louisiana Correctional Institute for Women Drama Club—Randels through research for a solo performance about her own untapped rage; AmorAmenkum as an extension of her pan-African community and spiritual values; and Mama Glo to give and receive communal healing through sharing and enacting personal stories after ten years' of solitary confinement and continued incarceration.

8. Opposite Sides of the Table 103
by Jess Thorpe and George Ferguson

Theater facilitator Thorpe and prison manager Ferguson reflect on how they arrived at a meeting of minds that made their collaboration in a juvenile facility possible, and how Ferguson came to support this work wholeheartedly. Subjects include rehabilitation versus punishment and both the benefits and risks of theater in carceral spaces.

9. At a Threshold Around Race 119
by Alexander Anderson and Kevin Bott

Anderson, who is Black, was a formerly incarcerated participant in Ritual4Return (R4R), which Bott, who is white, conceived to ease people's transitions from prison to a return to their communities. Bott and Anderson, now R4R's codirectors, explore their long relationship, focusing on how white supremacy damaged their collaboration, and efforts to repair that now.

10. The Lives We Lived 137
by John Bergman and Saul Hewish

Bergman and Hewish reflect on work they did together with Geese Theatre, one of the first companies to offer performances and workshops with incarcerated people in the United States and the United Kingdom, questions it evoked, and the effect of longtime work in prisons on all involved.

11. Unshackling the Body, Mind, and Spirit:
Reflections on Liberation and Creative Exchange
between San Quentin and Auckland Prisons 153
by Rand Hazou and Reginold Daniels

An adaptation of the authors' analytical essay about a workshop that Daniels, a formerly incarcerated Black American, facilitated in a New Zealand prison with the help of Rand, a Palestinian-Kiwi scholar-practitioner. Emphasizes links between liberation, creativity, and love.

12. Roundtable   171
with Ausettua AmorAmenkum, Alexander Anderson, John Bergman, Kevin Bott, Jan Cohen-Cruz, Saul Hewish, Kathy Randels, Jess Thorpe, and Gloria "Mama Glo" Williams

A discussion of themes running through Part II and the directions to which these chapters point that most stood out to these contributing writers.

Acknowledgments   *193*

References   *195*

Index   *199*

About the Contributors   *205*

About the Editor   *209*

LIST OF FIGURES

Figure 4.1	Finn and Jan on a visit in Trenton State Prison, 1972. Photographer unknown.	32
Figure 5.1	Flyer announcing performance of *The Trial,* Trenton State Prison, 1972. Created by workshop members.	55
Figure 6.1	"Wild Women, No Inner Checks?" Newspaper article by Kitty Hanson, circa 1973 (details unknown).	63
Figure 7.1	The cast of *Gifts of Our Ancestors.* Photograph by Libby Nevinger.	83
Figure 7.2	"Free Mama Glo!" postcard. Design by Fox Rich.	86
Figure 7.3	Tattoo. "Truth is in the Center of the Circle." Photograph by Kay Randels.	88
Figure 7.4	Ausettua AmorAmenkum and Gary Tyler. Photograph by Alexander Barkoff. Used with permission of Ausettua AmorAmenkum.	96
Figure 8.1	Looking for a Male Role Model. From MOTION. Photograph by Tim Morozzo.	105
Figure 8.2	These Men Used to Be Boys. From MOTION. Photograph by Tim Morozzo.	113
Figure 8.3	Blue Sky with Clouds. From MOTION. Photograph by Tim Morozzo.	115
Figure 9.1	R4R rite of passage, fall 2019. Photograph by Jonathan Brill.	120

Figure 9.2	Kevin facilitating an R4R workshop. Photograph by Alexander Anderson.	122
Figure 9.3	Alex and Kevin, the chapter's authors. Selfie by Kevin Bott.	135
Figure 10.1	Geese Theatre mask known as Buzz. Photograph by Saul Hewish.	140
Figure 10.2	The Geese Theatre van at a prison. Photographer unknown.	145
Figure 10.3	John Bergman facilitating a prison workshop in the early days. Photographer unknown.	151
Figure 12.1	Ausettua AmorAmenkum and Kathy Randels at the "Glow up for Mama Glo Rally," May 28, 2020. Photograph by Alison McCrary.	174

FOREWORD

BY SIMON RUDING, ARTISTIC DIRECTOR AND CEO, TIPP (THEATRE IN PRISONS AND PROBATION), MANCHESTER, ENGLAND

When Jan first approached me with her idea for this book and I set eyes on her exchanges with Finn, I knew immediately that I was entering a new territory in prison theater writing. They offered up no treatise for practice or session models. Their writing was different, an intimate exchange between old friends exploring something that is rarely touched upon in prison theater literature—the personal, human impact of prison theater on both the incarcerated participant and the facilitator/director/artist.

Sure, plenty of literature considers how our work impacts incarcerated persons, but it tends to consider bigger pictures and speak to other agendas, like how practice might impact criminogenic issues, assist regime management, or contribute to desistance. More often than not it speaks to the amorphous body of authority that Shakespeare in Prisons practitioner Curt Tofteland calls "the keeper of the keys" (Tofteland 2011).

Jan's and Finn's words are instead a microhistory: intimate insights into prison theater through human connections that also provide personal glimpses of the broader political and social structures of the early 1970s, when they met. Resplendent with its communes and political activism, seen through the window of prison theater, it transported me to another place and time. Their exchange, in its intimacy and raw honesty, offers a glimpse of a world that seems at once alien and also starkly familiar.

Jan's idea that her dialogue with Finn could act as the backdrop for a series of similar conversations between practitioner and practitioner, practitioner and guard, and practitioner and participant excited and intrigued me in equal measure. What emerges in the five subsequent microhistories is a new sense of the practice, each dialogue offering different perspectives on how the intimacy and connection of theater workshops impact all involved. It is a salient reminder of the importance of participatory practice for an understanding and appreciation of the other, which offers hope in an increasingly polarized world.

For this book is concerned with intimacy. I don't mean physical intimacy but, rather, Karen Prager's sense of the word as acts of self-disclosure and confiding, accompanied and underpinned by trust (Prager 1995). By this definition, the conversations, relationships, and histories described within this book are intimate acts, the trust and support evident in the words and subtext of the conversations between the contributors. It is there, too, in descriptions of workshop processes, in the detail of moments revealed and long remembered.

Drawing on Prager's ideas, Liesbeth Groot Nibbelink makes a case for the value of intimacy in theater. She suggests that intimacy, "when perceived as closeness within distance or difference," has the power to reduce emotional and psychological distance by generating "connectivity" (Groot Nibbelink 2012, 420). It is this connectivity despite difference that exists at the heart of any good prison theater workshop. It is this connectivity that leads people to say that during the time we spend together, we forget we are in prison.

Intimacy is often conceived as a state that develops over time through the types of long association and friendship exemplified by the dialogues in this book. That rapport is present here in the easy dialogues on challenging subjects. While memories are sometimes aligned, even if painfully so, as with Alexander Anderson and Kevin Bott, statements of "I remember that differently" are as readily accepted, with grace and reflection, by John Bergman and Saul Hewish, Jan and Finn.

There is another level of closeness at play within the texts, generated by the workshops, between participant and participant and participant and facilitator. It is an affinity born of the process and is at once a product and a by-product of making theater and performance. It is the connection we create when we share stories and make theater with people. It is shared moments of laughter, revelation, self-discovery, joy, sadness, and reflection. These little intimacies weave connections between prisoner and prisoner, prisoner and artist, artist and artist. Of course, such bonding can exist in any theater workshop, but in prison, where such closeness is frowned upon and considered reason enough for suspicion or sanction, it is felt all the more acutely because it is at once both transgressive and comforting.

Reading between the lines of all the dialogues, it is possible to get a sense of theater workshops and performance short-circuiting the slow, labored dance of mutual discovery and relationship building; in skilled hands, a theater workshop facilitates connectivity and trust. It is there in Finn's and Jan's descriptions of their workshop, in the poetry of Reginold Daniels's Auckland workshop, in Mama Glo Williams's memories of the LCIW experience, in John Bergman's reflection of the impact of the Motown singers in Texas, and is starkly present in the surprise of George Ferguson, the prison governor, at the changes in the young men who have worked with Jess Thorpe in HMP & YOI Polmont.

Intimacy is seminal to theater itself, and has been a central concern to theorists and theater makers as diverse as Strindberg, Brecht, Meyerhold, Schechner, and Bausch. In recent decades, it has spawned its own performance practice, concerned with developing what Josephine Machon describes as "practice that ensures the audience, their presence and sentient involvement within the work, is the central concern" (Machon 2013, 26). That same presence and involvement are the central concerns of my work, and of the makers and artists in this book. While stage and screen actors are particularly skilled at creating the illusion of familiarity, performance artists are concerned with creating it in the moment. We workshop practitioners are at it every day, sharing the same space, breathing the same air, generating closeness, and short-circuiting the long, drawn-out process of typical relationship building. If we think of interpersonal relationship development as a dance, the evolution of human connectivity is often a long, slow waltz; by comparison, a well-crafted and skillfully led theater workshop is a high-energy salsa.

Perhaps our practice as theater workshop makers is the most contemporary live art that exists. Our work is made in the moment, and succeeds as a result of relationships created in the electric "now" of the workshop. That liveness in sharp contrast with the carceral spaces in which it sparks up is the charge that creates the physical, emotional, and psychological connections and experiences to which this book bears witness.

PREFACE

This book sets out to solve a mystery—how the intimacy that I and many others have experienced in prison theater workshops is possible in that most dehumanizing of environments. Theater can be revelatory—seeing a person become someone else elicits hope that all of us can be other than how we are. And nothing is quite like watching someone emerge right before your eyes to make you fall in love, in its many forms. To see people take on fuller selves in prison settings is especially extraordinary, for both the persons seeing and the ones being seen, because how can such places house self-exploration?

The Trenton State Prison drama workshop, which I cofacilitated at the age of twenty-one, met for two hours once a week. Playing together, many of us were emboldened to revisit unresolved pasts, imagine aspirational futures, and reinvent ourselves in the present. The guys had no illusions that they could be that revealing during the rest of the week; nor did I have another context in which to explore my underdeveloped selves.

I developed a particularly deep relationship with Finn, one of the incarcerated participants. Accompanying each other as we tried on and cast off various selves marked the beginning of a love that, in the fifty-two years since, has taken many forms. What began as a glorious romance morphed into a lifelong friendship, and radiated out into a compassion for people in circumstances so unlike each of our own that we only first got there with the other as guide.

Finn's and my experience all those years ago initiated this book. It also serves as the backdrop for five pieces by other contributors, writing in pairs and in one case as a trio about their experiences together in prison drama workshops. They also wrote about love in its many manifestations without my even having asked. I am grateful to have had them as fellow sleuths.

Introduction

> Man wishes to be confirmed in his being by man, and wishes to have a presence in the being of the other.... Secretly and bashfully he watches for a YES which allows him to be and which can come to him only from one human person to another. It is from one person to another that the heavenly bread of self-being is passed.
> —Martin Buber, *I and Thou*, trans. by Ronald Gregor Smith

> The type of love that I stress is not *eros*, a sort of aesthetic or romantic love; not *philia*, a sort of reciprocal love between personal friends; but it is *agape* which is understanding goodwill for all men. It is an overflowing love which seeks nothing in return.
> —Martin Luther King, Jr., "The Role of the Church in Facing the Nation's Chief Moral Dilemma," speech delivered April 25, 1957

The Book's Evolution

This book is about theater workshops in one of the most maligned contexts of human life—incarceration—and about the significance of being fully seen in these collaborative spaces. It began in 2022 as a writing exchange between Finn and me as we revisited our experience in the Trenton State Prison drama workshop—I as cofacilitator and he as an incarcerated participant—which took place in the early 1970s. It grew to include five additional chapters, written in pairs and one trio—incarcerated participants, facilitators from the outside, and in one case a prison manager—members of the same secret club as Finn and I. This is not a book about outside facilitators changing, or "transforming," incarcerated persons. It is about profound connections between people collaborating in temporary communities in a spirit of love in its diverse forms.

I was deeply affected by the experience of the Trenton State Prison drama workshop, and by my relationship with Finn. We cherished the workshop as an ongoing laboratory to explore ourselves and create work that was bigger than all of us, within a small collective. Having the other with whom to go through it, face-to-face in the moment, on visits, and in an outpouring of letters, was vital. Indeed, we fell in love. Although our romance did not survive the complications of our circumstances, we reconnected a few years later, when he got out, and have written and emailed each other, on and off, ever since. In 2022, he suggested we write about that initial experience from our respective perspectives.

Upon completion of a first draft, I thought that Finn and I would decide together what to do with what we'd generated. But he chose not to stay involved, giving me his writings to do with as I wished. Finn's one caveat was that I not use his real name if I published it. Together, we chose the pseudonym Finn, because he wanted a name that would reflect his Irish heritage, and because I found Huckleberry Finn's rejoinder that he'd probably end up going to hell—often for admirable acts, like helping Jim escape, that were nonetheless against the law—reminiscent of Finn's only half-joking sense that hell was where he was headed.

Out of my desire to more fully understand how a prison workshop could be such fertile ground for what Martin Buber calls I-Thou relationships, I invited others with different kinds of loving relationships honed in prison drama workshops to read Finn's and my exchange and, if it resonated, to write together about their experiences. The enthusiasm and sense of recognition with which they received our writing was an enormous affirmation. Four pairs and one trio took me up on the offer. Finn's and my exchange became Part I, and their five essays, Part II of this book. They reinforce how profoundly we all need to be seen in our wholeness, in striking contrast to dehumanizing carceral spaces.

Prison Theater Workshops

As the writers recount, in theater workshops, we become more visible: (1) to ourselves, by getting to play out hitherto underdeveloped parts; (2) to one or more individuals whom we get to know more deeply than we are likely to have otherwise; (3) to the temporary community that the workshop participants create, where all recognize a purpose that binds them beyond self-interest. When evidenced in performance, hitherto hidden aspects of incarcerated individuals also become poignantly visible to some prison staff and, most certainly, to workshop facilitators. I've since learned that the way my eyes were opened at Trenton is not uncommon among prison arts workshop facilitators; whereas before I had not given caging people much thought, I now saw its cruelty clearly.

Moreover, developing relationships with the workshop participants, the first people I'd actually known who were incarcerated, tore to shreds preconceptions I hadn't known I carried. I learned that incarceration was more a result of systemic inequities than of character flaws as I came to see the connection between what the people I was getting to know had done to be incarcerated and the harshness, code of survival, and lack of options in most of their life circumstances.

The theater workshops anchoring these essays, in contrast to classes, are about collective exchange, not one-directional learning from teachers to students. Workshops are collaborative rather than hierarchical endeavors, environments where participants explore questions, identify problems, brainstorm ideas, and give form to real and imaginary possibilities. They are guided, not controlled, by facilitators. Workshops can be deeply affirming, recognizing each person's contribution to a larger goal and to what each knows through his or her experience. One can neither agree nor disagree with someone else's experience. The collaboration that takes place in a workshop is not about having to agree, as Finn recently wrote me, "but, instead, bringing our oppositions into the open and doing the difficult work of finding ways to join them in a creative vision."

Workshops are outside the routine of the day-to-day, rare in prisons—or anywhere, for that matter—where one can let down one's guard, try on different roles, reveal secrets, exchange ideas, ignore invisible boundaries, and be intimate. At their best, workshops offer spaces to practice living in community and be the self that one aspires to put out in the world, significantly enhanced, as in the examples in this book, by supportive personal relationships. Such workshops inhabit an energetic present, unlike much of prison life, when one is nearly always in a state of waiting.

Not all workshops are caring, healing, life-affirming spaces, for a variety of reasons. Most obviously, prisons are very dangerous places. The facilitators need serious collaborative, diplomatic, artistic, teaching chops to produce and maintain the creative learning and trust environment needed to make *communitas* possible. They need to let go of the reins so that the participants inhabit a nonhierarchical space in which to share experiences. They need to be conscious to do no harm and to refrain from judging the acts that led to participants' incarceration. They need to be generous about sharing skills, responsive to participant contributions, and mindful of how much they, too, have to learn in the process. Not all prisons provide a space where intimacy is possible, which often depends on either some authority's appreciation for the workshop's potential or administrative neglect, and not all groups gel even with courageous and skilled facilitators and committed and creative participants.

So while not necessarily writing about representative prison theater workshops, the contributors to this book share valuable mind-sets, principles, and practices for newcomers and veterans in the field of applied theater in prisons and elsewhere. Applied theater, broadly inclusive and emphasizing art's activist, therapeutic, and/or educational capacities, has proven particularly good at nurturing collaboration, providing tools to get to know and feel for people in a range of circumstances through playing and making things together.

Prison Arts Workshops and Abolition

Longtime activist Angela Davis indicts the prison system for blaming the individual without attention to the social circumstances that provide the context for transgressive behavior:

> Prisons do not disappear social problems, they disappear human beings. Homelessness, unemployment, drug addiction, mental illness, and illiteracy are only a few of the problems that disappear from public view when the human beings contending with them are relegated to cages. (Davis 2000, 51)

I would be remiss not to include Finn's perspective here:

> All that time in reformatories and prison helped, not hindered, me. Especially in Trenton, I settled into a creative way of life made possible by

the extreme conditions enforced by the old guard. They left me alone, making clear I could be myself in any way as long as I didn't violate rules of conduct, easy for me, and a great deal, heaven—never before was I left to find out who I am on my own terms, no restrictions, and be fed, housed, and clothed during the process. Under that cruel regime, I had more freedom than ever before in my life. Prison was definitely a blessing for me and many others, more than people can imagine. (Finn K. 2023, personal correspondence)

I wonder if Finn would have felt this way had the first twenty years of his life been loving and supportive.

Workshops that provide environments to align personal experience with large social injustices contribute modestly to the movement for prison abolition. They evoke the possibility of something other than incarceration to deal with and even heal misdeeds. Mariame Kaba writes that the abolition movement works to envision and build our way out of oppressive systems and "create the conditions for dismantling prisons, police, and surveillance" (Kaba 2021, 110). Indeed, the desire to abolish the toxic inhumanity of incarceration is a silent underpinning of this book. Abolitionist Patrisse Cullors emphasizes how interpersonal relationships, one-on-one conversations, and "a series of choices and practices" add up to an abolitionist ethos (Cullors 2021, xii). She notes that "[s]trong abolitionist work is born of strong communities, and strong communities are born of strong interpersonal relationships" (Cullors 2021, 235).

With each essay's dual or triple perspective on theater workshops, supportive one-on-one relationships, and participation in collectivity within the belly of the beast, this book occupies a small corner of work about the value of such projects, such as Lisa Biggs's *The Healing Stage,* William Cleveland's *Art in Other Places,* David Coogan et al.'s *Writing Our Way Out,* Nicole Fleetwood's *Marking Time,* works by and about Rhodessa Jones, Ashley Lucas's *Prison Theatre and the Global Crisis of Incarceration,* Liza Jessie Peterson's *All Day: A Year of Love and Survival Teaching Incarcerated Kids at Rikers Island,* and books by the late Judith Tannenbaum, one with Spoon Jackson, in the context of prison writing workshops. It is aligned with numerous organizations, including the Justice Arts Coalition, the Arts Justice Safety Coalition, the Prison

Creative Arts Project (PCAP), the Shakespeare in Prisons Network, the Medea Project, Theatre in Prison and Probation (TiPP), California's Arts-in-Corrections program, and *Visualizing Abolition,* a public scholarship initiative at UC Santa Cruz.

Angela Davis questioned early on if prisons had exceeded their value, if they ever had one, even given "how difficult it is to imagine a social order that does not rely on the threat of sequestering people in dreadful places" (Davis 2003, 10). My prison theater workshop experience and the relationship with Finn taught me about the gap between how people and systems appear on the outside and who and what they are inside. It made me more sensitive to societal forces that result in who, partly because of class and race, are most likely to face systemic life obstacles. Since my experience at Trenton, I have tried to stay aware of the limits of what I know about other people beyond my experience, and the necessity to frame what I learn about them socially.

While I have not continued to facilitate prison workshops, I have devoted much of my life to doing and writing about theater with people largely shut out of America's promise. I have also prepared and mentored students making theater with groups with which they have had little or no contact and about which they may otherwise have unexamined perspectives. I think of this as my calling, and see it as a way that theater makers do fieldwork, which anthropologists often describe as making the strange familiar and the familiar strange.

This book is a cry to see one another in our three-dimensionality, and for a world where we all get to live fully and develop into the selves that can lead to meaningful lives, contributing to and being nourished by the world and one another. Conscious of the inextricability of the political realities in which these personal relationships are embedded, the book points to how theater makers can use their art toward achieving social change. Once we have gotten to know people from a group hitherto outside of our experience, we may never look at others in unfamiliar circumstances in overly simplified ways again. Once one understands the environments from which most incarcerated people come, one may be more than ready to join the effort to shift the focus from punishing individuals to mending the world.

PART I

Intergalactic Travelers

In 2022, Finn proposed that we write, from our respective perspectives, about our experience together, grounded by the Trenton State Prison drama workshop. In what follows, he wrote the texts labeled "FINN"; I wrote the "JAN" texts and the reflective tissue (in italics). I think of this simultaneously as the story of a prison drama workshop, a love story, an essential part of my education, and a mystery.

1

Beginnings

FINN: Trenton State Prison is nicknamed "the Last Stop"; if you have grown up in New Jersey's criminal world and have done time in its reformatories and prisons, there is no place to advance to after Trenton. It is also known as "the Big Dusty," referring to a special detail formed decades ago that makes sure not a blade of grass is visible on the entire prison grounds, resulting in surface dirt turning to dust. The authorities occasionally spread oil across the surface of the yard, which turns the dust into a hard clay when it dries.

Trenton State Prison is where my involvement in theater life began in 1971, at age twenty-three. My closest friend, Tommy, and I returned from the mess hall, and on the tier bulletin board was an invitation: "A Drama Workshop will begin this fall. Any inmate interested, sign up in the Department of Education."

We stood there silent for a moment, and then Tommy said, "You think you could do that?"

"Definitely not," I replied, and then looked in his eyes. "But isn't that the best reason to do it?"

"Good point."

Within five seconds of arriving at the drama workshop in an education classroom, I grabbed a chair at the back of the room. I sat motionless, in fixed terror at the possibility of actually having to stand in front of a collective of judges who, with a simple utterance from my lips, would see deep into my successfully masked cowardliness and judge me with mocking laughter, or, worse yet, spread what they'd learned about my cowardice to the general population. The thought of getting up in front of people and speaking was terrifying, inducing what psychologist Karen Horney named as a fear worse than death—being found out.

Remaining seated and motionless, thoroughly hidden in the open, I perceived with depth the two characters who arrived with every intention of liberating us through what I viewed as Freudian Marxist theater life.

Richard, a soft-spoken, always wide-smiling Bertolt Brecht, introduced the workshop with a quote from Brecht himself: "Art is not a mirror to reflect reality, but a hammer with which to shape it," at which I shuddered. He was determined to conquer the oppressive world of patriarchal capitalism with a progressive—i.e., Freudian Marxist—ideology embedded in Wilhelm Reich's sexual-liberation principles. Reich made a mockery of everything that was grand in what Freud gifted to us as a moralist insisting on the Aristotelian mean, a balance between too much and too little. To Reich, liberating women and children into sexual freedom was the only exit from a totally repressive patriarchy.

Jan, the Jester, Inverted King, a psychoanalytic androgyne, moved about the room in a free-flowing mime-dance in worn-out black high-top sneakers, black jeans, a pirate-style white shirt encased in a firm-fitting black vest with gold stitching woven throughout in wild patterns. Her long auburn hair flowed ever outward, like flames, more like a young, enthusiastic anarchist than a staid, suffocating, power-obsessed Marxist. A mix of Janis Joplin, Susan Sontag, and a race car driver, she had willingly entered the worst prison in America on her twenty-first birthday, what would no doubt be for her a dying and being born into an identity distant from all she had previously known about herself.

I glimpsed her Jungian shadow side in a profound moment of her halting in a statuesque, steel-enforced gaze at Richard with incipient contempt. I was mesmerized, for it was clear: She was an idealist obsessed with moving forward in every second, whereas Richard came across as Degas's Dance Master, establishing himself as the centripetal force in everything that would transpire.

JAN: Yikes—I had certainly not arrived at Trenton with the thought of liberating anyone, except maybe myself. I had everything to learn from the experience and only my willingness to go where that took me, and some theater experience, to give in return.

It surprises me that Finn perceived me gazing at Richard "with incipient contempt." I recall above all my gratitude to Richard, the director of the street theater I was in, for inviting me to go with him into the belly of the beast. Reading Finn's words makes me reconsider my early perception of Richard as generous and collective-minded, to see if I find anything I'd overlooked. I am reminded of his relationship to his two dogs, Nick and Grusha.

The year before the prison workshop, I spent a lot of time at Richard's house on the Brighton Beach waterfront in Brooklyn, fund-raising and tour planning for the street theater. On breaks we'd take the dogs for walks along the ocean. He'd let go of their leashes so they could run and then he'd call Nick, who would grab Grusha's leash in his teeth and yank her back.

"Grusha's so dumb," Richard would say with affection. "Good boy, Nick!"

I wonder now if Nick's controlling Grusha and making her do Richard's will was a clue to Richard's way of being surreptitiously in control. Did he seek to dominate other situations as well in indirect ways? He had a nearly ever-present smile, which I first saw as kindly and knowing but later as controlling.

Did I ever sleep with Richard? Sure, but it was never serious. It was 1971; nearly all my peers slept with the people they were in close orbit with.

JAN: Richard and I drove the hour and a half from Brooklyn to Trenton, New Jersey. Although it was a maximum-security facility, the complex was, weirdly, in the midst of a working-class residential neighborhood. It had opened in 1836 and looked it: thick, bulky stone walls darkened with over a century of pollution and neglect; razor-sharp wire along the top; floodlights sweeping across the neighborhood all through the night; tall, dominating watchtowers.

"Why would they build such a forbidding structure in a family neighborhood?" I pondered out loud. "Do they care that little about the people who live here?"

Richard sighed. "Or maybe it's a warning."

We entered the edifice and went through a metal detector. On the other side, a guard walked us to "the star," where multiple corridors meet, leading respectively to the cell block, mess hall, infirmary, yard, and education wing. The latter is where the drama workshop took place, in a classroom with the desks pushed to the side and with surveillance windows along the wall adjacent to the hallway.

I had chosen my clothes with care, not because I was a clotheshorse— I've never been— but because, as one of the only females the inmates would encounter, I wanted to reinforce my personhood, not be seen as a potential conquest, while at the same time providing a little spice. I wore a loose shirt, a fitted vest, high-top sneakers, and, like most everyone else, jeans. I had long, unkempt reddish brown hair.

About a dozen participants greeted us warmly and introduced themselves. The energy level was high and people were clearly glad to be there, if for no other reason than as a relief from the boredom of a cell. The tall, muscular person, always moving with a spring to his step, whom we came to know as Kuwasi introduced himself to us as Donald, only later explaining that Donald was his slave name. We met Robert, his more serious but also warm and ready-for-action partner, whom everyone called "Nine" because he'd survived so much, it was as if he had nine lives, like a cat. Jackson, who was Native American, was softspoken, with keen, observant eyes. John was a white pothead. Winston was a deeply sincere young Black man. Coop, whom we later came to know as Kareem, was always ready to analyze a scene or text. Hakim, a light-skinned Black man, reminded me of how much race is social, not biological. Ted, the only Jewish inmate I met inside, had a "regular guy" vibe about him.

And then there was Finn, who moved me from the moment I set eyes on him, appearing so sensitive and tough at the same time. Finn had his own interpretation of everything, which later, when he allowed himself to come out of hiding with me, he shared, including background that illuminated it. He had a habit of bending his knees a little when we stood beside each other, to better equalize our heights, he being six or seven inches taller than I. He had green eyes, red hair with little fringe bangs like a Benedictine monk's, and seriously muscular arms. It was the first time I realized that guys in prison worked out not just because they had time on their hands but also to protect themselves; I hadn't thought about prisons as dangerous for the people there, only as places where dangerous people were locked away from the general population. Finn looked so fragile that the air around him trembled; how was that possible with those arms?

We began with warm-ups, some yoga-based, that the guys could do in their cells. We shifted to improvisations with simple structures. "Pair up," Richard instructed, "and decide who is Person A and who is Person B. Person A enters and sits. Person B enters and stands behind A. Person A exits. Now fill in the story." People came up with great variations on who these two people were and what was going on between them. One was a loop of constantly reappearing A persons and B persons, featuring something surreptitiously passed from one to another.

Moments before the first session was about to end, Donald said, "I got something. This takes place on a street corner. In Newark. Yeah." Little by little, people got up and hung out: sang doo-wop under an imagined streetlamp, shot the breeze, looked at the stars. It was a startling sensation, re-creating, more vividly than the thing itself, what I could do any day but didn't and they could not do any day soon. It was November 1, 1971—my twenty-first birthday.

2

Backstories

JAN: In 1965, I began on the path that brought me to Trenton State Prison in 1971. I was fifteen and leaving my small Pennsylvania hometown for a state-supported arts school in North Carolina. I had felt out of place at the local school, which valued sports and cheerleaders above all and where I felt I had to hide my love of theater. My parents thought that I was just going away to finish high school, but I never lived in their home again. One thing kept leading to another. I went from being lovingly molded according to middle-class Jewish American values to coming into my own by how I responded to what I encountered along the way.

My mother loved theater, as did I, as a way to experience feelings that were too strong for the place and people we'd been born into; but for her, this took place only in a fantasy world, and for me, there was the desire to integrate those feelings into the real world. Her dream was Broadway, with people and lights brighter than the everyday; mine was to reveal everyone's light. When I went off to North Carolina School of the Arts, my self-directed life began.

Leaving home released me from an overly circumscribed life, which my mother wrongly assumed was stardom-bound. Theater was nevertheless my bridge out. My life from age fifteen on, with theater as the through line, put me in touch with people and experiences I'd known nothing about, and in some cases about which I had wildly simplistic and mistaken assumptions.

Then there was the impact of the times seeping into my evolving perspective: the idealism, the polarization, the assassinations, the Vietnam War, explosive liberation movements on the political, social, sexual, and personal levels. As a child, I watched the turmoil on TV, but not much was said in my household beyond a general sympathy for the martyrs of civil rights. That context is part of this story.

Upon high school graduation in 1968, I joined a federally subsidized traveling theater company in New England, performing for broader audiences than just those who described themselves as theater lovers. I was thrilled when a community in the White Mountains paid their part for our performance, matched with a federal government grant, by holding a potluck dinner before the show, an event that drew the whole community. That dynamic—their food, our show—changed the actor/spectator relationship into an exchange.

I went to Paris in 1969 and taught English in a language school to support myself. My eyes were opened just living in Paris in the aftermath of the so-called events of May 1968, a period characterized by worker and student unrest and an unlikely alliance between them. There were skirmishes with the police in response to protests about wages and working conditions, and everywhere the graffitied slogan "The more I make love, the more I want to make the revolution. The more I make the revolution, the more I want to make love." Allying these two ideas stunned and inspired me, epitomizing a private and public life in sync with each other, for which I yearned.

I joined a group led by a guy who'd worked with the Polish director Jerzy Grotowski, whose "poor theater" was centered in what passed between the actor and the spectator, with no frills, emphasizing the holiness of the actor and theater as a spiritual path to uncovering one's deepest self. The work also emphasized following one's impulses, something I resolved to do more when I returned to the United States in 1970 and moved to New York. I also intended to look into street theater companies, like those I'd encountered in Paris, much inspired by U.S. companies like the Bread and Puppet Theater, which performed throughout Europe and the Americas.

However, back in the United States, at my mother's urging, and in a kind of amnesia vis-à-vis the path I'd been discovering on my own, I prepared my picture and résumé—an eight-by-ten glossy photo, to which I stapled my résumé, as is the norm in commercial theater—and sent this to agents. But I put no more effort into it, so of course nothing happened. Instead, I worked for free with Bread and Puppet, also back from Paris. They had a storefront theater that Nathan's Famous, the Hot Dog King, had paid to renovate, located in Coney Island, an amusement park on the Brooklyn oceanfront. Maybe Nathan's hoped a theatrical fun house would expand the customer base at their hot dog joint across the street, and they probably got a tax break of some sort.

I was drawn to Bread and Puppet's commitment to a broad public as well as to their aesthetics, a combo of popular entertainment and mysticism. Their fun house featured a two-story-high Uncle Sam figure with a papier-mâché head, animated by three puppeteers, one behind and the others on either side, moving its arms with bamboo poles. Other animated figures were as small as a thumb. A violinist and an accordionist accompanied a narrator, who told a simple, subtly political tale as the audience was led from one scene to another in the semidark. It was a bit like moving through a nightmarish living painting of the evening news.

One day, after I'd been with Bread and Puppet for about a month, I arrived early and the fun house was locked. Just then, a blue van with a cityscape painted on it and the words NEW YORK CITY STREET THEATER pulled up next door in front of its own theater storefront, also supported by Nathan's. People got out and started washing the van.

"Hi," I said. "Can you use another set of hands?"

"Sure," replied a man about ten years older than I was, with curly brown hair, wire-rimmed glasses, and a disarming smile, handing me a soapy sponge. "What brings you out here to off-off-off Broadway?"

"I met Bread and Puppet in Paris, where I was studying Grotowski's work, and came back to the United States to work with them."

"And how is it?"

"I actually prefer acting than, like, moving a limb of a great big puppet."

"Ah, yes. You don't want to be a puppet." He smiled, as if he'd told a cosmic joke. "Tell us about the Grotowski work."

So I did, and they invited me inside to demonstrate some of Grotowski's exercises that directed yoga asanas outward. Then they got busy packing things up, because they were leaving on a cross-country tour the next day. Curly Head invited me to stay in touch.

When they returned from the tour, the female codirector of the City Street Theater, clearly the stronger of the two, had decided to break with Richard of the curly dark hair, giving company members the choice of which director to go with. Everyone opted for her. Richard asked me to help him build a new company, raise money, organize a tour, and do a little of everything else. My sojourn in Paris had readied me to be more proactive, so I said yes.

That's how the NYC Street Theater/Jonah Project began. We hired actors and put together two shows, a short one based on a folktale and a full-length one based on the biblical Book of Jonah. We performed them across the country the next summer, traveling in a van, a car, and a flatbed truck that also served as our stage.

The story of Jonah goes like this: God told Jonah to go to Nineveh and warn the people that they were about to be wiped out for their evil ways. Jonah boarded a ship going the other way. There was a storm at sea because Jonah's god was angry at him, so the sailors threw him into the sea. He was swallowed by a whale and spat out on the shore of Nineveh. Then Jonah did as God had commanded. The Ninevites heeded Jonah's word and God forgave them. Jonah got angry, believing that he'd come for nothing; God was never really going to destroy them. On the next afternoon, hot and sunny, God created a shade tree for Jonah. The next day, God cut it down. Jonah got even angrier. God asked how Jonah could care more about that one tree than he expected God to care about all of Nineveh, with its many people and animals.

It was not lost on me that my path, like Jonah's, pulled me in unexpected ways toward what I think of as my destiny. Enacting the Jonah story for different audiences, my twenty-year-old self was alert to a calling apart from individual ambition.

Emblematic was a show we did in one of the Dakotas, in a town with a Native American and a white population. The white people never got out of their cars; they just opened the windows so they could hear the performance, and honked at the end instead of clapping. The Native Americans sat on blankets and picnicked during the show. They all seemed to take that arrangement for granted. It horrified me how easily they coexisted so close yet so separately. It was clear that simply bringing a show like ours with its humanistic content did nothing to change or even challenge that divide.

But it did something to change me. I saw people's lives closer up and got to talk with them, which had not been possible when I stayed on one side of the proscenium and the audience stayed on the other. When we performed for a Native American community, I, who had never ridden a horse more than a couple of laps around a pen, went on an all-day trip on horseback at the invitation of a couple of tribe members who'd seen the show. It opened time for a long conversation about their history and the land that had been taken from them. We slept that night in a hayloft.

Performing that show again and again, all across the United States, in indigenous territories, inner cities, at migrant camps, and wherever we were invited, made me want a life in the theater that would allow me to continue to meet a range of people and exchange ideas. I was hearing people's own versions of their lives, and all this rang truer than the little I'd heard about unsung and struggling communities like the ones I was connecting with for the first time.

When we got back to New York and Richard invited me to cofacilitate a workshop in a men's maximum-security prison, there was never a doubt I'd say yes.

FINN: During World War II, my dad, from Ireland, married my mom, a gorgeous child war bride from Scotland, with raven black hair and blazing blue eyes. After the war they immigrated to America. Dad became brutal and unrelenting because of a severe gambling addiction maintained not only by denying his children basic food, clothing, and medical care while caught up in the incurable fever of placing a bet but also by becoming indebted to Irish gangsters as his debts escalated, at one point receiving a $100,000 bailout. He bought and lost three homes during my childhood, one of them a palatial brick house with vineyard and wine cellar but no food in the kitchen cabinets.

When I was five, I was bedridden because of a severe chest deformity that looked likely to end in an early death, possibly within days. The doctors had pressed my parents to leave me at the hospital to die, but my hysterical mom insisted on taking me home. She kept me alive by constructing a decongestant tent to constantly clear my lungs and increase what little breathing capacity I had. My dad had had enough of Mom wasting her time 24/7 to keep me alive, seeing my frail existence as no life at all. Postmodern, not encumbered with ethical systems that would prevent him from doing what was right for the nuclear family and the larger culture itself, my dad agreed with the doctors. He perceived my mom as an emotional lunatic, possessed by a flawed feminine sentiment, and a weird sadistic, maniacal desire to keep me alive to constantly suffer.

The only ontologically deep intimacy I had with my dad in my childhood was when we entered a realm governed by Lady Death. After putting up with my mom's absurd efforts to keep me alive for years, my dad took me to the basement to snuff out this horrid condition and tried to drown me in the utility sink. But my mom stepped in. Not long after, I was one of four children in America chosen to participate in a new experimental surgical technique involving massive bone grafting, building me a chest.

My dad's ongoing war against my existence continued after I was cured. His daily gambling losses painted him as a total loser as a husband and dad. He attributed this to my vampiric clinging to the health of others to save myself, draining the life energy sustaining the family unit. But now his escalating losses locked him into a frustration he could not shake from his burdened soul other than through beating my brother and me for instant relief, which became the norm.

At age eight, with my restored body, I intuited that there was one way I could defeat him during the brutal beatings, an epiphany: *If I don't cry, he will be robbed of his power. I could beat him!* One night I forgot to do something he requested. He ordered me to go to the kitchen and remove my clothes. This time, my fear was displaced by a rabid determination to beat him at his own game. I wanted the beating, was anxious for it. I wanted to win.

I stood there naked. Already he could sense something had changed. I was not cowering on the floor, sitting with my arms wrapped around my legs and shaking, my head buried in my knees. The first lash from his construction belt landed against my upper left arm and back. But instead of falling to the floor and protecting my genitals as I had always done in the past, I just stood there, defiant. His fury and concentration intensified as blow after blow of the belt cracked across my back, arms, and legs. Then he punched me hard in the face with his right fist, my body crashing to the floor.

The lashings quickened with greater force, his face turning red, white spittle collecting around the corners of his mouth, his lips curled up tight into the gums of his false teeth, the muscles of his face contorting against his skull. He *knew* what I was doing, and screamed, "You bastard! You'll cry!" But I didn't, the belt tearing at my flesh but losing its sting... and then I moved—out of my body. I was hovering over and looking down at my body and Dad's twisted face, his mantric "Cry, you fuckin' bastard!" hanging softly in the air. I was calm, silent.

And then it occurred to me: *I'm going to die.* That thought connected as if through a lazy thread to my body below, and with a jolt, like an electric shock, I was back, letting loose a long and piercing scream. It was as if it didn't come from me at all, but from some distant place below me, now traveling up through my legs, intestines, stomach, heart, throat, and out the top of my head. When the scream stopped, so had Dad; but with a crazed deliberateness I screamed again, a futile attempt to capture *that* scream, to *know* it before it left forever, leaving me alone in this final submission—my body now belonging to him.

The final death dive my dad initiated was when I was fifteen. I had been homeless for some time, mostly on the streets of New York City; my family lived in New Jersey. But a snowstorm hit while I was in Jersey, dealing drugs five miles from my parents' house. I sat down against a large oak tree in a park, and woke up at about 5:00 A.M., covered in snow. I brushed the snow off and began my trek to get a bus into New York. But within two hours I entered a delirium state and found myself standing in the kitchen of my parents' home, hallucinating my brains out and not knowing how I got there.

It was a Sunday morning. My entire family was sitting in the living room watching television. Light was crashing into my visual space from every angle, even from the dark spaces between cabinets. And then I began to pontificate loudly to each family member on why our family was lost in hell, starting with my five-year-old baby sister and ending with my dad: "And you're the one who destroyed all of us, turning us as best you could into your image and likeness, all of us conquered and forced to participate in your living nightmare."

Then I saw Dad's bulky self, walking fast toward me from the dining room. With no intention, I looked at my right fisted hand, which was moving on its own without consulting me, driving itself with full force into my dad's face while I leaned against the kitchen cabinet, lending more power to the punch that stunned him. I grabbed both his ears with my hands, gripping tightly, my fingernails tearing into his ear flesh, and began pounding his head into the aluminum lined cabinet, blow after blow, his knees buckling and him falling to the floor. I would have pounded his skull into the arms of Lady Death if my brother hadn't come to his rescue, putting me in a hammerlock while my dad recovered from his daze and began throwing devastating punches at my body and head until finally saying to my brother, "Let him go." Then he grabbed my body and threw me down the cellar stairs, where I remained for three days, unconscious. He allowed no one to call 911. When I awoke, my mom was staring into my face, and said, "You're going to have to leave, and you can never return. Do you understand?" I slightly nodded yes.

So life began on my own, no reprieves. I found myself celebrating this arrival. I bought a new comic book that caught my attention immediately, *X: The*

Man with the X-Ray Eyes. The store owner said, "You know, they released a film based on the comic at the same time the comic book was released, first time ever they've done that."

"Do you know where it's playing?"

"I'm sure it's in one of the theaters on Forty-second Street." And sure enough, it was, made by the genius B filmmaker Roger Corman, whom Hollywood insiders rightly bestowed with the title "the Pope of Pop Cinema."

The story is about an acute empath physician who suffers terribly at the suffering of others. Being a doctor, he sees far more human suffering and death than most. He develops a drug he can inject to see more deeply into the origin and endless varieties of human suffering. His obsession eventually lands him in nonstop visions of human suffering on every level, with not a single break in the action. Having no respite from this dreadful consciousness drives him, like Oedipus, into tearing his eyes out.

I headed over to Central Park to kick back and ease into a Quaalude high to reflect on a simultaneously triadic matching experience in a comic book, film, and my lived experience. The story was identifying my destiny, before I understood what destiny was, but would prove true over a lifetime of reflecting. Without my ever having used the word *empath* or understanding its dynamics, the film was a perfect rendition of an extreme empath's life dressed up in a science fiction tale, an analogous fable on the human condition.

I knew that story was my life, but because of my immaturity, I was not able to see that my destiny involved seeking out and entering theater life, where the mysterious questions related to human suffering and death would be answered. If I attempted to avoid that destiny, it would end in prolonged and unnecessary suffering—what would turn out to be the most terrible affliction of all in sidestepping my destiny.

JAN: *Reflecting now on Finn and me at fifteen, I see us both breaking from our families, he for literal survival and I for figurative, he without support and I with misguided support, but both in pursuit of our destinies. Both of us Jonahs. "In the arms of Lady Death," Finn wrote of his interactions with his father, later explaining to me that death worship always stimulates a desire to kill the pain of meaninglessness. I wanted to escape meaninglessness, too, but had the option of going to Paris instead of using heroin.*

Finn recently wrote to me about my upbringing, even while understanding what was also suffocating about it: "You were brought up in a middle-class family where you were loved, affirmed, and prepared to go out into the world with an abiding confidence." What a contrast to his childhood, where he was nearly killed by his father, denied a place in the family home, and left to fend for himself.

3

The Workshop

FINN: Upon reflection, I understood exactly why I signed up for the drama workshop: to come out of myself, a requirement if I was to ever have a real life. I had mostly lived interiorly, in my many fear centers. I began to obsess on a Rolling Stones phrase that kept stabbing into my mind: "suicide right on stage." I signed up for the workshop to die the most important of the many deaths I would experience in Trenton: to exit my coil position, a tight bundle of nerves leaving me always on the lookout, ready to spring. If I accomplished this, I would for the first time in my life be free from my crippling fears.

I had known myself to be a coward at heart since the age of seven. This concerned me most when I entered the criminal life at age eleven, joining my older brother's gang. I was terrified of getting caught. He said to me, "You're worried about nothin'. You only got to remember one thing: Fight at the drop of a pin and you will get respect. If someone kills you, you won't be aware of it, so it's not an issue."

Over the months, turning to years, the fears remained, but like an alcoholic in rehab, I could fake being heroic, and faking would make it real. That was my plan, more frightening than any criminal job I pulled off in life. To be successful in theater life required the assassination of every solid yet deceptive persona I'd developed over the years and then to be born again into a fearless lifestyle. Theater life for me could only be real by being real. And that meant a war unto death with my many selves reflected endlessly in the lives of others.

I knew from the start that theater was my only option to enter communal life, which would remain my central focus through life. Living in terror in the years before I came to Trenton had the positive effect of opening me to others, a way of hiding by totally listening to and understanding them, ensuring they were no immediate threat. It was the best cover I could come up with, my existence of total listening becoming an affirmation of every one of them.

When I arrived in the workshop, I came out of hiding for the first time in my life, requiring the slaughter of my many false selves in front of an audience, for, ironically, any persona created for a stage performance requires the infiltration of who one actually is to make it real to the audience. The great inversion begins: wearing masks as a method of destroying social masks. Killing off every persona I had invented and incorporated into my being over a lifetime of pure survival was the only therapy I imagined could actually help me break out of my self-created dungeon of loneliness.

During the workshop process, I met Jan. Totally trusting her, a first for me, other than my brother, opened a door where I could, for the first time, step outside the matrix of my cowardly foundation. You see how precious the love I shared with Jan was and remains. For it was in that relationship I first came out of hiding. That was a major event. I chose her as my one compadre in this new and exciting mission, to die as many deaths as necessary to be free from those terrors, to destroy my demons of fear by confronting them directly, with the stage as the final confrontation. I trusted her alone.

I had read only one book by age twenty, *The Complete Works of Edgar Allan Poe*. Then in my two years in prison before the arrival of the Jonah Project, I had read only literature and psychology books. I knew very little about Marxism, feminism, and the sexual revolution, and Jan became my only real guide through all of it.

JAN: Finn may have thought of me as a guide back then, but I didn't. I was reading Marx for the first time, too; Mao was in the air of the culture I inhabited in those days, but I had merely read, not studied, the "Little Red Book," and uncritically at that. When I think about the workshop, I am flooded with memories of scenes and exercises, many from the guys' lives, which in some cases included radical political activity but only minor references to political writers like Eldridge Cleaver and Huey Newton.

On the other hand, I was devouring feminist literature and aspiring to free myself from an internalized sense of women's inferiority to men. The workshop was an excellent place to practice being the kind of woman I aspired to be, because it allowed all our identities to be in flux.

FINN: The other prisoners in the workshop were an interesting lot. They joined for various reasons—to get out of their cells, score points in the rehab game, or become famous actors or writers someday. They hoped for help getting their needs met, by others smuggling in drugs, providing sexual favors, helping them escape, or finding a legal path to early release.

Kuwasi, ex-military, was a committed Black Panther, but in his heart of hearts he was an anarchist, which politically and personally suited him, for he was an adrenaline junkie. He believed the revolutionary rhetoric, but his focus was on having fun absent any restrictions, including robbing armored trucks and escaping prisons, at which he was accomplished.

John was the consummate con artist, focused on keeping a marijuana stash to stay high 24/7. When I found out he had conned one of the workshop volunteers, a beautiful soul and Vietnam veteran named Billy, whose charitable heart was as genuine as it gets, I lost what little respect I had for John. He imagined becoming a great actor so he could sustain his radical solipsism for a lifetime.

Ted was a young Jewish man who was also committed to staying high 24/7. He was drawn to opioids, for he understood, as I did, that life for the most part involved one of two choices: fit in to a sadomasochistic world and adapt to the inevitable inconveniences of pain and suffering that is endemic to living life, or, whether fitting in or not, constantly kill the inevitable pain, marijuana a temporary relief.

Kareem was a hypersensitive soul, a Black man with a serious conscience, contained in a coil position and trapped in suppressed, raw anger he couldn't totally conceal in his facial expressions. He was looking for a way to exit the debilitating anger through action, and because he was a moral man, most likely an empath, he desired a path of action where he wouldn't have to harm anyone. That's why theater opened a big door for him, a place where he could express himself without harming others; indeed, he would be assisting others exiting their sadomasochistic matrices.

JAN: The workshop was as much about us getting to know one another across our similarities and differences as it was about the theater we made. That's what theater is meant to do, open people to one another, whether it's through a play or a workshop. It's only now I realize how much went right past me in the workshop, like some of the politically active guys initially thinking that Richard and I might have been sent by the FBI to find out what they were up to. But their distrust broke down over time.

After a few weeks, it became clear through the scenes they enacted that Robert and Donald were Black Panthers, an organization founded in 1966 for self-determination among Black people, in reaction to ongoing institutional racism. Donald had renamed himself Kuwasi Balagoon, reflecting an identification with his African roots, as was popular among politicized African Americans at the time. But it expressed something else about his identity, too; say it fast and it sounds like "crazy as a loon," a conscious choice on his part. For Kuwasi was at the same time endlessly playful. Like a card he once gave me that said on the front, "A genetic bent for illegality may run in some families." Inside, one guy is rolling on the floor, laughing at the other, who is making silly faces. The caption reads, "Cain slays Abel."

Kareem could have seemed to be a self-serving "common criminal," based on his conviction for a B and E (breaking and entering), a charge that was not overtly political. But he was also a Black Panther, and through the scenes he performed, it became clear that his actions had roots in rage, his lashing out motivated by extreme alienation due to deep racism in America. Kareem went on to shepherd community gardens in Harlem, where he later lived.

John was a white guy who said he was busted for marijuana, which might have been so, but who knows. It was a *maximum*-security prison, after all. Attracted to theater that transgressed norms, I brought up tricksters, disruptive and playful characters found in folklore who cast doubt on business as usual. I later learned that John had understood me as saying *trucksters*, as if I saw myself as some kind of bull dyke truck driver. No, I did not, and anyway, bull dyke truckers—what kind of stereotype is that? It's as bad as the misconceptions a lot of people have about people in prison, thinking that the words *hardened* and *criminal* are inextricably bound together. Maybe all that weed addled his brain.

The range of guys in the workshop brings to my mind the sailors of many faiths on the ship Jonah boarded to Ninevah. Like in the Jonah story, each was following his own god. Some guys wanted the workshop to politicize the general prison population, others were exploring themselves, and still others were out to get whatever they could for themselves. Some were doing all three.

Sometimes before a workshop session started, Kuwasi would ask me to take a walk with him. We'd stroll up and down the room, talking about one thing or another. Some years later, when Kuwasi was out of prison, we were walking and talking late into a winter's night and came upon the icy, untouched beauty of a snow-blanketed Central Park. "It's not a good idea to walk there this late," I said. He grinned and said, "That's because of people like me. Nothing for you to worry about now." Simply enjoying the beauty of a snowy, moonlit park together reminded me of the scene in the movie *Butch Cassidy and the Sundance Kid* when Paul Newman and Robert Redford, playing outlaws, get a bike and ride around on it with Katherine Ross, expressing so much pleasure. Like Finn often said, we each contain many selves; we are none of us monolithic.

Kuwasi once cast me as a member of his gang in a bank robbery scene that was exhilarating. I could imagine being part of his life outside, which, as a Black Panther, seemed righteous and brave. I now think Kuwasi was trying to seduce me into a life of crime, seeing my weakness for collectives, be they theater companies or gangs, softening me up for when he would start asking favors, then escalating, but beginning simply enough.

"Hey," Kuwasi said with his inimitable grin. "It would be cool if Nine and me had matching earrings—could we have that set you're wearing?" Yes, of course.

One day, when he got to the workshop early, Kuwasi asked me to open my blouse. I didn't, but I wondered how much that was due to old-fashioned ideas. The conditions of imprisonment are insane. Why are certain body parts meant to be shared only in private anyway? Kuwasi's requests escalated, eventually to the point where he wanted me to help him escape, but I didn't do that, either. Nonetheless, he did escape a few years later.

As Richard and I drove home after a workshop, I'd marvel at something that had happened. "Wasn't Finn amazing in that scene with the psychiatrist? He really nailed it—the absurdity of separating personal responses from the politics around you, be they the family or something more macro. And Kuwasi—that poem he read was so funny and belligerent at once. Nine told me that Kuwasi ghostwrote some of Gil Scott-Heron's songs."

"Yes and yes. But why are you so surprised?" asked Richard.

Why *was* I so surprised? What misconception was I carrying around, without even knowing it, about people in prison? A misconception that books and articles I'd read hadn't punctured but this experience had.

Finn said that most people in prison put themselves there. It is a relief, a respite from a world that expects some kind of behavior from them.

I thought of the expectations that the world I came from laid on people of my class. My intense involvement in the prison workshop was breaking a taboo, seen as downward rather than upward mobility. My involvement in the prison workshop made my parents greatly distraught.

"You're on a road directly to hell," said my usually gentle and nonjudgmental father, a World War II veteran and the son of immigrants, who had never criticized me before, frustrated to the brink of his patience at what he saw as me squandering my talents. He had worked so hard to give his children the opportunity to become anything they wanted to be—what was I doing among what he perceived as common criminals?

"But Dad," I had tried to explain. "These guys grew up in a war zone of poverty and violence, right here in the United States. You know from being in a literal war zone that there are different rules."

A glimmer of understanding broke through the hardness that had been his face during the conversation. But then my mother put an end to it, stonily silencing my father and wordlessly making him choose his alliance with her or with me, an impossible position. I never got through to him on the subject again.

The relationship with Finn and the other participants was the most profound piece of my own education. What it was to understand that Finn became a child prostitute to survive his childhood, ironically ending it at the same time. And that drugs are not a root problem, but a solution to the searing pain from which the addict seeks release. I had entered the prison unconsciously expecting to meet people who were inherently bad in some way, not yet understanding that they were shaped by the complicated and violent circumstances of their lives. Paraphrasing Brecht from *St. Joan of the Stockyards,* "These people aren't bad; they are poor." What existential realities force us into the choices we make and the people we become? My workshop experience was the crucible that saved me from believing abstractions about all I did not know.

4

Intensification

JAN: One evening in February 1972, after the workshop had been meeting weekly for over three months, Richard and I got to the prison and were told that the facility was closed to outsiders "indefinitely." The guards would only say that there had been a fire. I was enormously agitated, wondering what was happening to people I had come to care about, locked in there. By then we had been visiting some of the guys outside of the workshop, in what were called "window visits," like in old black-and-white movies, the inmate on one side of a heavy plate- glass window, the visitor on the other, speaking to each other through telephone receivers. The abrupt loss of these connections, too, was painful.

FINN: The fire was one of the many outcomes of the new "progressive" guard at Trenton. I had been settled into a creative way of life made possible by the extreme conditions enforced by the old guard. They left me alone, making clear I could be myself in any way as long as I didn't violate rules of conduct, easy for me, and a great deal, heaven—never before was I left to find out who I am on my own terms, no restrictions, and be fed, housed, and clothed during the process. Under that cruel regime, I had more freedom than ever before in my life. Then in came a new progressive guard that would become my true enemy, seeking to transform me into their image and likeness, and unconsciously to rob me of my radically unique experiences.

Before the arrival of these progressive administrators, the only education the prison provided was basic reading and writing classes. The war against the old establishment began with a new education department, the prison's new heart and soul. The guards focused on destroying or at least discrediting that Alamo, to rob it of its expanding power and influence on politicians to support their mission with an army of educators, social workers, and psychologists. The guards defeated them through the tried-and-true methodology of divide and conquer.

At this particular moment, the guards had identified all the members of two violent Black factions ideologically at war with each other, and shipped one of the factions to another prison to avoid a bloodbath. The guards' first major assault on the Alamo was bringing the transferred faction back to Trenton and giving them an office in the education department, sanctioned by the education director in his eternal quest to be politically correct regarding racial discrimination. He would not permit this newly arrived Black faction to be discriminated against. But the guards never alerted him to the ongoing war between these factions, so the progressives were stunned when a fire destroyed the faction's newly acquired office.

JAN: A few days after the fire, Richard and I each got an identical letter from Finn. The underlying cause of the fire, he explained, was due to different factions of inmates that the administration set against each other, through the bestowing and withholding of privileges, a divide-and-conquer strategy to make it easier for them to keep order in the prison. The fire had been set in the office of the group that edited the prison newspaper. Finn suspected that it was set not by an enemy but by someone wanting to bring attention to the favors that led to all the infighting, so it was a good thing. It revealed that any inmate group's power was actually held by the prison administration.

Finn wrote that his perspective came from what he had learned about power from an inmate who held ongoing conversations with a circle of men. Finn likened that group to Plato's dialogues with his students, asking and answering questions to develop critical thinking and draw out ideas and underlying biases.

The letter floored me, providing insight into the workings of prison life. I was surprised that the learning circle Finn described existed in a prison, which I'd always imagined as antithetical to free intellectual exchange. I was moved that Finn saw the fire as a good thing, even though it meant he, too, was locked down in a five-by-seven-foot cell. I was struck to discover how someone who grew up without books, schooling, or encouragement of any kind could be the deep thinker and articulate writer that Finn was.

I wrote back, thanking him. I commented that the prison power dynamics, with its trading of favors for certain kinds of behavior, reminded me of gender relationships, like women who get privileges by cozying up to powerful men, habits that were being challenged at that time.

I sent him *The Dialectic of Sex,* by Shulamith Firestone. He wrote back immediately, pulling out lines from the book that especially spoke to him, like "Thus the 'natural' is not necessarily a 'human" value." He sent a check to pay for the book. I wrote him that the check was unnecessary; it was a gift. He thanked me, writing, "The check doesn't negate how beautiful it was of you to share it with me. I believe you are 30th century enough to dig that money is just a practical matter so the really important things can run smoothly."

And so began a deluge of letters. We wrote to each other about books, movies, politics, and philosophy. We wrote how we felt moment by moment. We took apart our childhoods. He never trivialized the relative ease of my childhood in relation to the harshness of his own, taking my formative years as seriously as his. We wrote about our everyday lives. We shared our takes on the workshop and the participants.

We fell in love.

We wrote outpourings of our love to each other. As anyone who has had a long-distance love affair before the existence of the internet knows, letters become a space to be together. I focused on him and my consciousness curled into a place inside me for just the two of us. Every thought I wrote him went toward making two chairs alongside each other, a room where we could sit, a little house where we could live.

Time slowed down, so careful were we both to find fitting words to carry our feelings and thoughts to the other. I hadn't known how to take time in a romance before, but now time was what we had most. Holding the paper he had written on was touching *him*.

After a few weeks, the prison reopened to outsiders and the drama workshop resumed. Finn and I were energized in each other's presence, inspiring us to go further in the workshop than we had before. I had long fantasized a partner who passionately shared my work and intimate life, and amazingly, I found that in Finn, who cared as much about the workshop and the street theater as I did. He loved hearing about the people we'd performed for and spent time with, the idea that theater could be available to everyone, free and in public spaces. The prison workshop was a natural extension of the street theater, both reaching

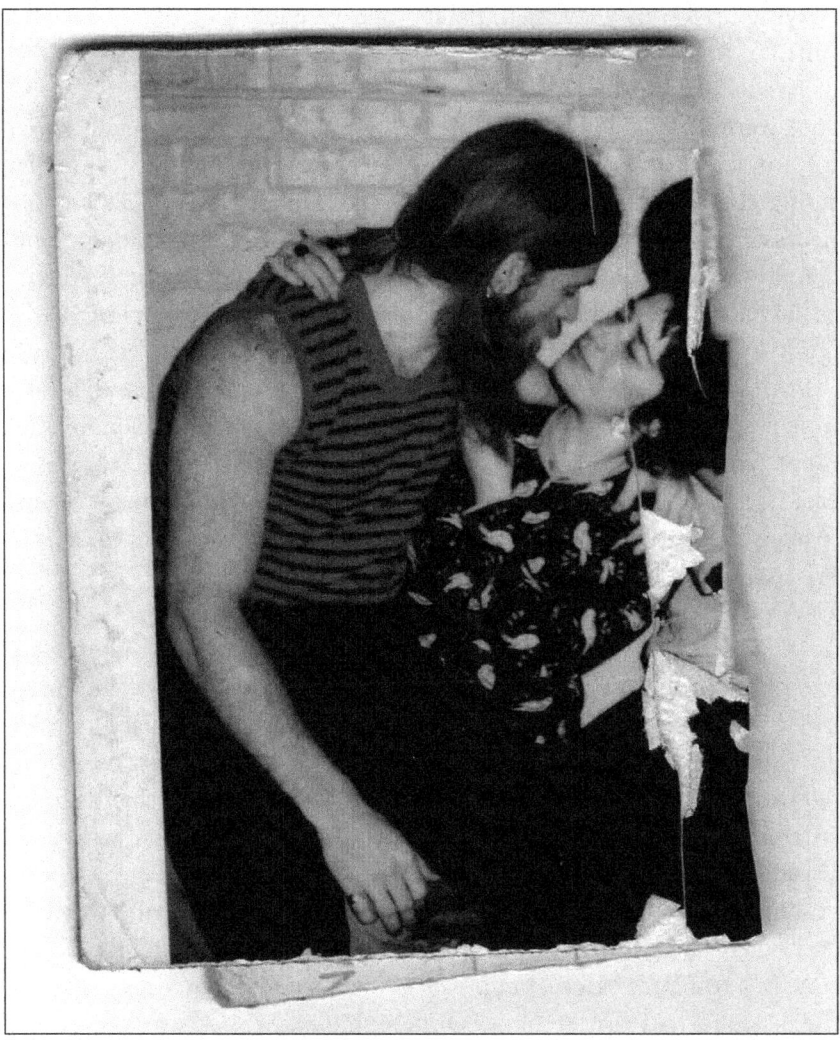

Figure 4.1 Finn and Jan on a visit in Trenton State Prison, 1972. Photographer unknown.

more people as performers and audiences than was the norm. Our letters intensified, energized by our weekly collaboration, and a way to be together between workshop sessions.

At the same time, much of what held meaning for me before the workshop no longer did. My aspirations, most theater on the "outside"— dust to dust. I could hardly understand what anyone saw in such a life, which seemed terribly self-involved and impervious to the conditions of so many people, often unseen but all around us. I was Jonah and believed that I was learning what I'd been sent there for.

The workshop, the letters, my daydreams of a future with Finn, street theater planning, the visits—those were the parameters of my life. They all bespoke the possibility of living in a beloved community, ever expanding, with a loving mate and meaningful work. Finn and I lived together in the alternative universe that we little by little constructed, grounded in the dynamic space of the workshop and extended through our letters and visits, practicing being the selves we aspired to be in the world.

FINN: I've always had a deep sense of destiny. Inevitably, clear affirmations arrived that kept me moving on a mission and sidestepped the spinning off into nihilism. When I saw Jan on that first day of workshop, I felt in the core of my being she was part of my destiny, what would be the greatest adventure of my life if we could somehow find our way to each other. Her movements declared she was committed to adventure, ever moving forward, the only pace that I ever found had any meaning. My *Iliad* with no *Odyssey* was to fight with no guarantee of winning anything, knowing there is no return to any hearth, all of life unfolding only in adventure. In that light, along with a singular desire birthed in my mind from my body at age seventeen—to coalesce as one with a woman into eternity—it's clear why she was the first woman I fell in love with. Never again did it go that deep. It became one of the many great blessings bestowed on me in being true to my destiny.

But all of this was taking place in a new prison arena that began two years prior to the Jonah Project's arrival and made it possible in the prison—the new academic way of saving criminals. The director of education glimpsed how powerful the Jonah Project would be, wanted his name on it, and guaranteed that he would lend his full weight in ensuring its success. The academic progressives infiltrating Trenton warred against the old regime run by prison guards with a new Alamo, an expanded education department.

The historical Alamo was part of the Texas war for independence from Mexico. The people who lived in that part of Texas had over many decades formed a real community of love, compassion, and mutual respect among peoples of all shades of skin color. The Tejanos, the Mexicans who first settled in that region, got along with Texan Americans in true communion. This, by the way, is how Billy the Kid survived and didn't get caught for so many years: He lived among Tejanos most of the time, and they protected him.

The Texans and Tejanos of that region saw themselves as distinct from other regions of Mexico and the United States. That's why the Tejanos joined the Texans as communal friends fighting off the Mexican military invasion of their territory, shared in common by Texans and Mexicans as one, what the Mexican militarists sought to annihilate. Yes, the annihilation of a true communion that defied negative racial stereotypes.

The Alamo is my metaphor for resistance by a group in defiance of any force seeking to destroy their communion. I saw the workshop as an Alamo.

JAN: Richard and I began planning for the next street theater tour. The previous summer, we had performed all across the United States, on city streets, in parks, on reservations, in prisons, never staying anywhere for more than a few days. "We should only go to three places next summer," declared Richard, "and stay three weeks at each, instead of going place to place like we did last year. We want to have impact! Then based on where we feel the most likelihood that something could happen, spend the entire next summer there."

I loved this idea, agreeing that simply doing our show and moving on was not the best use of our energy. We needed to build relationships, find people who saw a role for our shows in what they were doing beyond the stage in specific locales. By staying three weeks, we could begin to build relationships, do participatory workshops as well as our own shows, and support local efforts beyond our own.

We were also doing prison workshops at the Rahway and Clinton facilities. One day Richard said to me, "Now that we're offering so many workshops in New Jersey, I want to get a house on the Jersey shore. It'll make our commuting easier. As the people who are most committed to the work get out they can come live with us."

"And become part of the street theater."

"Exactly."

As Richard assumed, I wanted to live in the house and was happy to pay rent toward his mortgage instead of to the landlord of my studio apartment in Manhattan. At the time I didn't catch the contradiction of calling the house a collective when he alone was responsible for it and, without ever questioning it, making all the decisions about it, beginning with choosing the particular house. I found the house rather unattractive, but on the plus side, it had a bunch of bedrooms, a good-size kitchen, and was within walking distance of the beach. One of the other actors from the street theater, a sweetheart of a guy and a Vietnam vet named Billy, who facilitated the workshop with Richard at Rahway and sometimes went with us to Trenton, moved in, too. My friend Kate, who was beginning to facilitate workshops with me at the New Jersey women's prison in Clinton, was considering moving in, as well.

Doc, Richard's boyfriend, joined us next. I don't know when I realized that Richard was bisexual and Doc was his paramour. More surprising was the particular person that Doc was. It was hard for me to see the attraction. Doc had a job in medical technology that he was in no way passionate about. He had no interest in theater or social justice, so far as I could tell, and although he called himself a musician, I never heard him practicing, albeit he occasionally came to the prison workshop to accompany scenes with his electric guitar.

Doc was Black, which meant a lot to Richard, like some sort of badge of good politics. And he was much younger, so Richard was very comfortable always teaching him about various writers and political thinkers. The conversations did not generally last long before Doc put on his headphones and zoned out on his portable cassette recorder.

Amadi, a new guy in the workshop, put his girlfriend, Amina, in touch with us. Amina tricked for a living and had gone through a slow patch and lost her apartment. Amina, Richard, and I went for coffee just before the workshop one day, when Amina was visiting Amadi, to see if she might move in with us.

Richard began by saying, "The first thing to know is that the house is a collective, Amina."

" Do we each get our own room?" she asked skeptically.

"Of course," he said. "It's up to you who you share your room with. A collective means that we all contribute to and share what we have and support each other. It's like socialism, but instead of the state owning everything, we do, together."

Amina: "That's what socialism means? And here I thought it was some terrible thing! Yeah, I'm down for some collectivity." And she moved in.

I liked getting to know Amina the way you do when you see each other bleary-eyed before coffee, hear each other's music seeping under the bedroom door, cook together, and get into impromptu conversations over the dinner table.

One day Amina asked me, "What's the deal with Doc? Is Richard his sugar daddy?"

I knew Doc liked Richard's money, but I assumed he liked Richard, too. Amina gave me pause for thought. "I honestly don't know," I said.

Little by little, the small print of Richard's vision came clear. He hoped I'd have "a lot of babies" with Kareem, a very engaged workshop participant and possible future resident of the house, because Richard liked the idea of the collective including a racial mix. The idea was pretty crazy, because though I cared about Kareem, I was in love with Finn. Richard would make such comments with that inscrutable smile, so I was never certain if he meant it. I feel sure he would have denied it if I'd challenged him. I just rolled my eyeballs at him at times like that. But it was actually a very bad sign that he was trying to direct our lives as well as our plays. For me, collectivity never included becoming a baby-making machine. But Richard saying that did not make me less enthusiastic about the house. Maybe it was because he never pressed, just planted not so innocuous seeds.

The idea of collective living was not new to me. In Paris, a group of us practicing the Polish director Jerzy Grotowski's techniques rented a large apartment together that had a vast studio in the cellar. Living collectively was motivated by the practical need to afford the studio, aligned with our desire to live within a countercultural ethos. Materialism loosened its grip on us as we organically began sharing what we had with one another. When my mother sent me four sweaters, I gave three of them to others in the group.

For some, an aspect of collectivity was sexual experimentation, in the spirit of nonownership of the people one loved. One morning I knocked on Micheline's door to borrow something and she invited me in. There she was in bed with Jean Marc and Jacques, the three of them looking like sleepy kittens flopped on top of one another. I was really surprised; the three of them were serious intellectuals. This reaction made me realize I had a stereotypical idea of people either being more physically or more intellectually inclined. But they were both. Collective living also facilitated learning, both through largely political conversations over dinner and the English lessons I conveniently posted each day by the toilet.

For us in Long Branch, New Jersey, collective living was a way to build a street theater that could support people without the means to live on a shoestring, as so-called activist theater usually entailed. For ironically, despite the often sincere rhetoric that such theaters were for "the people," only the people with financial means could typically afford to participate in them.

Collective living was also a backlash against the insularity of the biological family, which made it morally acceptable for people to care only about blood relatives. For there was a cost to the many of the privileges of the few. As Kareem said, "Live simply, so others can simply live."

Reaching further back in my own history, I'd experienced collectivity within my family. For the first twelve years of my life, my mother's three siblings and their families lived within a one-block radius of our house, and my maternal grandparents just a few blocks farther. We ten cousins were in and out of one another's houses and the four families had many a meal together, especially on the weekends. While we were homogenous in many ways, every family is also different in important details, which I got to experience firsthand. And given that I found some of my relatives insufferable, I also learned that while you don't have to like your entire family, you do have to love them.

Finn's history with collectivity also predated the workshop. He had once been assigned to the prison bakery, and he and the other workers there had informally collectivized their tasks—instead of just doing their individual jobs, they shared all the labor and helped one another when their own work was done. But it didn't last. Some of the guys began taking advantage of the others and sleeping in, knowing their work would be covered, an example of the pitfalls of collectivity.

FINN: A major event occurred not long after the workshop started. Richard decided to buy a house with lots of bedrooms close to all the prisons where they led workshops—and within walking distance of the beach—with the intention of forming a permanent commune that prisoners could join upon release. Right away I had a vision of Jan and me being part of a true creative community, what I viewed as a permanent adventure. It was a utopian vision I latched onto, and it was my singular focus for the future, the only one I had ever entertained after understanding that chances were I would end up in prison for the rest of my life.

JAN: As soon as the prison reopened to civilians, my visits with Finn intensified. It was a great joy to drink each other in with our eyes and talk uninterrupted for an hour, adding to the time we could be together. We began to have contact visits, too, an hour to be physically together twice a month in a doorless cell in what used to be the wing for inmates with death sentences. We embraced, kissed, and held hands. Though guards patrolled the corridor, surveilling us, we reveled in our relative privacy and physical contact.

But one day when we were sitting close together on a contact visit, Finn said it was time to tell me why he was in prison—that he had killed a man. The floor beneath me sank into the earth. This gentle, loving man killed someone? I went cold and hot at once. And I despaired that it meant he must have a terribly long sentence—two, actually, I was to learn, one imposed by the state and one by himself.

FINN: I'd been involved with a criminal network that included a woman named Judy, whom I'd known since we both were teens. Back then, when she was homeless, I let her stay where I was living until she found somewhere of her own. I never took advantage of her, even when she offered sex, which I saw as her falling into self-deprecation, even though in her conscious mind it was no doubt an expression of gratitude. She paid me back in spades, being the only person to ever bail me out from a reformatory.

When I was twenty years old, I decided to go whole hog, master bank robbing and truck hijackings, and, with a new identity, move to Scotland, never to return to America. In the meantime, she and her boyfriend, Danny, gave me an apartment to use, money for food and clothes, and the use of a car until I found employment. They told me I could use their business as a job reference. In those days, employers freely exchanged *all* information about prospective employees. What I didn't know was that Danny and Judy would give horrible references, telling employers they'd caught me stealing and had to fire me. I was in a strange kind of dark place and couldn't even get jobs on manufacturing lines or doing janitorial work—never a return call. All of it was a setup to drown me in a rabid sense of indebtedness towards them, heightened by Judy knowing better than anyone my empathic nature.

Just then a member of the criminal network that Judy, Danny, and I were involved with got arrested, and although he was out on bail, everyone was certain he would turn state's evidence on all of us to escape a jail sentence. The gang wanted him dead. Because I was leaving the country, Judy begged me to be the one to do it, saying he was an absolute obstacle to her and Danny's happiness. How could I do otherwise? I was 100 percent opposed to it in every fiber of my nervous system, but I agreed to it, out of an endless sense of indebtedness to Judy.

Killing the man was definitely a cowardly act of suicide, for I did die totally inside, and I did seek to die in the electric chair, a lot like what Judas went through. I investigated all the dimensions of that cowardliness, sometimes with massive doses of LSD, psilocybin, or cocaine. My first conscious dive into the darkness to assemble a purely psychological (not spiritual) understanding of my condition was seeing all the dimensions of how Judy was my mom and her boyfriend Danny was my dad, now transfigured into a mom and dad who would support my efforts to break away from a matrix of crime and drug consumption. But that was later.

I eventually found out that the man I killed was innocent, that he came from a solid nuclear family, where he was loved, and was entering adulthood, about to get married and have children. I destroyed him, at the same time destroying his entire family, all because a member of our gang used to be in business with him and was scared he might report something to the police, on ethical grounds, after he left the business. It had nothing to do with a threat to our network of thieves. And that gang member had a fifty-thousand-dollar business-partner insurance policy on him. The man I murdered face-to-face, hearing his voice, made him real in every sense. His death removed me from any possibility for life in any fulfilling way for the rest of my days. That space became a ground to my constitution.

JAN: What I remember next is going to a close friend's apartment and dropping acid. In that state, I walked through the crime as Finn had described it to me, and I had the distinct impression that on one level his crime was about killing his father. The guy Finn killed was keeping a woman down, the way his father had always suppressed his mother. His mother was the only one in the family who looked after him; the woman, Judy, was the only one who ever got Finn bail. He could not deny her anything she asked of him, for she had never said no to him. What had the state ever done for him? And his father and brother had often broken the law. The important thing, they'd said, was not to get caught.

I don't remember feeling any differently about him, knowing what he'd done. I had slipped into another world that now made more sense to me than the one I was from. All the guys in the workshop had done terrible things to end up at Trenton, but they had had terrible things done to them, too, and they were my life at that time. I wanted to embrace their norms; the norms from my world seemed hypocritical and stacked against anyone born without money.

FINN: I had imposed a sentence on myself after killing an innocent man. The collective house was a sign, the possibility of some kind of glorious reprieve, bestowed from the unknown. (Certainly it wasn't chance.) It was like how my death sentence in the electric chair was mysteriously revoked after I had discerned, in depth, why my electrocution was important for all involved, myself included, and I stopped fighting it, doing all I could to ensure it. Then on the day of jury selection, a miracle happened, and I ended up with thirty years instead of death.

I had never expected to get out. I never even expected to want to get out. But then the collective house appeared on my horizon, the universe offering me one chance to return to the land of the living. I thought the house, with Jan, could be a place to begin a new life.

The only realm of lasting joy is community grounded in love, not ambition. A love-bonded unity is at the heart of true community, whereas the postmodern man or woman makes the first priority getting his or her endless needs met. Then, if it is one's penchant, but not as an ethical requirement, one can attend to the needs of others. The postmodern ideal of radical autonomy has gripped our culture by its throat and imposes its principles on us. It is now a basic way of living one's life. Community, once the universal ideal, had been replaced with the ideal of radical autonomy, the two in a permanent adversarial relationship.

JAN: *Finn could only allow himself to live if his life could manifest values antithetical to the act that now defined him. He found it in the vision of* *the collective house—a hunger for community, for a meaningful and good altruistic life—which I shared with him. We nonetheless diverged in what we saw as the obstacles to attaining communion. Finn saw nearly everyone as only out to get their "endless needs" met. I've known many people who were at the same time committed to community and caught up with personal ambition and fulfilling individual desires.*

Why, to Finn, was it so absolute, one or the other? I believed that cultural conditioning glorifying individual ambition was an obstacle to community but that the two impulses could and often did exist together in the same person, including me. The counterculture was important for giving people a context with other than mainstream values. Values are a soil, part of an ecosystem. It's almost impossible to practice nonmainstream values without others who share them. My life has only confirmed that impression.

5

Performances

JAN: After a few months, the workshop had generated quite a collection of poems and scenes. We decided to perform them for the prison population. Richard and I went to Trenton two extra times a week for rehearsals. It was deeply satisfying for Finn and me to be able to do this thing we loved together, and have our conjoined lives less fully on hold. Having a context meant so much—the guys in the workshop picked up pretty soon that something had shifted between us. Finn was known as "Red"; the guys took to calling me "J. Red." My hair was never as red as his, but I loved that connection. Richard chose a new name for himself, too—Jack. It was more easygoing than Richard, maybe a personality he hoped to grow into.

Over the months, the scenes reflected how the prison workshop had deepened. We explored both what was and what might have been. Nine did a scene about always wanting to fight. He had to support his mother and sister, so he joined the marines. He was good at it all—hand-to-hand combat, artillery, explosives—and he was quiet. So he was surprised when his first assignment was as a server in the officers' dining room. When time came for reassignment, they kept him there.

The scene began like so:

Nine: Excuse me, sir, but the class behind me just shipped out. Why was I not among them, uh, sir?

Training Sergeant: Oh, Harris, no slight intended. You're as good a fighter as we have. But the officers like being served by Negroes and have gotten used to you.

Nine went AWOL and joined the Black Panthers. There he found other angry brothers wanting to fight, but not by picking on strangers overseas. They knew who their enemy was.

One of the guys asked me to do a scene with him beside a hospital bed, me giving birth, him imagining being there for his partner in a way that he suggested he had not. In my memory, the room got very quiet.

I somehow learned over the course of the workshop that having lots of kids was considered a proof of virility to some men, but actually helping raise them was a little wussy. That scene allowed us all to feel the miracle of bringing new life into the world and the tragic loss for all involved when fathers are discouraged from being involved with their kids.

Kuwasi set up a scene with me as a con woman, part of a gang liberating money for "the cause," by pretending to be a hostage they were taking in order to make an escape. There I got to imagine how far I would go and in what direction for what I believed in. Finn and I talked a lot about our multiple selves; I didn't like when I or anyone else got pigeonholed in the most obvious ways. I liked that, in Kuwasi's scene, my white middle-class character was an outlaw. I loved seeing something I hadn't expected in someone, slamming me face-to-face into my own preconceptions.

In another scene, based on an incident that happened at Rahway Prison, Richard and I were walking down a prison hallway, accompanied by a guard. Other inmates were passing in the other direction, one of whom my character recognized.

Jan: Bobbie! So good to see you. You haven't made it to workshop in a while. I miss your music!

Bobbie: Great to see you, too. And thanks about the music.

Jan: I hope you come back to workshop. We're headed there now. Take care. (*Unthinkingly stepping over the line between the two sides of the hall, she gives him a little hug.*)

Jan (*to audience*): And suddenly there were whistles blowing and lights throbbing as two guards grabbed Bobbie from either side and hauled him away.

(*Back in scene*): Stop! He didn't touch me! It was my fault!

(*Back to audience*): I sent a letter to an assistant warden, who wrote me back, acknowledging my letter and telling me that Bobbie had all privileges suspended for ten days for his "infraction." Then I wrote a letter apologizing to Bobbie for being so stupid and getting him in trouble. And he wrote back.

Bobbie: Don't worry. It meant a lot that you like my music and missed me.

In another scene that Kuwasi cooked up, he and I were living in a cramped apartment and had gotten into a rut. I was just falling asleep when he started fantasizing about us starting over somewhere else. I got all excited and also started imagining how we might do that. The scene ended with me turning to him and seeing he had fallen asleep.

Kuwasi read one of his poems:

> Tell her that the last time you saw
> Me I was heading west
> With a cloud of dust
> And the biggest horse you ever seen
>
> Tell her that I was putting stirs in his
> Ass like tokens fallin in the subway
> At going home time
> Which I really hated to do 'cause I know
> It did hurt him
> But it was either him or me

We did two performances back-to-back and both times got lively responses from the prison audience. The scenes were familiar, so it felt like our show was an affirmation that their lives were worth putting on a stage. It was certainly an affirmation that the workshop had value beyond us participants.

During the backstage preparations for our performance, Finn brushed my hair, an act almost too exquisite to bear. It was an example of what Lillian Hellman called "pentimento"— something that resonates with an erased thing that preceded it and gives it renewed meaning. For as a child, Finn had often brushed his mother's hair, she who was a child bride.

It was wonderful for me, in the beginning, to be romantically involved with someone where sex was off the table. Plenty of people in prison found ways to have sex, but Finn and I were engrossed in the slow pace of our courtship. I had left home at fifteen, which was unusual in a middle-class Jewish household. It was ostensibly to go to a theater high school in another state, but equally because I found my hometown so toxic—anti-Semitic, racist, the school valuing basketball players and cheerleaders above all else.

When I left, I was already plotting never to live at home again, for one thing to propel me into another. I feared that if I became sexually active, I would get pregnant and have to go home. Sexual abstinence for me was a condition of personal liberation.

Every touch, every look with Finn was full and deeply satisfying for us both. Around this time he wrote me a letter that said, "My mind fell into a stereotype today—I wanted to marry you. Don't panic. Papers are not necessary for us to prove anything. It was just a cultural thought because I love you so much." Now getting to be in the same room with him for the extra rehearsals, I thought, *My cup runneth over.*

JAN: *Revisiting some of my responses to workshop now is somewhat mortifying. Like how quick I was to identify with outlaws in the scene Kuwasi cast me in, I who had benefited so much by staying within the law. Was he stroking my ego, hoping that enacting such a role would lead to my willingness to go down that road?*

FINN: Personal, mostly romantic, relationships were forming between prisoners and staff. Richard and Jan, rightly, didn't see themselves and those they brought in with them as staff, because they weren't. They were genuinely attempting to form a lasting community, and personal relationships exist in communities. It was natural. I gladly succumbed to this with Jan, but unlike the relationships most others were forming, especially in the context of the sexual revolution, and knowing it wouldn't take much for the workshop to be destroyed, I tried to stay thirteen steps ahead of the guards, always trying to figure out what types of games they were playing to undermine the workshop.

A lot of the games involved what they were letting us get away with, including engaging in sex acts. Guards made jokes about the women being conned by prisoners into being their sex slaves, forms of sexual degradation justified as revolutionary acts, liberating male prisoners sexually who suffered sexual repression under oppressive fascist rule. How could any woman truly committed to the sexual revolution allow herself to take part in that fascist sexual repression? It would be cruel and inhuman punishment to participate in depriving these men of sexual freedom when it could be provided. That's why it became a duty of these revolutionary women. And I rejected every bit of it as denigrating women.

With Jan, I focused 100 percent on not becoming involved in any form of sex, outside the sexuality that is present in the emotional life of loving another. This included my decision to refrain as best I could from having lustful thoughts about her, even though I was as sex-crazed as any other man in the range of normality. After all, I had committed to a hermit's life with ferocity, settling in to living in prison the rest of my days, a metal and cement dome of mind providing a peaceful containment inside interior landscapes that are endless and never boring, what monks everywhere no doubt become joyfully accustomed to.

At first, I had totally adapted to it as the punishment I deserved. It was a hell I was destined to arrive in. I didn't fight it, and then realized it was actually the best heaven I could possibly be in. Like a monk who leaves a violent, wretched life and gratefully embraces the monastic cell he is assigned to for the rest of his days, once I accepted Trenton as my permanent home, no restraint stopped me from contemplating the higher things, within and outside religious thought. I could travel anywhere, with no journey/adventure being dictated by external demands. Endless books led me into realms of truth that resonated with what I had witnessed in life. But later I understood that I chose that life, in the depths of my being, based on my empathic conclusions about the world outside.

With Jan during the many hours of preparing our first showcase inside ever-deepening affection, I fell all the way in; and the irony is that through it, something beautiful, even magical began to unfold, something that I could never have imagined. One night at workshop, Jan and I took an extended personal break together off in a corner, sitting in schoolroom chairs with attached little tabletops. We traveled all the way in, the classroom disappearing, and at one point either Jan or I placed the tip of an index finger on top of the tip of the other's index finger, and as those fingers rested there, a magnificent flow of libido energy began to flow at rapid speed throughout my body, yet never finding a concentration at the genitals, no conquering, no proving anything, no providing needs fulfillment, sexual or otherwise, and thus no hell of reciprocity present in the Fair Exchange Act of consumer culture. It was an unrehearsed, unprepared gifting of each to the other in a constant flow, being totally open to each other in love and trust, united inside a libido out of control, a roller-coaster ride: relentless sexual energy equally distributed throughout every molecule of my body, an experience I would never trade for an orgasm. For in that rabid, directionless energy, I experienced Jan and I becoming the biblical one flesh. And when I returned to my cell, my speculations went wild.

I had been absorbing all of what Marx and Freud had to say, but the first flaw I detected was a result of my encounter with Jan. The sexual revolution was ontologically powered by their notions of libido. Their principal claim was that all neuroses, psychosis, and other psychological maladjustments, including forms of hysteria found only in women, were caused by sexual repression. Later the cause would be correctly attributed to the existential repression of women's true identities, connecting with the unique missions they are called to, and the gifts they possess to be successful in those missions.

I came to understand this because I experienced libido truly freed, not culturally restricted to focusing on being fetishlike, groin-specific, nor on fulfilling a rabid desire to get one's sexual needs met inside the arena of a sexual circus that most often ends in disappointment. Instead, it was allowing the libido to move freely through all the affection centers, which then grew strong and made possible a complete union capable of influencing the larger culture to true communion, the micro to the macro via deeper affections for one another, never the reverse, for macro imposing on micro only breeds cruel, bitter bureaucracies.

I learned through experience the body will adapt to the decision not to live in lust, deepening one's bond with the other through deepening the affectional life, with the assistance of libido freed from a primary focus on genitals. Then when genital orgasms occur, they will be an outgrowth of an affectional life, a gestalt union, not confined within a sadomasochistic factory where the man and woman work on an assembly line providing sexual titillations, always leading to disappointment, and usually to divorce.

I was lying on my cot one late evening soon after, totally absorbed in thinking about Jan and our life together in the commune once I was released. Then a vision appeared of us walking down the beach, relaxed in the presence of each other, a relaxation in love I had never known—not permitted in the coil position that I usually adopted. There was nothing to say, just relaxing in love. It turned out Jan was walking down the beach near the house during the exact time I had my vision.

During our first showcase performance of skits and poetry, I had the confidence to be present onstage but not to speak. Kuwasi had come up with a skit about a shooter randomly killing people walking down the sidewalk. I asked him if I could be one of the victims, to which he agreed. He understood I didn't want to speak. I chose to stand at a bus stop, holding an armful of books all the way up to my chin. When rifle fire shots were heard (created by Doc, Richard's boyfriend, with an electric guitar), I stood rigid and let one book fall at a time, until all the books hit the ground, and then I fell to the ground. We got a loud ovation for that scene.

My idea for this involved my new life after dying to the world, a world of literature and exploration into my endless tortured path that brought me to the worst prison in America. Like a dedicated reader of the *National Enquirer*, I simply wanted to know all of it, and who needs Satan to provide this knowledge when one has a lifetime of exploring anything one chooses to explore?

JAN: *I'm all for sexuality that is not centered only in the groin, but I am still a fan of sexuality. Did being a child prostitute ruin the possibility of sex as a joyous, free experience for Finn? Did his crime require that he not have too much pleasure? I sense now that he equated deep affection with love, whereas sex had, in his experience, been horribly coercive and without affection. I don't doubt that his analysis of his actions was his truth; but what was mine? Might we ever have reached the point when we could have had both deep affection and sex?*

FINN: After the success of the first show with skits and poetry readings, Richard announced, "We did great, and we are now ready to move on to a major production, exploring the one thing all of us here share, a radical sense of justice, always sensitive to injustice when it rears its ugly head. I have learned about most of it through history and political theory, but all of you have learned it from experience. In fact, you are living it now, which positions you as vanguards for the revolution to bring about true justice for all, a good life not just for those in power basking in wealth. I chose a book we can adapt to the stage, exploring the phenomenon of bureaucratic injustice better than anything else I've come across. It's Franz Kafka's *The Trial*.

"The novel is about a bank clerk, Joseph K., whom the court has charged with a crime and is certain of it before Joseph K. is even charged, the court not caring to engage in any reflection on the matter. No crime is ever officially named, pointing to what goes on in our judicial system. Anyone who appears before the court is guilty of anything they choose to name. That's the nature of America's criminal justice system: Everyone charged is guilty, that bogus refrain "innocent until proven guilty" giving Kafka a good chuckle in his casket.

"Josef K. is the central character. The court and its administrators work out an understanding of his guilt inside the snail-like pace of its bureaucracy. The court trials are all for show, engineered to reassure everyone that although justice is no longer available, we still have proceedings to go through the motions.

"We know absurdity exists as ground throughout the criminal justice system in America. There is no real justice. The entire system is based on a patriarchal hegemony dating back thousands of years. Leaders only saw the suffering masses as ignorant servants or slaves, convinced these lowly ones were genetically programmed to live in sloth, with no appetite for intellectual advancement. They accuse all of you of being criminals as a means of locking you away in prisons to exploit your labor. They are responsible for generating the conditions in impoverished cities that force kids to find mentors in the criminal world that they grow up in, that forms their surface personality, masks, and ambitions, having no option but to become criminals and end up working in prison factories.

"What we're doing here is waking prisoners up to all this, and once free from those mental chains, they can turn their justified anger in the right direction—no longer against themselves, their families, and their neighbors, but against the Man, the patriarchs who for centuries in America locked the impoverished into a prison service industry. Prisoners will see the time has come to redirect their energy into overthrowing the patriarchs and bring about justice for all. At that point, we'll have no need for prisons."

Richard pulled out copies of Kafka's *The Trial* for everyone and continued.

"As familiar as all this is in a boring sense, it is a strange landscape nonetheless. One can't escape the feeling of being suffocated by a system that is one big prison with endless tiers and cells where one is forced to consult with bureaucrats in seeking a way out, only to discover these professionals could care less about you. Those people outside prison who read Kafka's works feel they are in unfamiliar territory, too, in all its familiarity—no one gets away. It's not about the surface but how we, absent power and a voice, respond internally to systems of oppression that have us on a treadmill going nowhere, at all kinds of speeds, to escape ourselves as the only way to escape a system of oppression, usually in criminal drug use—precisely how the oppressed end up in prison.

"That's the patriarchal matrix of our culture rotting away in absurdity. We must prepare for the day of its utter collapse, when we will renew revolutionary awareness that there can be no standing still. For the revolution is permanent, progressive, as long as it stays active and never succumbs to bourgeois containment. Only the sexual revolution is capable of breaking out of the suffocating dungeon of repression the nuclear family insists on, the last stronghold, the cornerstone of patriarchal oppression.

"What I want everyone to do is read the book at a comfortable pace. It's going to take time to build this production, and I don't want you speed-reading the book like an assignment. *Listen* for any response that is paralleling an experience from your past. Then make a note of that experience, and when we get together, we can start improvising with those scenes, following familiar threads to construct a narrative reflecting the oppression of prison life and how that connects to Kafka's story, which is evidence of its universality."

When we prisoners started to leave, Richard called to me.

"Finn—can I talk with you a minute?"

"Sure."

"I was thinking about the best way to integrate personal experience with the scenes in the novel in the structuring of the play. I've read your writing and think you could help with that."

"If you mean taking notes during the improvisations and linking it to the Kafka narrative, I could do that."

"That's exactly what I mean, and thanks for offering!"

It was an epic event in my life, something that rarely arrives. I had been purchasing prison-related literature and blindly purchased a book of collected stories titled *In the Penal Colony*, by Franz Kafka. I had inadvertently walked into a landscape of mind that went deep beyond my imagining, but I caught the drift and pushed forward. I was rewarded in reading another Kafka story, "A Hunger Artist," experiencing a recognition that our tortured lives, whether chosen as exhibits on the world stage or something we loop around in unconsciously, can have meaning in artistic expression, and acting is primary for everyone.

In other words, when all else fails, even when camping out in a death wish, the creative spirit can conquer. (Think how Sylvia Plath played with Death to keep her at bay.) It's spiritual warfare of the highest order, what Kafka, Proust, and Dostoevsky exhibited with brilliance. It harmonized perfectly with my situation in a prison cell, just like the Hunger Artist in his little cell. I realized when a guard or anyone walked past my cell, passed me in the mess hall, in the yard, or when I was sent to a hearing, that sense that I was in a movie and playing the role of a hardened criminal was always there. Forty-three days in the hole and hunger strikes came easy as long as I was in performance mode.

It was all theater. It was the same on the streets as a teen, selling prostitutes who didn't exist and other adrenaline-soaked scams, petty thefts, and getting arrested to perform in another play. It was all theater, from beginning to end.

I had entered Kafka land, never to leave. And here was Richard, telling all of us that we would be entering Kafka land for our major production. It could go on forever, continuing on the outside when Jan and I, in a creative commune, entered our Paradise. It was one of those cosmic intervention moments where the sense is that all is in order, what I would later understand as an affirmation of destiny.

From day one, I saw in Richard a soft-spoken, slow in his motions kind of man, not setting out to dominate anyone, but simply to gently lead us all into fulfilling what he had envisioned. While always generous in working with us, he did seem to enjoy standing when he had something relatively profound to relate to us, a singular desire for self-ascendancy becoming visible, Napoléon with a wide, gentle smile. I saw him as beautiful, good, and true, and also saw his egocentric pursuit of power, making his claim in the world and a permanent place in history.

I had picked up on Richard's solipsism from day one, but so what? We live in a solipsistic culture, surpassing its narcissism to ascend the heights, reaching for the status of überman or überwoman, becoming radically autonomous, the principle that destroys communion in every instance but dominates as a working principle in this postmodern age grounded in nihilism. I saw him as just one more victim. He truly did have good intentions for us, and I went with that.

My ire against Richard only ignited after he tried to convince me to engage with Jan sexually, knowing I had never engaged in sex with women or men. (I don't count my child prostitution as sexual engagement on any level, as popular hebephile literary artists like Ginsberg and Burroughs kept insisting about us.) I experienced a tinge of rage at his effort to fit me into his sexual revolution vision, into a role he had designed for me.

This rage that lurked in my soul after that encounter with Richard only plunged me into reflecting how he, Jan, Kareem, Kuwasi, and others engaged in sexual relationships saw me as sexually repressed. It was easy for them to see me as some type of lunatic turning down sex in prison when it was freely available, no doubt suspecting my rabid Catholic upbringing had a role in this. I took all of this seriously, for freedom in every context was my obsession, and if my being sexually liberated in the manner Richard was prescribing was necessary for freedom and I was resisting it, it was easy for all to see my reasons as a cover for my sexual repression. That's what I was being told by those who really cared.

I signed up for counseling with a four-foot-three Indian psychologist with a huge Afro combed backward, looking like he was always running at a hundred miles an hour. He had been trained in India, worked in London for five years, and came to work in Trenton to catch the wave of prison reform going around. After some months in therapy, I asked him outright if he saw me as sexually repressed.

"Why would you say that?"

"Look at my life. Ever since the onset of puberty, I had lots of opportunities to get sex, but I turned them down every time. I would always see in the girls' faces a desperation and possibly a terror about the territory we were about to enter. I was a criminal on the run, with stacks of warrants out for my arrest, and had no idea of how to find a way to settle down with a woman I might fall in love with, absent which I would always be putting her in danger. If I were arrested and put in prison, she would be abandoned for my own selfish pursuits, and so I'd always exit the situation."

"Where I'm from we consider that thinking and behavior honorable. Besides, I've gone over all your psychiatric history, and I'm certain not you or anyone in your family are sexually repressed. Your problems are obviously existential, not sexual."

With that news, I ended therapy. And when leaving on that last visit, Kamal reached into a lower desk drawer and pulled out a stack of papers.

"When you started therapy, I asked you to type out as much as you could about your past and present, and this is the collection. Just wanted to return it to you."

"Just chuck it. I have no use for it."

"Well, let me ask you: Is what you wrote here all true, or did you make it up?"

"All true. Every bit of it."

JAN: Richard's cajoling Finn to have sex with me was yet something else I didn't know at the time. I didn't perceive Richard as a controlling kind of guy, so why would I have suspected that? More troubling is that Finn didn't tell me for fifty years. And in fact, I was not having sex with anyone in or outside of the workshop at the time.

JAN: "Someone must have been telling lies about Josef K., he knew he had done nothing wrong, but, one morning, he was arrested." And so Joseph K. spends the rest of the book going from one office to another, encountering one person after another, even a laundress whose appearance erases the line between the world of government offices and domesticity. He's in a nightmarish landscape, trying futilely to find what he is charged with and get out of the absurd predicament.

Richard got a few things right—not only was this text a great vehicle for a story we in the workshop wanted to tell but its power would rely on integrating our personal experiences into Kafka's vision. Richard had mostly done productions of plays written as dramatic lit or stories adapted into dramatic form, but not with the actors adding to the narrative from their lives. He somehow must have known that we couldn't do this play without the participants' stories, a practice that took the alternative theater world by storm a decade later.

The next week, having read the book, Kuwasi said, "How about if in our version, Josef K. is a sociologist, and he comes to the prison to get a job? An assistant warden interviews him and then tells him, 'Okay, the next part of the process is simulated treatment; we lock you up in a cell so you can feel what it's like.' Then the assistant warden goes on vacation. Meanwhile, Josef K. wonders why they are keeping him locked up so long. He calls a guard and says, 'Hey, I don't belong here!' The guard says, 'That's what they all say.' Josef K. says, 'No, I mean I really *don't* belong here'—but the guard has already left. And like in the book, he spends the rest of the story trying to get out."

Kuwasi was chuckling as he described the scene, and the rest of us were right there with him. Finn added, "But everyone he goes to is there to keep the system going. That's their bread and butter. And they must have people to feed the beast."

"Yeah," said Kuwasi. "It's a hellified thing."

The room went quiet.

"We gotta have a preacher, a jailhouse preacher," said Winston. "Who always tries to get you to their meetings and shit."

"And a psych," said Finn.

"And arrogant, power-hungry guards," added Kareem.

So that's what we did. Finn outlined the scenes and we all improvised, adding the character types we each wanted to play, wanted to expose, and the part of our own story to which we wanted people to bear witness. Finn saw *The Trial* as an entrance into actually performing onstage and speaking, the result of which he believed would determine if he would be able to function as an actor in a theater community.

Kuwasi played a guard. "Wolf-Gang, Wolf-Gang, Wolf Gang-Green!" he would howl when announcing himself; you could almost catch the scent of rot. Kareem played Captain Beefheart, representing a cadre of sadistic officers—"White Hats," they were called—who loved to lord it over the inmates. Kareem got particular pleasure in giving his character an itchy butt.

We added a prologue, outside the story proper, to set up that the story was as relevant now as it had been in 1914, when Kafka wrote it. In it, I played the sister of a guy who'd been unfairly imprisoned and who had gotten nowhere in proving his innocence. Now she had come to the warden to plead his case again. I wanted to play someone on the outside who loved someone who was locked up and would do anything to help free him. In another scene I played a sadistic nurse, which deepened my understanding of the abuses of power common among the professional class, of which I was a part.

The next scene was the job interview between Josef K. and the assistant warden, and from there, the whole play unfolded. After the play proper, we returned to the sister leaving the warden's office, her clothes askew, making it clear that she had traded sex for what she hoped would be justice, but it didn't look good.

It was uncanny to have found in Trenton, New Jersey, this group of people motivated to make theater for an audience that so-called political theater makers yearned for—spectators actually in the situation that their peers were enacting. Not in Manhattan, not with some famous director, nor a well-trained group of actors who'd all gone to some university program together, but somehow our ragtag collection of people whose paths crossed, there, and who made a space where we all wanted to tell something that we suffered over, related to injustice, and found a way to tell it together through Kafka.

When time came to perform, the guys circulated a flyer that began: "ATTENTION COMRADES IN THE STRUGGLE. ON THURSDAY, AUGUST 2ND, SOME OF THE KAPTIVES IN THIS PRISON WILL PRESENT A PLAY—*THE TRIAL*." The flyer explained that false rumors had spread when we did

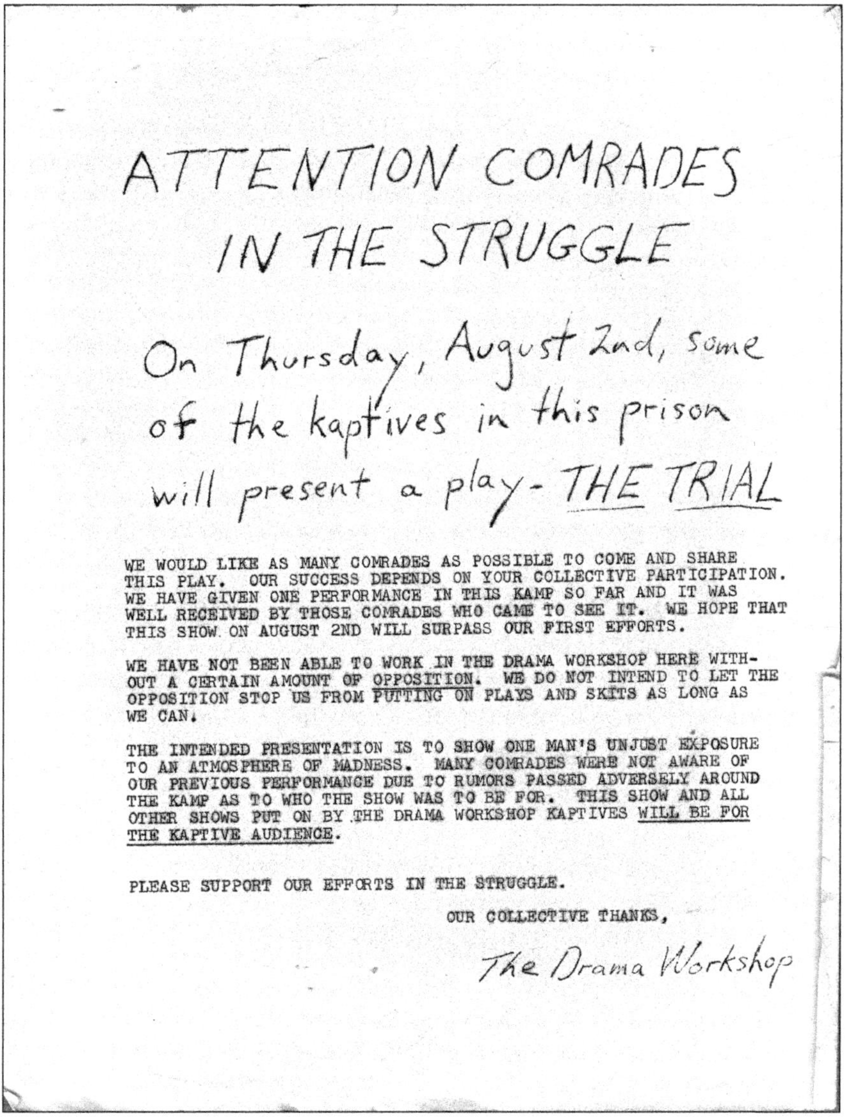

ATTENTION COMRADES IN THE STRUGGLE

On Thursday, August 2nd, some of the kaptives in this prison will present a play - THE TRIAL

WE WOULD LIKE AS MANY COMRADES AS POSSIBLE TO COME AND SHARE THIS PLAY. OUR SUCCESS DEPENDS ON YOUR COLLECTIVE PARTICIPATION. WE HAVE GIVEN ONE PERFORMANCE IN THIS KAMP SO FAR AND IT WAS WELL RECEIVED BY THOSE COMRADES WHO CAME TO SEE IT. WE HOPE THAT THIS SHOW ON AUGUST 2ND WILL SURPASS OUR FIRST EFFORTS.

WE HAVE NOT BEEN ABLE TO WORK IN THE DRAMA WORKSHOP HERE WITH-OUT A CERTAIN AMOUNT OF OPPOSITION. WE DO NOT INTEND TO LET THE OPPOSITION STOP US FROM PUTTING ON PLAYS AND SKITS AS LONG AS WE CAN.

THE INTENDED PRESENTATION IS TO SHOW ONE MAN'S UNJUST EXPOSURE TO AN ATMOSPHERE OF MADNESS. MANY COMRADES WERE NOT AWARE OF OUR PREVIOUS PERFORMANCE DUE TO RUMORS PASSED ADVERSELY AROUND THE KAMP AS TO WHO THE SHOW WAS TO BE FOR. THIS SHOW AND ALL OTHER SHOWS PUT ON BY THE DRAMA WORKSHOP KAPTIVES WILL BE FOR THE KAPTIVE AUDIENCE.

PLEASE SUPPORT OUR EFFORTS IN THE STRUGGLE.

OUR COLLECTIVE THANKS,

The Drama Workshop

Figure 5.1. Flyer announcing performance of *The Trial*, Trenton State Prison, 1972. Created by workshop members.

our first show as to who it was for, and stated clearly that all our shows were and would continue to be *"for the kaptive audience."* It alluded to opposition we'd encountered in the workshop and asked for the population's support. It ended, "OUR COLLECTIVE THANKS, THE DRAMA WORKSHOP." I knew nothing about the rumors the flyer referred to but had sensed the guards' attitude that the workshop was too much fun. Did other inmates see it as a reward? For what? I hoped the flyer would quell any doubts anyone had about us.

FINN: The night we performed *The Trial*, I saw clearly how Richard would sacrifice Jan and anyone else. It was etched in his face when he confronted a guard who went to complain about us as we were setting up. Richard was excited about the possibility of a riot, and purposely naïve.

I immediately told Jan the danger of a confrontation with some of the guards that could get violent. She looked at me with concerned, sympathetic disbelief about what I was saying. Then I had this thought that Kuwasi might use a riot to escape (I would if escaping was my penchant, and it certainly was Kuwasi's; a riot would be a gift for his intentions). It would be a perfect opportunity, so saving Richard or anyone else from the outside in a riot would not be his first concern. I see my apprehension as valid then as now, no mistaking it. I remain an extreme empath, another reason I'm alone, and that's not a lament. It's my destiny.

JAN: Our performance of *The Trial* did not set off a riot; on the contrary. Not only did we get no substantive pushback from guards, but I felt the tension of the prison audience release as we performed and was gratified to hear much laughter—that of recognition. Seeing experiences that the spectators knew to be true enacted on that stage did not make audience members angrier; it affirmed them. They did not need us, despite Richard's rhetoric, to show them the truth of incarceration; they knew it very well. Our contribution was to reflect it back to them in a room where we witnessed it all together. We knew that everyone else knew this, and that included the guards as well as the inmates. What anyone does with what he knows, if anything, is a next step.

I recently asked Finn why he thought the show might have led to a riot. He said he didn't mean the audience would have risen up but, rather, that by provoking the guard, Richard might have been setting him up to make sure something happened to punish us for being there in the first place. But that didn't happen, either. The show was a true testament to the power of theater that is by, of, for, and about its intended audience, and we all felt high for weeks.

6

The Year of Living Way Too Dangerously

JAN: In 1972, my individual passions aligned with my collective ideals and my actual life to a degree that I had not experienced before, nor have since, in one concentrated year: the street theater company, the prison workshop, the collective house, the effort to be part of progressive activist politics, Finn and my love, and soon the experience of loving multiple people simultaneously. For my intense feelings for Finn spilled over to a mutual attraction with another workshop participant and with Finn's sister Lee.

A few years later, I found an explanation for my state when I read Vivian Gornick's *The Romance of American Communism,* which traces the idea of all-consuming passion back to the ancient Greeks. They defined sexual passion, in which I include love that is all-consuming, whether sexual or not, like mine and Finn's, "as a disease: something that strikes from without and touches a source of human need so deep, so hungering that the rational and humane faculties are rendered helpless before the mad, distorting behavior that follows . . ." (Gornick, 1978, 3).

Gornick acknowledges several stable human hungers that can flare into passion "once brought to expressive life." One is the need, "not of the flesh but of the spirit," for a life of meaning. She writes, " [I]t is possible to live an entire lifetime without encountering the people, ideas, or events that will trigger into conscious life this primeval hunger. But once met [. . .] For the law of passion is such that it is all; and when a thing becomes all, people do terrible things to themselves and to one another." (3)

What became "all" for me was the drama workshop, the perception of the United States as a gravely unjust society, and Finn. In some cases, I only almost did terrible things. Kuwasi asked me to transport weapons across state lines to Georgia—for "the revolution," of course. Luckily, I told Finn, who talked me out of it, explaining that it was a federal offense that would have definitely landed me in prison. It's not that I was impervious to the risk. Rather, that kind of passion is powerful because it makes the immediate moment so all-encompassing that nothing else matters. Since Finn was ever present to me, he could get through.

Then there was his sister Lee. I met her on a day I happened to go to Trenton for a visit, when she also stood up when Finn's name was called. She was tall, with long black hair and ever-changing blue eyes–dark, clear, cloudy, incisive. I quickly found out that both Finn and Lee had gotten calls that morning that their mother, who was in a downward spiral in California, had purposely walked onto a busy highway, been hit by a car, and killed. Lee lived in New York City, and after the visit I drove her back, making two stops along the way for her to borrow money to attend the memorial.

FINN: Through my years in reformatories and prison, I had never put anyone on my visiting list. I reasoned I was the one who got me there, and I wouldn't burden anyone with the results of my decision. And I just couldn't bear the anguish I would see in their faces. So I was more than surprised when I was called out for a visit through a one-square-foot bulletproof window with a phone, and Lee sitting on the other side. I thought it was Jan, because she was the only person who I expected to be visiting.

"Lee. What's going on?"

"You must know about Mom dying."

"Yeah."

"It's been rough. I'm really at a loss. Can't focus. I'm going to have to leave where I'm living, and I've got no place to go. I'll be homeless."

I knew she was looking for help and that she had burned all her bridges in using people to care for her. With Mom's death, she gave it a shot to visit me and see if I could help.

"I'm involved with a theater group, and the director bought a home by the beach with lots of bedrooms. I can ask if they can help, at least temporarily."

"That would be great."

That was one of the biggest mistakes of my life. I hadn't communicated with Lee in many years. And now, looking at her face, I could clearly see her abandonment to a life absent love in any form. It doesn't get more tragic than that. It was in my utter heartbrokenness for Lee that I gave her the phone number of the house. And the next thing I saw was Jan and Lee on a window visit. Lee was solidly situated in the house, not taking long to get there. What

I didn't know was how violently manipulative she had become, seeking the only escape she knew from her utter emptiness: pain relief, and the drug she chose was alcohol.

I began to see Lee through a new lens after having a serious nervous breakdown following our Mom's death. I was literally living inside a multitiered hallucination, my unconscious thoughts running amok in consciousness, which I concealed from those around me. I perceived at least six different possibilities of what was true in any second, each seeming to have equal significance, rendering me speechless.

JAN: Over time, Lee made frequent visits to the street theater house. Our closeness grew quickly as together we made food packages to take to Finn and did whatever else we could in support. She soon moved in.

Meanwhile, Finn had befriended Harold Jane, a jailhouse lawyer. The two of them were focused on Finn's friend Lennie, whose sentence was about to end but who'd been slapped with a new charge that they were trying to get dismissed out of court on the basis of "irreparable mistaken identification." According to a precedent that Jane had researched, it meant that Lennie had been denied due process. To exacerbate matters, Lennie was seriously ill, and Finn feared that he would die in prison.

FINN: I had a friend, Lennie, who I trusted more than anyone else inside, a Black man right out of a gangster novel. Lennie had the appearance of a Black Mr. Clean with his muscular frame and shining bald head. He was the only prisoner I knew who was committed 100 percent to the convict code seen in forties gangster films, with solid principles and a steadfast ideal: Be no man's servant, never stool, and never hurt the innocent—if at all possible. He was the James Cagney character in *Angels with Dirty Faces,* pure evil for many, but possessing a courageous, loving heart he kept well hidden. Lennie was in an advanced stage of sarcoidosis and would certainly die in prison if convicted on an armed robbery he didn't do, for it would be his third strike, meaning life without parole.

JAN: Lee and I found a lefty lawyer on the outside who agreed to help us pro bono, using Jane's research and instructing us on next steps. I strongly felt that Lee's striking good looks played a part in his willingness. Lee and I contacted coworkers who knew that Lennie had not been at the crime scene and would attest to it, remembering him at work at the time the crime occurred.

So when the lawyer casually asked us, like an afterthought, "By the way, did Lennie do it?" I was shocked.

"Of course he didn't do it," I replied, flummoxed. "Why would we be fighting the charge if he did it?"

He said, "Don't worry, I'm going to defend him either way. It just helps to know. But I'm a lawyer—my job, no matter what, is to prove my client's innocence."

I was horrified. His job was not to search for justice? To get to the truth of what happened and prove it, reveal the bias, get to the facts?

It was great doing the legal work with Lee. We were both tireless and utterly committed. We more than once put aside a personal disagreement so we could appear as a united front with a lawyer or potential witness. Though Richard was sympathetic, he was busy with his own activities and did not offer much concrete support. Lee, in fact, became a partner. I was fascinated with her perspective on the different issues that came up, having grown up in the same family as Finn but then somehow going on to college.

My love for Finn extended to my relationship with Lee. It was great learning that I could be drawn to particular people, regardless of sexual categories. I was deeply attracted—intellectually, emotionally, and physically—to Finn *and* Lee.

Lee had a way of describing people who seemed to embrace an ideal but then interpreted what came down in a way that undermined it—she said they had the "right experience, wrong conclusion." For example, Kate, a friend whom I had brought into the workshop, fell in love with one of the overtly political inmates, Hakim. They were the exact same color—what we called olive-skinned—but he identified as Black and she as white, and they had lived their lives that way. They were emotionally, politically, and intellectually compatible, but after some months, because she was "white," he ended the relationship. I believe that for him, loving a nominally white woman was at odds with his core identity as a Black political prisoner.

There was a derogatory expression at the time, "vanilla fever," referring to a Black person who was attracted to a white person, suggesting it was an illness; that Black people ought to give their attention to "their own." Was how fellow Black radicals saw Hakim more important to him than the discovery that he could truly love a white woman? Kate accepted the breakup as politically necessary and that was the end of it. But I felt it was an example of "right experience"—love initially undeterred by racial difference—"wrong conclusion"—that the political exigency to "support one's own" meant a personally loving cross-racial relationship must be squelched.

I was having the right experience and making the wrong conclusion with Lee. I recently ran across an old journal entry about the instability of our relationship. I went on to write, "But how could I leave when I have so much to learn from her? Her actions come out of her freedom from social norms." The prison had turned my world on its head, making me question every norm I'd grown up with. Right experience. But taking care of Lee, as I was increasingly doing, because I had had a more privileged upbringing, was the wrong conclusion.

I eventually learned that she had been the favorite child in the household, which caused its own kind of suffering and which she tried to escape by finding a well-to-do family to take her in while she was still in high school. It took me longer to recognize her manipulation, which I believe grew out of her neediness, like the times she tried to keep me from visiting Finn, feigning chronic back pain and other ailments to keep me with her at the house.

I was also caught up in the spirit of the times. The women's movement was in full swing, challenging norms of gender behavior. I was uncertain how to express my own feminism and unsure how far to take political action in a world with so much injustice. My political confusion was epitomized in my mixed feelings about the kidnapping of Patty Hearst, the heiress to a newspaper fortune, by a group of people calling themselves the Symbionese Liberation Army (SLA). They were women and men, Blacks and whites, and anarchists and extremists from various walks of life who wanted to incite guerrilla war against the U.S. government and destroy the "capitalist state."

Kept in a closet and inculcated with radical ideas, Hearst befriended her kidnappers. Some months after her capture, an image of her wielding an assault weapon as part of a San Francisco bank robbery was widely publicized. The next day, she released a taped eulogy for several SLA members who died in a shoot-out with police in Los Angeles. She

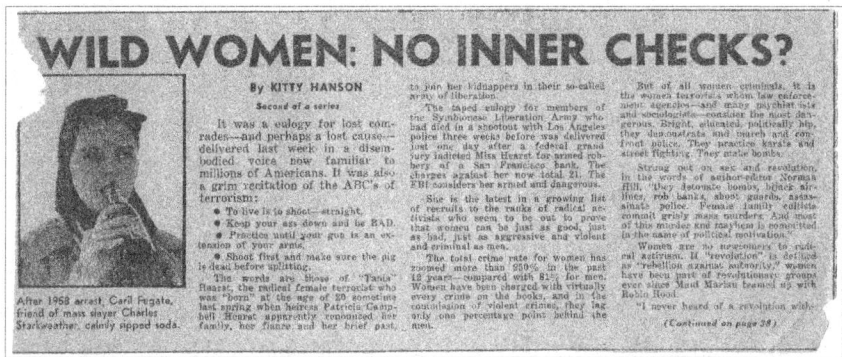

Figure 6.1. "Wild Women: No Inner Checks?" Newspaper article by Kitty Hanson, circa 1973. (details unknown).

had ostensibly renounced her family, fortune, fiancé, and past life to join the SLA, which she had come to believe was indeed an army of liberation. She served twenty-two months of a seven-year sentence before President Carter pardoned her. I still have an article about Hearst from back then entitled "Wild Women: No Inner Checks?" It was sensationalist, lumping women involved in a range of justice-seeking organizations into one category, albeit the SLA's methods were misguided and also harmed people who were not their enemies.

It seems painfully naïve now, but I truly did not see how physically expressing love for Lee could be hurtful to Finn, or how she might feel jealous of him. Neither of them had let me into the complexities of their relationship, given their family history, in which she was raised to believe everything should be hers and not her siblings'.

FINN: I was still adrift in the nervous breakdown in response to my mother's suicide, in a newly discovered dimension of Dante's Hell. I was lost in endless inner space with no borders, intersecting nightmares, an inability to get stable inside any thought, idea, or purpose, with the avalanche of information from the Abyss crashing into my mind every second. I was possessed by a fear of total disintegration inside and outside the wilderness of my mind, with no visible marker for a safe return, no lifeboat to travel anywhere other than to Kierkegaard's 70,000 fathoms to drown in the Abyss, with not a thread of hope of being reborn into who I truly was outside my fear-based imaginings.

It was then that I executed a major assault on the communal ideal. At that time, a workshop member's girlfriend was staying at the house, and she had a connection for China White, the purest form of heroin on the market. She agreed to purchase the heroin so I could sell it to cover our ongoing expenses on Lennie's case.

I went blindly in and arranged for Jan and other workshop members to be involved in smuggling the high-grade heroin into prison. It would mean more time in prison than if busted for smuggling guns across state lines, which I had objected to with moral insistence when Kuwasi had approached Jan. I was now even worse. A Dylan refrain kept piercing my brain, "You see, you're just like me."

This signified I was already preconsciously stepping away from the workshop ideal and into my own subjective pursuits, as I perceived others doing inside the prescribed behavior and language of sexual revolution mandates—a worldview I could not abide—which is no excuse. For it is undeniable that the heroin escapade was a major assault on the drama workshop that could have easily destroyed it in an instant, an immoral act of the highest order.

JAN: The possibility of Lennie dying in Trenton ate at Finn. Though Harold Jane and Finn were doing background work from the inside, and Lee and I were doing footwork, there were still plenty of expenses, with documents to obtain and filings to be done. Our pro bono lawyer signed off on documents but did not cover our material expenses. The way that Finn knew how to make a chunk of money fast was by selling drugs, which at the time, he could do in prison.

During a private moment in workshop one day, Finn said to me, "We've got a way to get the money for Lennie's case, but you'd have to do something that I don't really want you to do. And you don't have to—we could think of another way." He looked ill and spoke low.

"What is it?"

"There's a guy who could meet you at the train station in Trenton. He'd give you a package. You'd bring it in and pass it to me on a contact visit."

"Don't they check you pretty carefully at the end of those visits?"

"Yeah, but there are ways around it."

I was all in.

I barely knew Lennie; Finn had arranged for us to meet once on a window visit, but he was not part of the workshop. My willingness to go out on a limb for him was a way to fight what I saw as the system's injustice—the success rate for defendants with paid attorneys far exceeded the rate for those with court-appointed counsel. Plus, Lennie was Finn's close friend. What better assessment of character did I need? And I wasn't willing to compromise my commitment to Finn in any way. The answer to anything he asked of me, which was extremely rare, was yes. I said yes to this, too.

That was the moment I crossed over. I had come to understand that people in prison are usually there because of circumstances so impossible to remedy legally that they do what they have to do illegally. This is not to justify such acts but to say how I came to believe that any of us might have ended up in prison, given the circumstances that our lives presented us with. I nearly did.

FINN: After I had settled into seeing my future with Jan and the theater community by the beach, Harold Jane agreed to work on my case, which was riddled with constitutional violations, including an arrest with no cause, no search warrant, and kidnapping. Just as he was ready to take the final step toward securing my release, he told me he wanted to engage in sex before he did that last filing. So I dropped the case. That was the first major sign that my life was about to fall apart. The second sign was Lee's growing involvement in my life, and Jan's.

I started to see what I had done, unleashing Lee's unfathomable propensity toward destroying everything around her out of jealousy (convinced she should be receiving *everything*, including Jan). I realized I had cowardly committed a horrible act against Jan when I succumbed to Lee's manipulation.

What got me most, and drove me into endless guilt, is how I would plead with Jan to help Lee, honestly seeing it as Lee's only hope in life—finding a creative way out of the family hell by committing to writing her poetry, the best and only way out for her. The house could provide space for her to do that. Jan was smart but young and naïve. She became a victim inside our familial nightmare. Many years later, in her forties, long after Jan had freed herself from Lee, Lee finally destroyed herself when, like mom at that age, she committed suicide.

JAN: When Finn shared with me in 2022 that he'd had a nervous breakdown after his mother died, I felt terrible that I hadn't known it at the time. Did he hide it so well? Did we see each other for such relatively short time slots that I had not recognized his distress? Was the depth of understanding between us more limited than I realized? Was his habit of solitude that impenetrable, with the closeness we had experienced up to that moment the extent to which he could let down his guard? Only seeing each other in such contained periods, we could control what we shared of ourselves, unlike relationships in the messy outside world. I doubt that I looked closely enough at his pain at his mother's suspected suicide, having no clue of how to help him handle it.

JAN: The boundless love I felt that year, released through my relationship with Finn, extended to another workshop member, Kareem (expressed sensually, never sexually). I only later thought about the fact that Kareem, Finn, and Lee had not had the same desire to enter into multiple amorous relationships as I did. So the same beautiful love that was motivating Finn to want to get out of prison, and the two of us to live together as part of an alternative, beloved community, was also generating jealousy and pain. This was complicated by Finn's and my commitment to an abstract idea of "freedom." Wanting me to be "free," Finn did not tell me what he, in fact, needed, which was threatened by the situation I created. I believed that Finn was glad Lee was part of our love.

FINN: The principles of the sexual revolution were now an ideal in the workshop, and I was totally outside that matrix, without Jan being aware of it. I had no confidence in what I was feeling, being so uncomfortable with most everything being promulgated, which is why I didn't discuss those feelings, a cowardly response.

Then one day, Jan arranged a meeting in a classroom with just her, Kareem, and me. She explained she had deep affection for Kareem and wanted a sensual relationship with him. She truly and rightly saw this as no problem in the context we were all living in and agreeing to, myself included, with the counterculture also in accord. So I couldn't make judgments. I just retreated into my coil position and began drifting away from what turned out to be a delusion. Not the love. That was real. It was just that the communal world that I had committed to was falling apart. I thought of a reflection I wrote down when workshop first began, titling it "Misquoted Fragment": "The whole world's a stage, and everyone is a principal actor as well as playwright and director, and, most especially, one's own editor."

Drifting away I began to hear that familiar call from Thanatos. (I'm in or out with life and death.) There was only myself to blame, my cowardliness. Now late in life I'm still amazed at a remarkable gift among many I got from the workshop: *losing all desire for heroin,* what had sustained me from age sixteen to twenty, always a blessing because it was the most potent force, removing from my nervous system the relentless view of suffering all around me and within. This loss of desire for heroin was not founded in fear; I had just found something better to addict myself to.

JAN: It's excruciating to see now that I was still flying high with the workshop and my fantasy of boundless love, while Finn was going deeper into the depression that began with his mother's death, which seemed certain to have been a suicide, and worsened as I embraced the sexual revolution and he perceived the workshop falling apart.

At least we got Lennie out. He was paroled to the care of his mother, who gratefully invited Lee and me to Christmas dinner. Lee and I got to the house, dressed in our holiday finest, at the designated time in the early afternoon, and rang the doorbell. No one answered. We must have eventually awakened Lennie's mom, because finally she came to the door in her bathrobe and apologized profusely, welcoming us in. But Lennie did not appear. His mom warmed up food and sat with us while the two of us ate, keeping up a steady stream of conversation. Lennie's stepfather stuck his head in to thank us, but we never saw Lennie or anyone else from his family, that day or ever.

Trying to pierce through the haze of all the years that have passed since, I see the almost predictable depression that follows the high of a great achievement, like postpartum depression. We had made The Trial, *a piece that really spoke for us, and our audience got it. And all within the confines of a maximum-security prison. Who would have known that all the limitations could provide a laserlike focus on our goals? However, with the workshop reconvening after that production, what now?*

An unfamiliar impatience pervaded the group. New people joined, which us old-timers acknowledged as good, but they also threw off the intimacy of our group dynamic. We never discussed how to integrate them into our work other than just welcoming them. At the same time, some longtime workshop members got antsy. We'd done the show, and the audience dug it, but so what? Nothing changed. We didn't have tools other than making plays; none of us had a vision of how we might build on that production. I've since learned things we could have tried. Pairs of guys could have facilitated workshops for other inmates. We could have made a play portraying an ideal environment for people who'd transgressed, what real rehabilitation could mean. We could have focused on the house as a post-incarceration reality. But we lacked leadership and never figured out how to move forward as a collective.

JAN: Hegel points out that something new is born in the collision of opposites—that's dialectics: thesis, antithesis, synthesis. Charlie Chaplin said that Hegel was the funniest philosopher because he couldn't conceive of a thing without its opposite. Nor could Chaplin, describing comedy as an idea going one way meeting an idea going another. He loved collisions of very pompous people brought down by their opposites, like the dowager who gets a scoop of ice cream right in the cleavage when a child eating it on a balcony above her accidentally drops it. Or when people read the same image two totally different ways, like Chaplin's Little Tramp picking up the red flag that falls off an extra-long truckload of lumber passing a factory just as the workers have stormed out in protest. They think that Chaplin's character, running to give the flag back to the truck driver, is the revolutionary leader, and follow him.

In our case, ideas going one way meeting ideas going another led to collapse. For example, one day Richard told the group that a prison administrator wanted a video made about the workshop as an example of rehabilitation. Some of the guys in the prison were firmly against what could look like "fun and games in Trenton State Prison" and would have none of it. That made perfect sense to me. The workshop at its best was a space where we could try to be the selves we aspired to, in the context of a collective ideal, not as pawns in someone's game or each of us only out for himself or herself. These two ideas of the workshop went in opposite directions and led to the terrible conclusion that we either had to preserve this space and be used or give it up—which may have been the only way to preserve it. At the same time, some of the prison old guard resented the diversity of our group, since "divide and conquer" was one of the ways they kept control.

Finn identified the workshop's undoing as our focusing on individual desires rather than upholding the collective ideal. For me, this is always an active struggle, not either/or. We were so young, the majority of workshop participants in our twenties, and didn't know how to balance individual and collective needs and desires, which even *trying* to do in our self-centered culture means swimming upstream.

To me, the workshop's undoing was the lack of vision to take it to the next level. Making theater together for ourselves and the inmate population continued to be meaningful. But absent a way to go further than making and presenting shows, jealousies festered, the perception that someone was getting more—attention, love, praise—than someone else. And finally, prison conditions are inhuman. After the high of the show, all the inmate participants returned to their cages. A couple of hours a week in the workshop couldn't balance out the wasted hours that prison conditions impose.

My multiple romantic relationships caused the undoing of my relationship with Finn. In the beginning, the conditions that the prison imposed had been weirdly conducive to our relationship, and to the workshop itself, making each moment together matter. Through our letter writing, I learned that the power and intimacy of words between two lovers can be far greater than I'd ever imagined, an invaluable lesson about the many forms that love takes. But finally it was not enough, given everything about our lives that brought us to that time and place and that followed.

One factor was that Finn was in prison for killing a man whom he later found out was innocent. He said that he'd seen that man's face every day since he did the deed. A therapist once told me that there are some things you cannot fully heal from, and killing someone is one. I wondered if she included the killing done in war. The man I eventually married had killed in Vietnam. I was troubled by the immorality of killing in a war being treated so differently from what Finn did. But my point is what it did to Finn to have taken that man's life. Though he never actually agreed with me that the act of killing a human being had caused him to terminate his right to certain pleasures in life, he never denied it, either.

Another factor was that Finn felt Lee's suffering as his own and therefore could not try to get her to back off from me. Plus, the pull of family is formidable, even if relationships have been tortuous. He could not both fully support Lee and allow himself to express his need for a monogamous relationship with me.

Then the administration canceled visits between inmates and people who worked in the prison, even if the prison didn't pay them, like Richard and me. We got grants to do the workshops, which covered expenses like travel, and, I later discovered, gave Richard a fee for service. But it didn't matter; we still worked there. The loss of contact visits with Finn twice a month put me through intense withdrawal. Contact visits took place in cells of what had been death row before capital punishment was abolished in New Jersey. Though in the summer we sweated, I remember the feel of those cells as icy-fingered. But it was worth it.

Finn and I talked about the choice we faced: I could either continue in the workshop or continue to make visits. It took us no time to opt for the workshop. That was what we needed more. But in fact, we lost both and suffered doubly. Because ironically, someone else's contact visit led me to be banned from the prison entirely.

The girlfriends of two of the guys in the workshop, one a woman who had never attended the workshop and the other someone who occasionally did, disguised their appearance in order to make a contact visit. It appeared to have worked without a hitch until a few days later, when I went to the prison for the workshop and was surrounded by eight guards and taken into a little room. I was terrified of what they were going to do to me. Guards had often leered at me as I came and went from the prison, and now in that little room I thought, *This is it.* But they did not touch me; they made an accusation.

"You disguised yourself as a Puerto Rican and made a contact visit this past Sunday!"

"That's absolutely ridiculous. And what does that even mean—disguised myself as a Puerto Rican? And if you thought I was there, why didn't you stop me on the spot? And who was I supposedly visiting? You've named someone I never even wrote a letter to or visited. And anyway, I was in Pennsylvania visiting my parents, whom you can contact for proof."

"As if your family wouldn't cover for you. You're done here!"

And I was never allowed to be part of the workshop again. Richard continued for a time, but things were pretty rocky with him by then. There was no sense of how to move the work forward, and the gap between the heights we'd reached and the repetitiveness of the same old theater exercises was untenable. Some of the guys wrote me that a drama workshop continued but that it lacked the vision and energy we all had brought to it. None of the core members stayed with it.

Then the collective house collapsed. Richard's boyfriend, Doc, did not like that I had any say in what Richard gave him and where the money came from—too often, I was sure, from the grants we got for the workshops or the street theater. One day at breakfast, Doc and I got into an argument about it and he came up behind me and hit me over the head with a cast-iron frying pan. That was the end of our collective living. Lee and I packed up our belongings.

My relationship with Richard also ended. Why was I, the person Doc had attacked, the one to leave, rather than Doc? Richard was totally exposed at that moment, sticking with Doc, who fulfilled his individual desires, rather than telling Doc such behavior was unacceptable. Why was there no collective process to decide how to move on from such a very low point? Richard and I never spoke again.

Finn and I continued to write to each other for a time, but the relationship suffered without an actual way to manifest the collective ideal that had brought us together. I didn't take in that he had already left, and because I couldn't let go, I couldn't believe we wouldn't find a way to continue our relationship. He looked for more and more direct ways to tell me. Finally he sent me these words, which struck hard: "If you want to torture me, just send me a letter containing a blank piece of paper." Just seeing my handwriting on the envelope and imagining what I had written was enough to send him into a maelstrom.

So I stopped.

That was before I realized that he had been withdrawing ever since I took up with Kareem and Lee and that he'd had a nervous breakdown as a result of his mother's probable suicide. That was before I knew that he saw the workshop as devolving into individual desires and neglecting the collective. That was before another woman had slipped into the picture, someone who could easily fit into the life he'd led before Trenton.

Lee and I needed a car to move our things back to New York City, so we borrowed Kate's. Kate also kept Lee's cat, Zelda, during the housing upheaval. Lee felt we still needed a car after the move and refused to return Kate's, as if our need somehow justified keeping it. I was convinced Lee was correct, that going back and forth to Trenton was a reason to take something that was not ours. Kate, rightly, wouldn't return Zelda until we gave her back her car. So we did. It's astonishing now to think how I could ever have thought we were justified in keeping—no, stealing—Kate's car. That incident ruined my friendship with Kate for good, a loss I continue to feel. I made several attempts over the years to resuscitate it, but without success.

I see in my journal that by late September 1972, I was pulling back from Lee, given her drinking, demands, and the derailing of the life I had been so fervently building. Finn was no longer in the picture, and she had been part of that whole, not someone I chose to be with one-on-one. Without the work on the court cases, I no longer felt we were traveling on the same path, and cut the relationship off for good.

FINN: I'd been camping out in the depths of hell ever since I found out that the man I killed was innocent. I assimilated to its conditions to the point I no longer feared a permanent place there (why I could live in a prison hole for the rest of my days), deciding the only imperative was to be honest at all times, to always tell the truth as one knew it, come hell or high water, whether right or wrong by the standards of truth delineated by the larger culture. I resolved to learn firsthand what Pinocchio learned, what made him a mythological hero for all time—letting his conscience, not the dictates of self-aggrandizement and pressures to conform to groupthink, determine a path to success in life—recalling as I often did Dylan's lyrics about failure as both a very particular kind of success and no success at all. The ultimate conundrum.

To live in truths one has personally witnessed and understood through conscience is the only ground to true freedom. Anyplace else is a living lie, for a life is determined at ground, what we call destiny, and most of the horrors of life have their origin in fighting our destinies, what we go to war against most. And there's the biblical promise that we would all at some point hear the unspoken truths hidden throughout history in inaccessible darkness and light, now shouted from rooftops. And it seems we have arrived. And I'm on board.

JAN: Now I wonder: Even if Lee had never entered the picture, and if I'd never taken up with Kareem, puncturing Finn's dream of one man and one woman in a perfect union, could Finn have let himself be with me on the outside? Could he have put down the weight of having taken a person's life? And if not, could I have lived with that heaviness? At some point, wouldn't his sense of truth have conflicted with my sense of truth, such that he saw our paths diverge?

And there'd always be invisible threads tying him to a past I was not part of. At any moment someone else from his family, someone he'd known in prison, or in his younger criminal life, could appear on the scene and shake the stability of what we were trying to build together. Could we ever have controlled the circumstances enough to make a life together?

Coda

AFTERLIVES

JAN: After the demise of the workshop and back in New York City, I did alternative theater and finished the BA that I had abandoned while at Trenton. Four years after I was removed from the workshop, I received a letter from Finn:

> June 23, 1977. Dear Jan, Here I am surprising myself. I am not only typing out a letter to you, I am doing it with certain knowledge that I will be mailing it. Yes, there have been many attempts at writing letters to you before, painful experiences. This writing is painful also, it is impossible to be otherwise, yet I am compelled to continue. I have a parole date, and although I know that we will be living separate lives we have connections, a bond, that will never be undone. And I know you loved me as I loved you—in the best way we were capable.

He later told me that he'd gotten a scholarship to study acting with Lee Strasberg in NYC. Those of us in the street theater had studied with Strasberg. But on the day of his release from Trenton, his parole officer, without whose permission he was restricted to New Jersey, would not allow him to go to New York, assuming it was just to make drug deals. So Finn jumped parole but nonetheless lost the scholarship. The parole officer would have gone looking for him at the Strasberg studio first, and Finn had no intention of being rearrested. Though I didn't know it, Finn did go to New York and was part of Alec Rubin's Primal Theatre. He later told me that he sold drugs to support himself but never himself used anything heavy again.

Another year passed. I met a man at a big event celebrating the recipients of a grant for artists to do community-based projects. Neither I nor he had even applied for this grant; we were both there to celebrate good friends who had. We talked, or tried to; the noise level was piercing, but he later said how much he liked my voice. We danced, or tried to, but the room was packed; he later said he loved the way I moved my arms.

He came for dinner one January evening. That year the snow was something mythic; his van got stuck outside the house. He couldn't leave for eight days. The relationship deepened, cocooned together. A few months later, he and I got a loft together.

That spring, it must have been 1979, over a year after his release, Finn came to see me. It was a great joy, beholding him in natural light for the first time, sitting on the rug as the sun poured in through the high industrial windows of my boyfriend's and my loft. I was still pretty knotted up by the whole relationship with Finn—the haunting feeling of something unfinished. But what? I remember him stripping the paint from a wooden trunk I was using in a show, so he must have hung around for a few days. He did not want to get in the way of my relationship. But I felt the need to know who we were to each other by then.

At my behest, we went to a friend's apartment and made love, the one and only time, but it was strained. At the time, I thought that at last connecting sexually would be a completion of sorts, pulling together the other ways we had been so close. But I could feel, once we were in the act, that he was not experiencing it that way at all, and so of course I didn't, either. Then he was gone again. Only years later did he tell me, when I asked, that it had been futile; it couldn't restore the grounding we'd shared years before in prison and our paths did not lead us back to that ground.

I next saw Finn maybe a decade later. He had moved to the West Coast and tried to break into the movies, but the effort was undercut by his girlfriend at the time. He then settled in Seattle, got married, and had a daughter. I had also married, after a tumultuous five year on-again, off-again relationship with the guy whose van had been stuck in the snow. We had twins. I had gotten my PhD, was teaching community-based theater and related subjects at NYU, and was writing books about socially engaged performance, which had so come alive for me through the prison workshop.

Finn had been diagnosed with a terminal form of cancer and came east to say good-bye to three people he loved, including me. We met in a café on the Upper West Side, near a bus that would get him easily to La Guardia Airport, where he was heading after our visit. He talked a blue streak, the sort of thing one could say to anyone, which I found really unsatisfying. I said very little, until finally I asked if we could just sit quietly for a moment, and we did. I felt that the silence frightened him, but there it was. It was a great relief just to look at him. Then we spoke slowly, haltingly, but to each other. I felt a little of the old communion, that the love persisted for us both despite the distance and respective circumstances. And then he was gone again.

I found an undated journal entry where I'd recorded that I'd seen him once when I was visiting a friend in Seattle. I think his wife had left by then, the reasons being, Finn said, that he wasn't into sex and wasn't ambitious. He was doing some spontaneous street theater in coffee shops and once guerrilla theater on a TV talk show when political prankster and egomaniac Abbie Hoffman was the guest.

The next exchange I remember was years later. He was cured of the worst of the cancer but still had a condition that was very expensive to treat in the United States and was practically free in China. Years earlier, he had befriended a Chinese woman when they were each the primary caregivers of their kids in Seattle. Now she was retiring, returning to China, and asked him to go with her. He was planning on doing it. I wished him well and hoped it would be great for him, but I was secretly sorry to see him going quite so far away.

Then a few hours later, I got another email, which began "Dearest darling." My heart stopped—how could he be writing this now? Then I realized it was intended for her and he'd accidentally sent it to me. He ended up not going to China, perhaps because his daughter and grandkids lived in Seattle, although they were estranged.

Time passed.

Around 2015, Finn took his abusive son-in-law to court and got custody of his twelve-year-old grandson. Finn raised the boy until he reached eighteen, when he and his girlfriend got an apartment together.

FINN: Over the years I put a lot of my energy into the Church, which throughout her history has had many models of true communion, almost always founded by women and men, like Saint Francis and Saint Catherine of Sienna, out of love. Theirs were powerful acts dedicated to restoring true communion to the Church, and they were successful, and will be successful again, unlike anything we've seen since the death of Martin Luther King, Jr. I've collected enough info to write out a methodology to restore true communion to the Church, but I realize I'm no saint, and a saint must arrive who can take the methodology and apply it.

I take a five-mile walk most days. Though I never leave my apartment with the notion of talking to anyone, I've somehow been gifted with it just happening. From my street, reformatory, and prison lives, I fit right in. This morning, a young Black man came up to me all happy, telling me about his new job and apartment, and how he appreciated my advice. I didn't recognize him at first. He was looking great, a former street kid who'd been in really bad shape.

People from the streets, from all walks of life know me. Like a woman who had been psychologically and emotionally destroyed by her parents, a lawyer and a doctor. She has been clawing her way out of that abyss slowly but persistently. Presently she can only afford a room in a drug house with a horrid shared bathroom, but she's into celebrating life for the long haul, and she is going to make it. She somehow miraculously escaped from a predictable doom, in a mental milieu that was destroying her piecemeal right into the grave. She turned her little room into a paradise—one feels the joy when entering that space. Truly an inspiration.

It's a natural and a good way to spend my time waiting on that last train out.

JAN: As Finn once wrote, "You and I resided in two different galaxies that briefly touched as they passed going different directions." Yet I had never gotten over the abrupt end of the intense phase of what we had. Rain is the medium of longing; when someone is gone from your life prematurely, you think you see them in the rain. That is why you walk in the rain when you are melancholy, an emotion with no apparent cause because it comes from another time.

Writing this exchange together brought that other time into this one. I have been able to hold it, see it from the perspective of distance, and accept that Finn has always been with me, since I made that little space inside myself with two chairs during the height of our romance, though I've barely been in the flesh with him at all.

Through our love, I discovered that what the physicists said was true: There *are* no boundaries between *your* atoms and molecules and those of a chair, a lake, another person. But it took love for me to know this. And as Finn has written—and he really likes having the last word—"Our love abides."

PART II

Expanding Universes

My 2022 writing exchange with Finn opened up questions and feelings I had tucked away years before. Now I wanted to know more, if not about Finn, then about prison workshops and how places characterized by dehumanization could be environments for such profound connections. So I reached out to people who've developed different kinds of loving relationships in the context of prison drama workshops that had a profound impact on them. Some were people I knew; others were friends of friends or colleagues of colleagues. I asked them to read Finn's and my exchange and, if they found resonance, invited them to contribute to this book. Four pairs and one trio of writers joined me. Those exchanges follow.

7

Life and Love in the LCIW Drama Club

Gloria "Mama Glo" Williams, one of the core participants, and facilitators Kathy Randels and Ausettua AmorAmenkum each recount becoming part of the Louisiana Correctional Institute for Women (LCIW) Drama Club and its impact on them.

Mama Glo

Before I became a member of the LCIW Drama Club, I had many dark, hidden secrets. Through drama I learned to find a place in myself where I felt safe enough to share all things that held me back from my destiny. Through drama, I and others learned how not to let the system incarcerate our minds. People were able to tell their stories and release things that they were dealing with that they couldn't find peace with. Drama is needed in every jail, prison, church, and school. If you allow drama to help others uncover the tools they need to move past the pain in life, they can become free within themselves. I could never find the right words to express just how much I appreciate Ausettua, Kathy, and so many others they brought into my life. Thanks a million to a new family. Drama is IT.

I joined the Drama Club right after spending 1985–1996 in solitary at a maximum- security facility. Sherall Kahey and Mona Rhodes kept telling me about it: "Mama Glo, you speak so well, you should join the Drama Club!" They wouldn't let up on me. Sherral and Mona were on the board that interviewed people interested in becoming members. I was voted in, and from then on, I fell in love in with drama.

I am still grateful to Mona and Sherral because I learned so much from them. Sherral was a teacher in the vo-tech area. Your diction had to be excellent for her, and you had to dot all the *i*'s, make sure all your *t*'s were crossed! She was such a powerful and rare breed of woman. You would learn a lot simply from watching her and listening to her.

She told a unique story of wanting to be a midwife, because that ran in her family. Her time was cut short here on Earth from cancer. But her memory lives on through us.

Sherral told the midwife story in the first performance I did with the Drama Club, *St. Gabriel's Nativity*. We mixed our own personal birth stories with Mary's story of Jesus' birth; LCIW is in St. Gabriel, Louisiana. We did the performance at Christmastime, and we set the story at the LCIW. In it, I worked for the warden, and Mary was pregnant. I did not want Mary to give birth to baby Jesus on the inside of the prison. So I came up with this brilliant scheme to mix Mary's release papers in with other papers the warden had to sign.

That didn't leave a good taste in the actual warden's mouth when he watched the performance. If I remember correctly, that kinda took us down the pit in the club. For a minute he would not approve the Drama Club to do anything. After Lorraine Gibson, a social worker, left, Assistant Warden Jordan became the prison's representative for the club and opened the doors again for us to do the performances we wanted to do.

The next performance we did was *Gifts of Our Ancestors*, after Ausettua joined us. Sherral Kahey and I made all those yellow skirts and I ironed all the costumes y'all brought. I remember that cuz you have to have your room in compliance, meaning everything had to be put away. But I was in a room that had an empty bunk. I had ironed all the skirts and I had them on the empty bunk so the guards couldn't see them when they passed by.

I remember the sounds when we were hitting the floor with the sticks. It was a dance to call the ancestors when you pound the sticks on the ground, and something happened: There was a guest there, who was none of us! The person who came to visit us—her skirt was in a perfect circle, completely flared, so many panels in it that it covered the whole floor. And it wasn't no one from the circle. To this day I believe it was one of the ancestors who came to celebrate with us. I hope Kathy or Ausettua finds that picture. The face was blurred. I thought it was Sandra Starr, but she said it wasn't her.

I remember when Ausettua first came in. Kathy told us she was bringing her friend, who was a teacher of different types of dancing. Ausettua said, "When Kathy invited me, I was like okay, I'm going. I'm

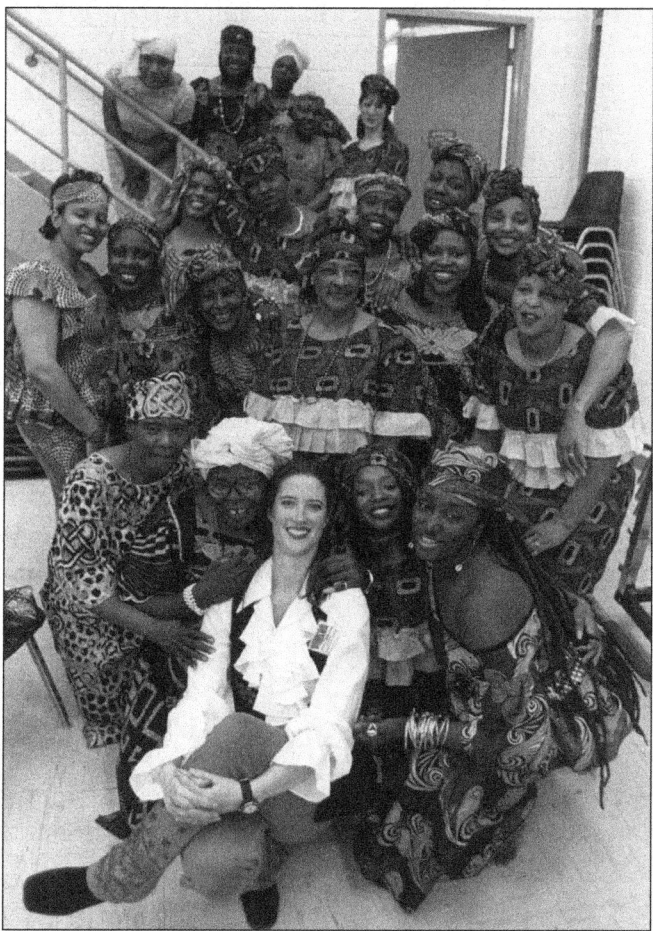

Figure 7.1. The cast of *Gift of Our Ancestors*. Photograph by Libby Nevinger.

gonna have to come back." Guess what—she stayed because she became addicted to the Drama Club and us! Because we are free-spirited people. We are easy to love and show love. We've been hurt so much in our lives and have had to suppress so much, until that suppression comes out to anybody and everybody. When I love somebody, I don't care what you do to me. Ausettua is a rare breed of woman, because she speaks what she feels, and if it hurts your feelings, so what. Sometimes I wish she would not be so blunt, but, guess what, you have to meet her and love her, but you can't change who she is. That's who she's been all her life.

Kathy's the type of person you meet once in a lifetime. When God made Kathy, He broke that mold. Kathy makes sacrifices for people. She cuts herself short. Her time is dedicated to people. She's in love with people, and that is rare. The world is so hard, people don't care about anyone. I love Kathy as my daughter, as if I gave birth to her. The most powerful thing that happened between Kathy and me was when she put the cross that she gave her mother around my neck. For somebody to do that, they not only respect you; they accept you totally for who you are. That spoke volumes that no words can express. I will carry that day in my heart 'til the day I die. I can't find the words to express what that day and entrusting me with that gift, how much that meant to me.

I don't want Kathy ever to think that what she does is not appreciated and not making an impact, cuz it is. I pray God keeps giving her the strength that she can keep doing this 'til the day she go meet Jesus. It's embedded in her. I remember when she did the one-woman show with the storm. She did the whole show by herself on the table and chairs. It was so profound. I was so taken aback by her covering that whole stage and playing all those parts. I was so impressed that she could remember them. That was one of the things that enticed me to join the Drama Club. I was always drawn to drama in school. It wasn't until I was an adult that I was able to learn it. I thank Kathy and Ausettua and the wardens for allowing us to be able to do it.

We are a family in the club. We became a family. It was a healing place. I protected the club with my life. One thing I know: If I spilled my guts about the ugliest thing that happened in my life, if you told somebody, they'd say, "Mama Glo gonna get you!" What went on in the Drama Club stayed in the club. That was the place we could come and talk about the ugly things that happen in life. Jackie Williams said, "I walked into Drama [Club] and found the strongest woman on the compound crying and sharing and I knew that's where I belong!" I'll never forget those words.

In the club, you could be your real self, but before you walked out that door, you were able to take out the phony mask for the compound and put it back on. Drama was my sacred place and it became many others' safe place. If we chose to share it, a lot of our performances came from our pain. That's where Jacqueline Bloodworth said we are the sacrificial lambs. We sacrifice ourselves. We put our pain out there to try to heal someone else and release them from the pain they're going through.

Drama became my healing place—where I needed to be to free myself from the monsters that held me back from my true destiny. Drama should be used throughout the world to help people uncover tools to free themselves from whatever happened in the past. Whatever bad things come our way in life, we have to move on. If not, it holds you prisoner to that spot and you don't grow. I'm so grateful to them. I'm free from the monsters. As long as we have stuff that holds us rooted to that spot, you give that person the power to hold you to that spot in your life, to dictate your future.

We did so many performances. The most powerful one I remember was *Behind the Wall*. At that particular time, I had lost my mother. I didn't have time to make amends. We did a performance and I released some of the pain and guilt that I felt by apologizing to my mother for the pain I caused her and the disobedience, 'cause that's the not the way she raised me.

I was able to release some things from my own closet. I shared things in Drama Club like "the monster in the yellow house," about the man who molested me from a child until I got married. I didn't know how to tell my mom. At that time, nobody would believe that this Black child was telling the truth. And I didn't want to put my mother at risk from negative reactions from the community. So I held that demon inside until I was able to create a character in Drama Club to release it. I had to take back the power by forgiving him. The world needs to learn more about forgiving. If you don't, you continue to give power to that person who took from you.

Drama was part of my cleansing. I was able to show love to others throughout drama and our performance, and nobody called me weak. Until this day, I still pull on those things that I was taught in Drama Club to heal myself now, because the club helped me uncover tools that I needed. People don't have to know you're talking about yourself. You can create characters to free yourself, and I am so grateful that I am a member of Drama Club to this day.

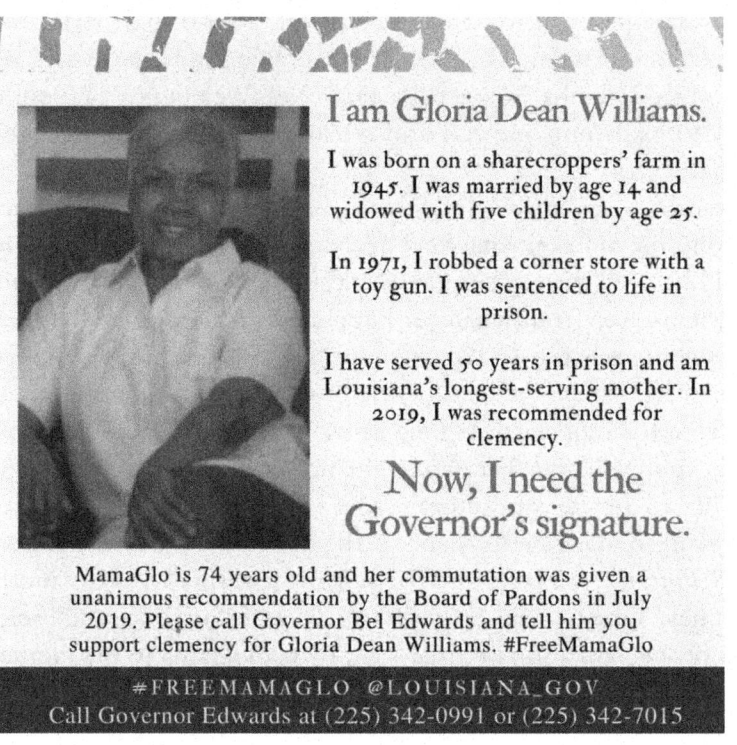

Figure 7.2. "Free Mama Glo!" postcard. Design by Fox Rich.

Remember *LIFE*? Warden Jordan came to that performance. It was a parole hearing. In the show, I was going up for parole and I had to convince the board to release me. I had to go through the line, just like Minnie McCallan, when her family came to get her on a white bus and all dressed in white. They made a line and she had to walk through it. We did that in our performance. All were dressed in white. When I was granted parole, Sandra Starr came though that line to get me because I was really crying. And Warden Jordan said, "Somebody's going home!" Two months after that, Jackie Collier, the one they said would never walk out of prison, went home! And about ten years later, so did I!

Oooo, I've got so much I could add. My sisters call me "Dean." They told me recently, "One thing, Dean, Momma never let us forget, 'Your sister's coming home.' She said it every day. 'Y'all can stop that mess; she's coming home!' She said that on her dying bed, 'Your sister's coming home.'" Words have power! If you speak it often enough, you speak it into existence!

And that leads me to Fox and Rob and PDMNOLA (Participatory Defense Movement New Orleans, Louisiana], who fought to get me out of prison after fifty-one years! I never saw their faces. I heard Fox a few times on the phone. But I found out about the sacrifices they had made to fight for my freedom! They didn't know anything about me. I didn't know anybody else really gave a damn besides Kathy and Ausettua, David and Zohar. But to find out there was a village out there fighting? And that village didn't stop fighting until I was free!

I remember talking to Fox, who said the governor said it was going to take a Damascus experience for him to sign Mama Glo's papers. And Fox said, "Well, here come one!" She was willing to buck the system for me. They did everything humanly possible to set me free. Had it not been for that village knocking on that door? The justice system sentenced me to life in prison, but God had another plan, cuz I'm free today.

Now I'm barred from Louisiana. I hate that because it still hurts my heart that I can't go bury my daughter. My daughter's ashes are still sitting in the house where I live. I would like to grant her request: She wanted to be buried by her grandmother. I can't go do that, and the state of Louisiana is giving my son and them a bunch of baloney in order to put her body to rest. That is insane. I can't heal because it's right here with me and it lives with me. I was just strong enough recently to be able to hang her picture over my bed, and put the blanket on that bed that matches the picture that's on the wall. I can't rest until it's done, so my question is, how long are you gonna make me suffer? You can escort me in and escort me out. I would be in total peace if they'd do that. But because of their stipulations, it's not gonna ever happen.

KATHY: Forgive me, Mama, but I remember a wise woman—namely, you—telling me during the Free Mama Glo campaign, "Never say never!"
MAMA GLO: That's right. They said they were going to bury me in prison, but I said that would never happen.

Kathy

Dear Jan and Finn,

Thank you for writing so honestly to each other about an intense time in both of your lives. For letting us peer into your relationships to yourselves, each other, theater, and the criminal legal system. Reading your exchange brought up a lot of thoughts and feelings from my own work in these realms. Thank you, Jan, for inviting me to dig deep with this chapter. I believe that when we receive bold ideas from the divine, and follow through with them, it is similar to the magic of the story

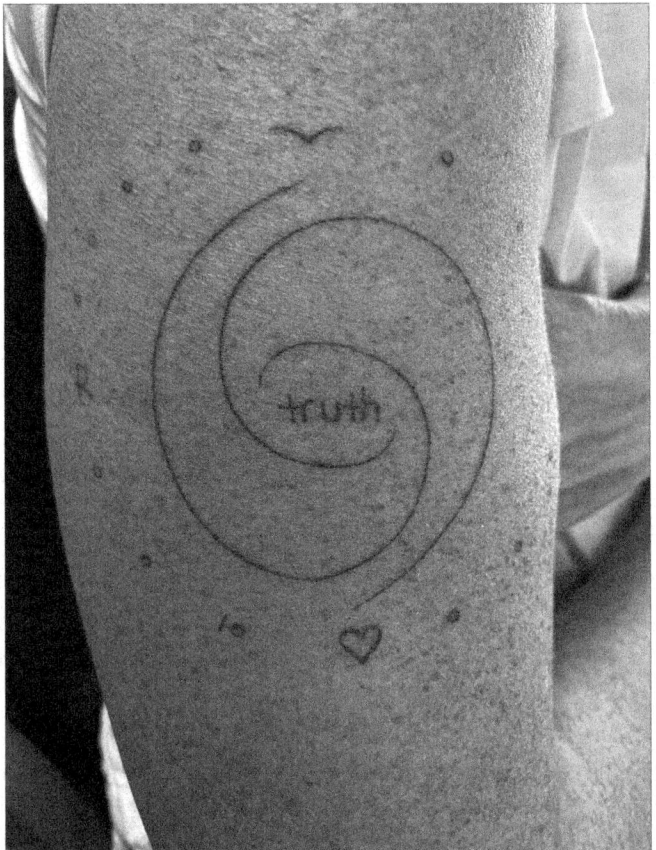

Figure 7.3. Tattoo. "Truth is in the Center of the Circle." Photograph by Kay Randels.

circle that I learned from John O'Neal: The deepest story that comes to you in the circle is the one the circle needs to hear. So share it, let it out, put it in there. I believe this so certainly that I incorporated it into my first tattoo, a fiftieth birthday present to myself. Truth is not anything that any one person knows, can hold, or own. Truth sits in the center of the circle of those who seek it. Here is my part on the spoke of the wheel of the truth this book seeks to illuminate.

Dear Reader,

I work for The Universe! The Divine. My instinct. The world's need. The place that needs me the most. The place that I need the most. The Truth. The center of the circle.

In other words, I'm an artist.

Some artists will concur with my guidelines, and some move from a completely different place. But, on the cusp of turning the age reflected in a deck of face cards with two jokers (fifty-four), here am I!

The LCIW Drama Club has been one of the major training grounds for my work, relationships, civic duty, and paradigm shifting. And "Nothing But GOD" sent me there. And nothing but those women (channeling GOD!) have kept me there.

Our art teaches us a lot. Our research brings us new knowledge in whatever realm the work calls for. The stories that spill out when we're working on a piece surprise us. When we share them, we see our own lives through someone else's lens, and that can help us to reframe our story. It can help us move from a stuck place to forgive someone or something. Clearing out mental and spiritual pathways is like riding rapids to healing, to the cool, calm, big body of water at the end of the roiling river.

Being dumped by my first lover after two weeks (at eighteen, finally throwing virginity away and some part of the faith of my fathers with it) led me to connect to the deep, raw heart of every woman who has been wronged by a man. And more than that, it led me to want to talk to women who actually killed the men who wronged them—wondering if murder appeased the rage inside. All that culminated in a solo performance, *Rage Within/Without*, which I created in college and toured throughout the world for twelve subsequent years.

My first contact with women who killed was in 1994 through the Illinois Clemency Project for Battered Women. One of those women asked me why I was so intrigued. This was long after the first lover and deep inside the first marriage. Another of those women, whom I told I was leaving my husband and going back home to New Orleans, said, "Well, keep working with women in prison down there."

I didn't have to listen. But I did. A door to the unknown.

After the first six-month workshop at LCIW, which was supposed to be the end and I was going to go on with my life, one of the participants, Sherral Kahey, said, "You know you can't leave us, right, Kathy?" Right, Ms. Sherral.

I started the Drama Club in my mid-twenties. A few years later, I was across the world, traveling through the war-torn former Yugoslavia for the love of a theater goup from Serbia named Dah Teatar. When I left the safety of Belgrade to travel on my own throughout Croatia and Bosnia, I kept getting the same question. Throughout my years in the Drama Club, I've been asked it, too. Sometimes out loud, and sometimes not. From security and the women; from folks on the outside, too. Here are some of my answers through the years, looking back.

> Why are you here?
> Cuz nobody told me I couldn't be.
> Why are you here?
> Cuz I was curious.
> Why are you here?
> Cuz all the doors opened to let me in.
> Why are you here?
> Cuz I have healing to offer.
> Cuz I need healing.
> Why are you here?
> Cuz y'all being locked up here ain't right, doesn't sit well with my spirit.
> Why are you here?
> Cuz you asked me to come back.
> Why are you here?
> Cuz you pray for me and my well-being when I come.
> Why are you here?

Cuz the performances here are the best on the planet.
Why are you here?
Cuz I hate violence, and what it does to us, and I know that the majority of y'all are in here for committing a violence that ended a life, and I know that behind your violence was a violence that you received. A hurt. That NOBODY. EVER. APOLOGIZED, much less atoned, for.

Multiple streams landed me in the well of healing that is the LCIW Drama Club.

My father called the Drama Club my "mission work." He was a Baptist preacher, so he used his words, and recognized his own impulse, in me. The same seminary that brought my father to New Orleans, and had me and four siblings raised here, has brought a wing of its school to LCIW. My relationship to my Baptist heritage is complex. I've written three performances about it and I still love Yahweh and Jesus despite the fact that I also worship divine beings from multiple cultures—especially the Hindu goddess Kali, who saved my life by giving my locked-up anger a divine feminine playground in my psyche; as well as Oya, Yemaya, and Oshun, whom, thankfully, Ausettua introduced me to.

Dear Ausettua,

In a 1997 talkback after my performance of *Rage* at LSU, I asked if anyone would be interested in volunteering with the Drama Club. Brave, quirky Mary Katherine Politz stepped forward. Mary Katherine held down the Drama Club with Laura Pattillo during the summer of '97, when I worked with Dah Teatar, and then fall into spring of 1998–1999, when I returned to Belgrade. She was our dedicated codirector until a stroke kept her homebound in 2015.

In 2000, Roscoe Reddix, Jr. (my codirector of a youth theater ensemble, the Positive Outreach Leaders), told me I should invite YOU to work with me at LCIW. Mary Katherine was white, like me. The majority of women in the prison were Black; and there were things that I, as a young white woman, could not provide for many of the women in the Drama Club, despite having been through two Undoing Racism training sessions with the People's Institute for Survival and Beyond. So, yes, I did reach out to you because you were Black, like you wondered, but not because I thought being Black meant you automatically knew everything about incarceration!

I was terrified to call you. I had seen your amazing performances all over the city since I was in high school and had taken some of your West African dance classes in the community. You command every stage, with every movement of your body. You used to spin your head and superlong dreadlocks around so fast, it was dizzying just to watch. Call HER? But there I went again. Acting bolder than I felt. Following a spirit that gave me the courage to face giants. And you said yes.

The first performance you did with the LCIW Drama Club was *Gifts of our Ancestors,* a title I subconsciously stole from one of Dah's early performances. It felt right in terms of what Kumbuka (meaning "remember" in Swahili)—you and drummers Zohar Israel and Brotha T—had to offer the Drama Club, especially the Black women. As African American women in Louisiana, they all at some point were traumatically separated from their ancestors by the transatlantic slave trade. I didn't fully understand the connection between slavery and mass incarceration until Michelle Alexander put words to it in *The New Jim Crow.* But I felt like I was stepping back in time to the antebellum South every time I went to the prison. Even though there were a few white women, and one or two Latina, Indigenous, and Asian women throughout my twenty-six years, the majority of the women serving time there have been Black. I couldn't look at that and not see it, question it, and challenge it.

Dear Mama Glo,

Did we first meet in 1997, through the show *St. Gabriel's Nativity*? Did you play one of the three wise women who convinced the warden to release Mary from prison? I need your impeccable seventy-eight-year-old memory to tell that story! I got to know you through the Drama Club. You became MY mama, along with so many women on the compound. And even some of the guards! I think you were the first woman in Drama Club that I trusted that deeply. Your giving spirit and ability to love unconditionally is astonishing. Your manifestation of the Christ you love and serve is humbling to behold and receive. One of the greatest gifts of your love, faith, good works, and deep relationships is that we, your children, strive to emulate you and follow your footsteps!

You were always devoted to Drama Club, but the turning point came when you shared the death of your mother. It was terrifying. Your voice was so powerful. It was clear that you were reaching through the veil of this world to the next and really begging your mother's forgiveness. Everyone in the room felt it. You touched an elemental part of human experience. We all came through a mother. And while not all mother-child relationships are healthy, we could all feel the truth of your spirit in that piece, and it freed everyone in that room. That's the sacrifice we speak of. You were IT that day.

You always called me your angel. Words have power. You brought out the best in me. You were certainly my angel. Encouraging me, asking me to share the stories of my life and work. You would always say, "When you tell us a story, it takes us outside of these walls. Carry us with you. If my body can't leave, I can leave with my spirit, through you."

I was invested in your freedom! So when Sherral Kahey got out, why couldn't you? And when Mary Turner became the fourth Drama Club member to DIE in prison, I said, "Hell NO, Mama Glo's coming home!" So when Fox Rich got her husband, Rob, out of Angola (the Louisiana men's prison) after twenty-one years, through clemency from the governor, and they took on your case through PDMNOLA (Participatory Defense Movement New Orleans, Louisiana), I got myself and everybody I knew on the "Free Mama Glo" Train! And after constant heat, vigils, protests, and quiet meetings, on January 25, 2022, you were finally released! Ausettua and I sang and danced and threw rose petals at your feet.
Hallelujah.
Amen.

What happens when we make theater out of our rage and our pain; what gets transformed? What can move or be learned? So much pain leads to folks' incarceration in these United States. Many are innocent. Many are "guilty." I bring it back to my tiny, personal connection to this mammoth story of anger, aggression, and violence in women, and ask where we put it. Where do we put the hurt that has been done to us because we were born in a woman's body? Where do we put the pain of sexual violence, or our innocence in incest? Where do we put the harms we commit because our own harm has not been held?

There is a well deep inside LCIW. We call it the LCIW Drama Club. It sits in the center of every story we tell, every time we gather. It gives us pause.

                                      Space.

                                              Respite.

                                                        It heals us.

Sometimes, just to say IT, whatever IT is for each of us:

"I watched my father murder my mother when I was nine years old."

"I was forced by my husband to have sex with my son."

"My grandfather, who was a preacher, made me suck his penis, outside in the woods, when I was a child."

"The white man at the store fondled me every time I went [there] from ages nine to twelve; and he did it with all the little Black girls in my small town at that exact age, and moved on to the next one once we looked like women."

"I took my own child's life. My neglect. My anxiety. My drug-induced haze. My inability to manage my own emotions. My inability to extract myself from an abusive relationship with my husband, or lover, or baby daddy, or dealer, or love bomber, or narcissist, or manipulator, or mind controller, or the person who once made me feel like a divine queen and then, throughout the course of our relationship, somehow that shifted to making me feel like his slave, worse than that, his dog—that he can beat however and whenever he pleases."

Breathe. Pray. Listen.

"I dreamt of fish last night, Kathy; that means a baby is on the way!"

"You have the key to the gate to your freedom!"

"Meow!"

"Get the holy water!"

"Surrender, Dorothy!"

"Spread your wings and fly, right now."

"Love, love, love, love is my medicine, my medicine."

Those are phrases, encapsulations of some of the tears, some of the stories that live in the well of healing that we all found deep inside our own hearts when we gave ourselves permission to meet in a little group called the LCIW Drama Club.

Amen.

Ashé.

Love,

Kathy Randels

Ausettua

> We are the willing doing the impossible for the ungrateful; we have done so much with so little for so long that we are now qualified to do anything with nothing!
> —THE ANGOLA DRAMA Club mantra, Louisiana

> Man can't give life; only God gives life.
> —MAMA GLO, LCIW Drama Club

> The greatest glory in living lies not in never failing, but in rising every time we fall.
> —NELSON MANDELA

My journey to work with incarcerated community members began in the 1980s with my dance company, Kumbuka, a Swahili word that means "remember." Kumbuka African Drum and Dance Collective consists of artists who are also nurses, lawyers, 911 dispatchers, schoolteachers, A/V technicians, jewelers, and accountants. It is committed to the preservation, documentation, and presentation of African and African American culture and folklore. We are committed to ensuring that the *entire* community had access to learning about the significance of the relationship that African culture has to Black Americans. Our community includes the elderly, the young, the working, the retired, and, yes, those who are incarcerated.

Majeeda Snead, a founding member of Kumbuka, and Mary Howell were the primary attorneys for convicted murderer Gary Tyler. Tyler was a young man who was tried and convicted, as an adult, in the shooting and killing of a student in St. Rose, Louisiana. It was October 17, 1974. Tyler, sixteen years old, was headed home on the school bus. As the bus was leaving Destrehan High School, it was attacked by an angry mob of between one hundred and two hundred whites, mostly students who were angry about integration at the school.

The racially charged atmosphere had been heightened by the arrival of David Duke to Destrehan. He was emerging as a leader in the Ku Klux Klan and neo-Nazi politics in Louisiana and the United States. Timothy Weber, a thirteen-year-old boy standing outside the bus with other classmates, was shot and fatally wounded. He later died. Police searched the bus more than once, but no gun was ever found. The bus driver said he believed the shot had come from outside.

All the students from the bus were taken to the police station and interrogated under extreme pressure and abuse. Tyler was arrested for disturbing the peace when he talked back to a police officer; he was soon charged with Weber's murder by an all-white jury. He was the youngest person to be on death row and served forty-one years for a crime he did not commit.

While incarcerated, Gary Tyler was an active participant in the Angola Drama Club. He eventually directed the Drama Club, a position he held for thirty years. He used drama to promote civic responsibility

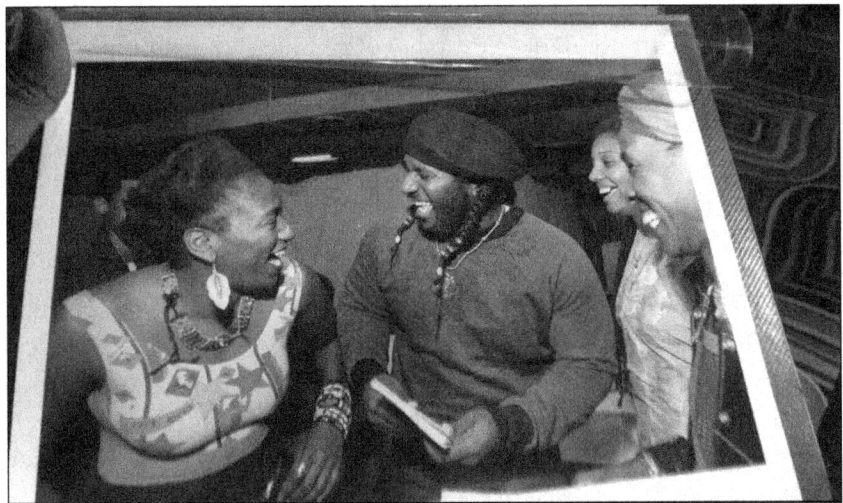

Figure 7.4. Ausettua AmorAmenkum and Gary Tyler. Photograph by Alexander Barkoff. Used with permission of Ausettua AmorAmenkum.

and hope. The Angola Drama Club hosted several presentations, and invited Kumbuka to perform on several occasions, through Tyler's connection with his attorneys, Snead and Howell. We were the first traditional African dance company to perform at the prison and left quite an impression on all who were there to witness. The power of the drum and the dance left an indelible mark on the land. Music awakens the ancestors; and the land where the prison now sits was once a plantation. Our performance opened a portal for the ancestors, reclaiming the land, even though we didn't realize it at the time.

Kumbuka was overjoyed to perform at the prison. We were not financially compensated, but the benefits were very clear. By giving of our time to the inmates at Angola, we were manifesting the concept of *ubuntu*: "I am because you are." We understood that our destiny was tied to their destiny. The African concept of life extends beyond the present. It includes those of us who are living now, those of us who have lived and transitioned (ancestors), and those souls waiting to be born. In African culture, the community is where all three of these existences are actualized and observed. The individual is born into the community and, even after death, will always be part of the community.

Interdependence, communalism, and sensitivity toward and caring for others are all aspects of *ubuntu* as a philosophy of life. The principles of *ubuntu* include humanness and social justice. It is a core African value to treat all living things with dignity and to acknowledge their humanity. Being a part of the spiritual and cultural journey for many of the brothers in Angola was so fulfilling. We observed their self-esteem and self-worth magnified. They were able to connect to members of society, not related to them, who took time to come and visit them. It was necessary to make that small contribution for our incarcerated brothers to ensure that they knew that they were valued, their life had meaning, and they were still a vital part of the community. African people understand community as a united group of people that work collectively to construct an interdependent society living together in harmony. Neither death nor incarceration stops *kujichagulia*: self-determination, in the sense one's personal and collective identities not being defined by others.

Years before, I had completed an undergrad degree in psychology and had attended graduate school to work on a master's in criminal justice. But I felt little gratification from an internship at the local parish prison, teaching male inmates basic subjects, nor did I feel comfortable working in a prison environment. The presence of the guards with loaded guns constantly hovering over my every move was very annoying and counterproductive. I always wanted to be a criminal psychologist, but I was sensing that maybe that wasn't my destiny.

That's when I received a phone call from Kathy Randels, inquiring of my interest in volunteering at a women's prison. I realized that in life you can plan your journey but that the route it takes is unpredictable and many times you must let Spirit be the guide. I must admit, I was a little annoyed at the idea that she felt that I could relate to incarcerated women. I had never gone to prison, I didn't know anybody who had gone to prison, and I felt like I was being stereotyped. Was it because I am Black? I never processed that I was on this trajectory academically with my desire to be a criminal psychologist. In hindsight, my decision to go with Kathy was the beginning of a twenty-year commitment to working with women in prison, completely different from the way I worked with the men in Angola.

I remember the first visit like it was yesterday. Entering the LCIW prison was similar to entering Angola: the long, winding road, checkpoints, and large iron doors that made a loud slamming noise as they closed. I remember the guard leading us to the room where the women were anxiously awaiting. I had no idea what to expect, no plan about what to teach. I simply went in as an open vessel, willing to pour what I had, and hoped that the women would be receptive. I brought my years as a cultural advocate, dance instructor, and the spirit of Yemaya with me into the facility.

As I entered, I was met with smiles and hugs and shouts of "Haaay, sister." The space felt so familiar to my being; I had entered a room filled with my aunties, sisters, cousins, and mamas. Among those women, I was honored to meet Gloria "Mama Glo" Williams, Sherral Kahey, Mary Turner, Michelle Allen, Carry Emerson, Taece Defillo, Selina Anderson, Demetricy Moore, Consuela Gaines, Ivy Mathis, Rhonda Oliver, and Sandra Starr. I was home and it was love at first sight.

The LCIW Drama Club uses performance to increase self-fulfillment and self-esteem, instill hope, assist participants in learning more about themselves and others, and introduce them to the concept of ancestor veneration. This reverence for their ancestors directly magnifies the connection they have to themselves, their family, their community, and the world. We made many productions using African concepts, dances, songs, and costumes for women who had never traveled to Africa, or even imagined that they were deeply connected to that ancestry and that culture.

We not only introduced African artistic concepts into the productions but also structured the drama club according to African cultural values. The elders are the leaders, but everyone has input on decisions that are made. Everyone is made to feel that no matter what their struggle or challenge, they have a safe space to express themselves, in which to be vulnerable, human, and loved. Whatever transpires in that space stays in that space. It is important that we listen to the participants and offer support to ensure them that they are worthy of our love and support. Core values have been established and are communicated to attendees orally.

The Drama Club is very inclusive: We rarely turn anyone away who expresses a desire to join. Often participants have made sure their prison behavior was perfect so that they could participate in the club and the productions. Because of the volunteers' and members' consistency and commitment, expectations have been agreed to, processed, and established by all. When violations occur—such as missing rehearsal (usually due to a prison infraction) or attempting not to be supportive of a sister's personal journey—consequences are implemented in a just and holistic manner. The women, especially the elders, take it upon themselves to discipline one another and keep the group in line. The women have felt empowered and have had a sense of ownership. They have internalized the core values and enforced a vow of discretion among themselves that has transferred to the entire compound.

A strong indicator of the Drama Club's success was the desire of participants to continue the work after they were released. This led to the formation of the Graduates, a performance group of LCIW Drama Club participants. The Graduates, all powerful performing artists, allow themselves to be used as sacrificial lambs as they share their personal stories with audiences throughout the United States. They powerfully demonstrate how performance can be a tool to educate and advocate for the thousands of individuals still existing in the prison-industrial complex. The Graduates were recipients of a Rauschenberg Fellowship. They created the Life Quilt, featuring the beaded names of 107 women serving life at LCIW in 2016, which was exhibited in the Ford Foundation gallery. They participated in a successful advocacy initiative that contributed to the release of Mama Glo, in 2022, after she had served fifty-one years, the longest time a woman in Louisiana has spent incarcerated.

I went into both LCIW and Angola with good intentions, bringing my skills and experiences, hoping to help someone. The reality was, I learned so much more working with those brothers and sisters, valuable life lessons. They taught me how to be determined in a seemingly defeated situation, to never give up on oneself. They allowed themselves to be receptive to learning and growing. They were not ashamed to speak their truths and be vulnerable *on a stage*. They were willing to take their spiritual walk with others, understanding that their paths were different, but through the use of the performing arts in prison they found their voice. They mastered how to make valuable use of their time out of the world, preparing for successful reentry as valued, contributing, returning citizens. It is so easy to remain focused and positive when you are in the free world, but how would *you* function if you were removed from the comfort and love of your family and home? For those participants, performing arts was the vehicle to self-discovery, forgiveness, and hope.

Their ability to remain positive and focused is unparalleled in my experience. Both Gary Tyler, the first juvenile sentenced to death row, and Mama Glo had faith, and allowed Spirit to direct their paths.

Mama Glo, Kathy, and Ausettua

AUSETTUA: I never asked you, Mama Glo: Do you remember the time the Free Mama Glo campaign went to the road out back from the prison carrying the signs and wearing the shirts?

MAMA GLO: Yes, one of the security people told me.

AUSETTUA: What was that moment like for you, knowing we had gotten on the grounds and were demanding that you be let out? What did the security person tell you?

MAMA GLO: She said, "Come step outside with me. There are people out there fighting for your freedom." It was so powerful—people who didn't even know me fighting for my freedom. I didn't know there was so much love in the world.

KATHY: Mama Glo's freedom was a shift for all of us—of course, biggest for Mama Glo.
AUSETTUA: That's right. We were no longer just sponsors in the prison. We were advocates. We had to go beyond the boundaries of the prison.
MAMA GLO: Now I have a question for you, Ausett. When you first came to Drama Club, you said you didn't intend to stay. What happened?
AUSETTUA: It was an ancestral connection. I felt connected to all of you. I didn't expect that at all. I was just coming for one Saturday. It was a pure example of how love just sprouts. Especially after going to the prison training, where everything was don't, don't, don't—don't touch them, don't this, don't that. And I got to the Drama Club and there were all these Black women, some my daughter's age, some my mother's age. It was love.
KATHY: On some level, calling it the LCIW Drama Club limited our thinking. We thought, *We are going to make theater*. The shift actually began in 2012, when we started the Graduates. Even before that, Ausett, you and I talked about doing something with women when they got out.

The Graduates became the mouthpiece for the Drama Club. When we got the Rauschenberg grant and finally had some money to work with, we went to a Formerly Incarcerated & Convicted People and Families Movement conference. And they asked all the formerly incarcerated people in the room to stand. We, of course, did not stand. But here was this huge room filled with formerly incarcerated people and they were all working for changes in the legal system, getting their brothers and sisters released, healing people as they got out, all sorts of things.
AUSETTUA: And we began to use the Drama Club for advocacy, too.
KATHY: Bringing it back to you, Mama Glo—even though it was a miracle, miracles do happen, hard work pays off, and the doors of the prison can be opened.
MAMA GLO: When you turned the key and I came out, a string of people came out behind me because of what you guys were doing.
KATHY: Ausettua, you have often said the work we do with the Drama Club and the Graduates is *life* theater—
AUSETTUA: Yes. Because it allows participants to evaluate their experiences via the stage. The self-actualization actually occurs in the process to get to the stage, although the performance is pretty powerful. In life

theater, everyone learns valuable life lessons—the audience, prison staff, and the actors.

KATHY: Mama, if you could sum up what you learned from the Drama Club in one sentence, what would you say?

MAMA GLO: Can't say it. Gotta sing it, sing our song: "Life is what you make it. Life is happiness. Life is where you're going. Life is where you've been."

8

Opposite Sides of the Table

A conversation between theater artist Jess Thorpe and prison manager George Ferguson, Scotland, UK

Theater maker Jess Thorpe's contribution to this book could have been about any number of meaningful relationships she's forged through prison theater workshops. She could have had an exchange with one of the dads in prison whom she was working with at the time, preparing to make a theater production with their children, or the trans man in her women's drama group who was exploring how to be himself within a system that misgenders him. She could have conversed with a friend she met in prison who is a survivor of domestic abuse and with whom she now collaborates on a podcast on the outside.

When Jess asked me if I had a preference, I leaned toward a conversation with prison manager George Ferguson, a close and important colleague of hers and the person who quite literally holds the keys. This exchange is not the place to bring up every feeling she has about the carceral state, but only the aspects that are strategically most useful in moving prison-based theater workshops forward. She is extremely grateful for George's willingness to have this conversation. I, as editor, am thankful to them both for distinguishing between a humane individual and a problematic system.

JESS: Tell me, George, about when we met. What did you think of me and the idea I was proposing to you—that we wanted to make a piece of public theater with young men incarcerated at HMP & YOI Polmont [His Majesty's Prison & Young Offenders Institution]?
GEORGE: Okay . . . Well, our partners from the charity Barnardo's told me that there was a meeting coming up about a theater project. And obviously I didn't know anything about performing arts and I just

remember thinking, *Wow*. I've got a vast prison background in operations, and when I first heard what the plan was, I was thinking to myself, *Oh dear. This is going to be a ten-month creative project for young people who have got, at best, a limited attention span.* I'm thinking, *God, do these performing arts people really know what they are letting themselves in for?* You and Tashi [Gore] came in and gave your idea. I remember thinking, *This is probably going to be a waste of time.* I never voiced that opinion at the time because I was keen to see what your approach would be, but I was very skeptical.

JESS: It was kind of the opposite for me. I was trying really hard to sell you the idea of making a professional piece of theater in the prison, and honestly, I did not know if it would work. I really believe in theater as process and I have a lot of experience working with young people and working in prisons, but of course there were loads of things I didn't know and possible challenges I thought might come up. It was an ambitious project. We were going to be trying things that are not attempted in prisons very often, like attempting to open the prison up as a venue and invite a public audience in to see the work as part of a national theater festival.

I was, honestly, a bit terrified when we first went into that boardroom with you, but I was not going to let you see it. I expected resistance and a bit of skepticism. I am used to it. I have been working with the prison system for fifteen years and most of my experiences have been with men in suits who have thought that I am naïve or idealistic or even that the arts have no place in this type of establishment. I have had to work very hard to develop a language and a set of skills to navigate this initial point of view in order to build what I want to build. I suppose I have learned that in these first meetings I just have to go for it, because if there is any evidence that I'm not completely confident in the idea that I am pitching, then we might not even be allowed to try.

GEORGE: I can understand that. I think it is probably because of a culture in the Prison Service. I'm sure a lot of other partners have experienced a similar thing. We need to think about the operational impact of any new project: How is this going to work? Can the people involved be trusted? How do we know it will work?

What actually altered my thinking in our meeting was that I had just come from another high-security establishment, where things were quite rigid. When I came to this prison, I just couldn't believe the facilities available. Polmont is the only prison in Scotland to have a purpose-built performing space, and although I knew they had hosted sharings and events in it before, it seemed as if there was still more we could do with it. So maybe about three-quarters of the way through that first meeting, I started to think, *Maybe this could work. We do have the resource here and maybe I'm underestimating you as artists to have the skill set to pull something like this off.* I started thinking, *Right, okay, let's try this.*

JESS: So we worked with a group of eight young men, ages between sixteen and twenty-one, for about ten months. We started with one three-hour session a week and built it up gradually over time as we moved toward production.

Together, we made a piece of devised theater called MOTION, exploring what it means to be a young man in Scotland today. It played

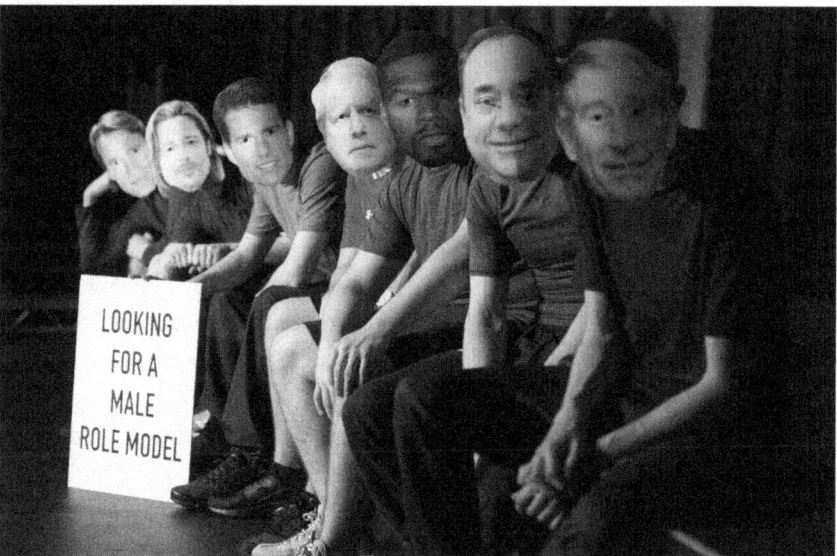

Figure 8.1. Looking for a Male Role Model. From MOTION. Photograph by Tim Morozzo.

for five performances for an audience of sixty members of the general public, each time as part of the Futureproof program, a festival of new work for and by young people, produced by the National Theatre of Scotland as part of the Scottish government's Year of the Young Person (2018).

GEORGE: I went to all five shows. I thought they did really well with the first show, but there were wee bits here and there that didn't go quite to plan, and you could see them getting agitated. When they did the second show, it was tremendous and I could see that they cared about it enough to keep working on it and making it better. That was a massive lightbulb moment for me.

I guess my experience on this project helped me to see the benefits of the performing arts as a tool for working with young people in the criminal justice system. Not only was it giving them an opportunity to create and perform and bringing them together as a community but it was also giving them a sense of agency and purpose. It was giving them a voice and providing them with a platform.

It also brought me back to the question of risk that we as prison management are always thinking about. We know that the risks are there, right? But we can and we do put processes in place to negate those risks. For example, when prisoners attend visits, or go to educational programs, or work in the joiner's [wood shop] or the builder's [construction] or the kitchen. We risk-assess these activities—we decide what could go wrong and we put things in place to make sure everyone is as safe as they can be. Why should a project like this be any different?

Now I look at things from the total flip side: What are the benefits of working in new ways? How does that outweigh the risks? If something does happen, then how do we just manage that risk? How can we think in new ways?

I have an example of what I mean. When you were in rehearsals for MOTION, there was a section where the young guys were going to wear superhero costumes as a way to explore masculinity and what young boys learn at an early age. Our head of operations was very opposed to allowing the superhero suits in the prison. I said to him, "Okay, then—talk me through: Why?" He said, "Because it's civilian clothing—it's a security risk." And I said, " I can totally understand security risks. However, do you not think that our staff might notice if Ironman or the Hulk or Captain America was trying to get out of the front door?" And he laughed and said, "I see where you're coming from," and we made it happen.

At the end of the day, you've got to remember that a performing arts project is run really different from the culture of the prison. This way of working was new to staff within their usual responsibilities, and some of these bridges hadn't been crossed before. There had been shows and events in the prison before, but not quite in this way or on this scale, and we didn't really know how to manage the conventions that came with it. We didn't know how to navigate things like blackouts when you were doing a lighting plot or a backstage costume change. We had to develop new ways of working and make everyone comfortable with them.

JESS: For me, it was a game changer when we started to collaborate on what we could achieve. I had done loads of prison projects before and was always met with "No, you can't possibly do that—this is a prison, remember?" When I worked with you, things started to shift.

I knew that this project was ambitious—we were making a show in a prison that people would pay to come and see, and it was going to be part of a national theater festival. We wanted to raise the bar aesthetically and illustrate the value of the work of the young people and what they wanted to say.

In previous prison theater projects, I was never allowed a blackout or a costume change. Officers' radios and alarms would be going off throughout because, you know . . . security was first, but you were like, "Actually, we can mitigate these risks and put other security measures in place. This is a show, so it would be kind of undermining if our radio goes off." So you made the staff in the theater space take the batteries out of their radios and you allowed a blackout and for the young people to change backstage. Honestly, I thought it was amazing.

I suppose in that sense you were trusting the young people to rise to the challenge, and they did. Because of that, they got more and more responsibility as the process progressed and of course they flourished as a result.

I was then able to use it as a precedent for planning other prisons arts projects to demonstrate that it can be possible to do things like apply professional theater production processes, invite members of the public in as audience, and document the work properly. Because it's about showing that we value the young people and their work. We see them as human beings; we believe in them. That shared humanity is so important to me.

GEORGE: It was a bit of constant battle from the start for me. I was lucky in that I was part of the senior management team in the establishment, but I was constantly being challenged by staff: How is this getting to happen? Why are they getting this special treatment? When we had an evening performance and I allowed them out of their halls past seven o'clock at night, it was a first.

JESS: That was an amazing moment. . . . That was their highlight. . . .

GEORGE: It was a major thing for them, right, because nobody had ever been able to access the activity buildings at night, but I asked, Why? It needed to happen. It felt important to challenge the status quo and start getting people to buy into what we could achieve together. I felt that I could recognize the benefits of an arts project of this size, but I just needed to mitigate the risks and put other contingencies in place to allow the smooth running of the performance.

We kind of handpicked staff who we knew would support the young people and promote them. I remember having a meeting with them and saying, "Your alarms can go on silent . . . so let's put them on silent, okay? We are trying to make this as professional as we can; the young people have been working on this for ten months. We need to ensure that they get the best chance at this." That was the ethos, because for the fifty minutes that the show lasted, I wanted it to be an out-of-prison experience, if you know what I mean. I wanted the guys to think, *I'm not actually in prison at this point.* Physically, they were, of course, but I wanted it to be an escape from that and a bit of reality for them. If an alarm were to go off or a radio buzz, then that would bring everyone straight back to the prison context. When the audiences, the community, came in, I wanted it to be as if we were at the theater down the road. Just at a show, not a show by young offenders.

JESS: Exactly. And we also made decisions about the content of the show based on that idea. One of the first things that happens in the show is that the young people shake hands with members of the audience and look them directly in the eye. That was so the audience would recognize that the young people wanted to connect. We wanted to convey a message that we are all human beings and we were breaking down the othering that happens when we view some people as "criminals."

I always speak about this idea in my teaching. . . . Every single time we do a show with a group in prison, we ask them, "Who do you think the audiences are expecting they are coming to see? Who do you want to show them?" The idea we seeded at the beginning of MOTION was if we just said hi and extended our hands immediately, then we would be changing the narrative and the young people could have power over the way the audience saw them in the space.

Rachel [O'Neill]'s design of the show supported this. She said, "Okay, the prison is concrete, it's barbed wire, it's gray, it's industrial, it is brick. We are going to have gold and metallic blue and we are going make it beautiful." We deliberately made these choices about the show to try to humanize it and find connection. And I suppose the combination of your choices and our choices meant we were working together to take the prison out of the prison, if that makes sense?

GEORGE: It does. I remember when you were doing the get-in and I was in an operational meeting. My colleague Grant came and found me and said, "All the theater kit has arrived. The curtains are up, George. You'll need to go down and see them, eh?" And I remember coming out of my meeting and throwing my book into my office, locking the door, and rushing down, because I was actually quite excited to see what it looked like. I went in and I was just thinking, *Wow, this is good*. I kept thinking that the young people would be thinking, *Look at the effort people have put in for us*.

JESS: It's all about value, isn't it? It's about sending a clear message: You are worth this. You have value.

GEORGE: It was really quite moving for me because my son was the same age. I kept thinking if he were ever in a similar position, where he was incarcerated, how would he be treated? I would want him to be valued.

JESS: It's useful to think in that way. How is this child my child? What is our responsibility to one another as human beings?

It reminds me of another of my favorite moments from that project. Before one of the shows, we had an audio desk set up and the guys were allowed to play music. It was an informal attempt to give them a little freedom, just being able to act as DJs and "be" in the space. Then one of them put "The Grease Megamix" on and we all started to dance. They danced. You danced. Other staff danced. Everyone in the room danced. It was such an abstract moment of being in a high-security prison in a room with disco lights on. It was just a beautiful slice of normality and they were all really joyful and content and I found it, probably of all the things, one of the most moving. That and when I was doing a speech on the last day and the group did not tell me I had lipstick on my face, when on the first day they would have made a laughingstock of me about it.

GEORGE: Ha! In moments like that I noticed that the young people had started to see you as part of their gang, if you know what I mean. Is that okay to say? I just mean that they cared about you.

JESS: I get it. We were part of their community. That was something we wanted and hoped for. But there is also something interesting that I want to dig into about that idea. I remember when I did a similar project in a different prison and a similar thing happened where the group was really emotionally connected to the work. At the end of that show, they did a big emotional speech about how much they cared about me and the project and one another and what they had achieved. A complaint was made by an officer that the display of emotion was inappropriate, and I found it hard to understand. I just kept thinking, *How can the arts communicate their worth properly without it seeming like we're crossing a line?*

The thing about drama is, we are dealing with emotions, right? Although I have clear boundaries about what material is and isn't for the performance. I recognize it's not therapy; we don't want to open boxes that we can't close, but at the same time, groups are offering themselves and trusting themselves, so we need to respect that. Because of course there are important emotional boundaries and we are professionals, so we have ways of working with safety and care. You can't share all your personal information. You have to keep yourself and others safe. You have to be respectful and trauma-informed and you have to think about what might be triggering. But where is the place for love and care in the work? This is the practice of the social. It is about being human. Feelings are involved. And that is okay, right?

GEORGE: Absolutely. Of course. There is a line—there will always be a line—but it's about where people perceive that line to be. I think to date the Scottish Prison Service has come a long way; however, we've got a lot of learning to do in terms of how we as the Scottish Prison Service look at things and say, Okay, what can different types of projects offer us here?

When people are sent to prison, their punishment is the loss of their liberty, but they still need to be engaged in opportunities for learning and growth. They still have that right. We still need to provide experiences for them to move forward in life.

JESS: There's a tension, isn't there, between punishment and rehabilitation? How can both things exist at the same time? What are we hoping will happen if we lock people in cages on top of one another and keep them alone most of the day? Is that going to make a safer society? What happens when they are released?

Last week I was doing a lecture with a group of students and one of them said that he didn't think that murderers, for example, should be allowed to do drama. I hear this view a lot, but I find it utterly perplexing. It speaks to this idea that drama is somehow a treat or an extra or even a luxury. For me, it's the absolute opposite. The arts are fundamental to who we are and how we process as human beings.

Maybe the problem is it looks "fun." And maybe it is sometimes; there can be something incredibly healing and pro-social about fun. But let's be really clear—it also requires a lot of bravery and a lot of deep digging. It needs a lot of communication and collaboration and to essentially out yourself in front of others. It is positivity and change and growth. Isn't that what we want?

I felt like replying to the student, "Are they allowed math? English? What are they allowed?" I guess it comes back to the idea of what prisons are for. We are speaking about Scotland, and in lots of other countries they will of course have different versions of this, but I feel like sometimes—and I see it in the general public as well as in the system—there's a tension between "Are we punishing or are we trying to support positive futures?" Essentially, these are two different things, and sometimes I don't think we know which one we are doing.

That and the fact that we know—we actually know—that most of these young people that we are imprisoning come from a handful of postal codes in Scotland. Statistically, they have experienced a huge amount of childhood trauma. They have already been let down by system after system. So as painful as it might be to the general public, is punishment even the right conversation to be having?

GEORGE: What would you rather have? Somebody who does ten years in prison but learns nothing and returns to the community? Or somebody who comes in, engages with projects and services to try to better himself, takes part in education, learns a trade, etc. That person has got more of a chance of surviving and being accepted within the community and never returning to prison. The difficult part isn't doing the time in the prison, but reengaging back into the community after a lengthy period of time or going back to the same situation he was in before. Because if that continues, then we have a continuous cycle of short-term offenders, you know? Doing life sentences in installments. It can be like a revolving door.

The Scottish Prison Service is definitely about rehabilitation and how we can better prepare individuals for release; as our corporate vision states, we are transforming lives and unlocking potential. What we have to remember is that the punishment for anyone in our care is that person's loss of liberation when sentenced by the courts; people are not sent to prison to be punished.

What I have come to recognize through being part of the performing arts is that it is all about confidence and communication and having respect for one another. There were certain individuals who could hardly look you in the eye when they started and were very quiet for a couple weeks. Maybe they were scared to get involved, but I watched their journey and how transformative it was for them.

JESS: It is fascinating to me how long-term change actually happens and how we as human beings support one another to grow. Because surely we are investing in our own society when we do that.

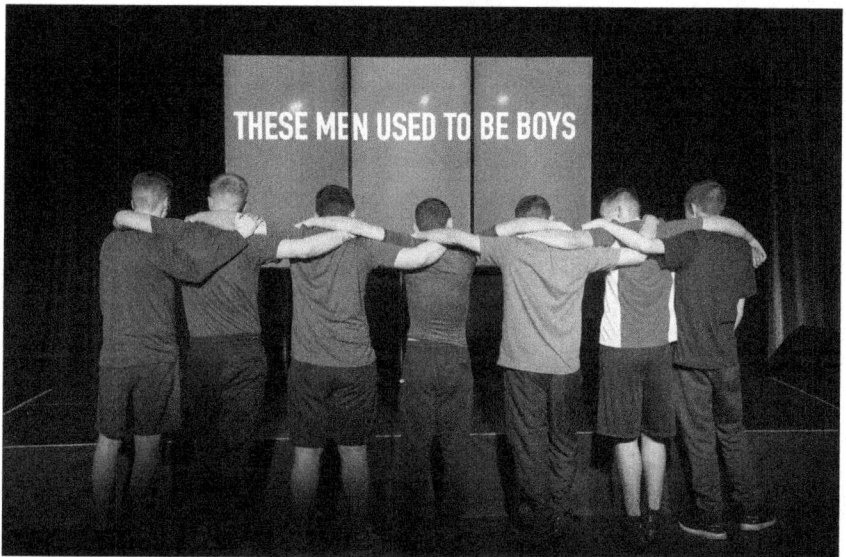

Figure 8.2. These Men Used to Be Boys. From MOTION. Photograph by Tim Morozzo.

GEORGE: So if somebody was to come back at you and say, "Okay, then. Tell me what performing arts have done to change individuals in prison. Does it impact their overall behavior or how they approach things? What actually are the benefits?"

JESS: I think it's about supporting people to explore their interests and develop confidence in themselves and the skills that they already possess. It's about encouraging them to use their voice and create a platform where it is amplified, heard, and valued. Some of the people I work with currently, especially women, didn't even know that they could have a voice or that anyone would want to listen to what they have to say.

For me, it's always been about creating opportunities for individuals to build a more positive version of themselves and to care—like care as a radical act—because I think it's super dangerous in our society when people don't care. If they don't care about themselves or one another or the society we live in, that's where we start to have a problem. What's really good about performing arts projects is that we have to work together as a group; it's not competitive. We have to be a community. I always work with devised theater, which means we are making a performance together from scratch, so there is always a dialogue involved. You get to share your ideas and test your opinions in a supportive environment. And it is not just about doing a show— it is about being human.

My big dream would be a cultural program in every prison. We have got only fifteen prisons in Scotland, so would it be possible to have an arts project in every single one? What could be our commitment to that? Not just from the prisons but from us as an art sector? How can we make sure that that the arts are really valued in all of the prisons, because if that's the case, that bleeds out into society, doesn't it? That could make a massive change.

GEORGE: If I were being cynical here, I'd ask what you would say is the benefit of getting everyone involved the arts for you as a professional. Some people will look at that and say, "Okay, she's trying to get an arts project in every prison. That drums up work for her and her company. Is it all a bit self-serving?"

JESS: Okay. Yes. I hear you. It's a fair question. Actually, it's a question that the young people in the group in Polmont did ask: "What's in for you? I bet you guys are just using us to further your careers. So everyone can say, 'Well done—you managed a show with dangerous boys.'" It's a bit painful, but of course that is because there is probably some truth somewhere.

I would say that I honestly feel very motivated by other people's personal growth and it brings me an incredible amount of joy to see groups succeed and to just love being onstage. I also make shows for mainstage theaters, and while I enjoy that, honestly, the high of watching a seventeen-year-old woman who has been told she is worthless, who feels she is worthless, get an award for her creative writing and cry with joy beats it every time.

It's moments like that which keep hammering the point that the arts should be for everyone. In our society right now, we are not really making them as accessible or inclusive as they should be. Not even close.

GEORGE: And that's why I ask that question, of course. Right now, you and I are having this conversation at the Royal Conservatoire of Scotland, in Glasgow. Look at all the students sitting on the steps. They just don't look like they've come from deprived backgrounds or whatever.... And if I'm honest, that is what I think is the general perception of the performing arts. Do you know what I mean? Somebody who has come from an affluent background whose parents can afford to buy them a cello? And take them to shows? And give them the money for tuition?

JESS: Obviously it's difficult to know about the students' lives just by looking, and there are certainly exceptions, but I take your point. It's a big tension for me, too. We had young people in our prison performance who were easily as good. They just have never had the opportunity to know it.

GEORGE: I always tell this one anecdote about our project to new officers starting at the prison. It was the time when the penny dropped for me about the value of the performing arts. It was the end of MOTION and we had a young guy in the cast who was hyperactive.

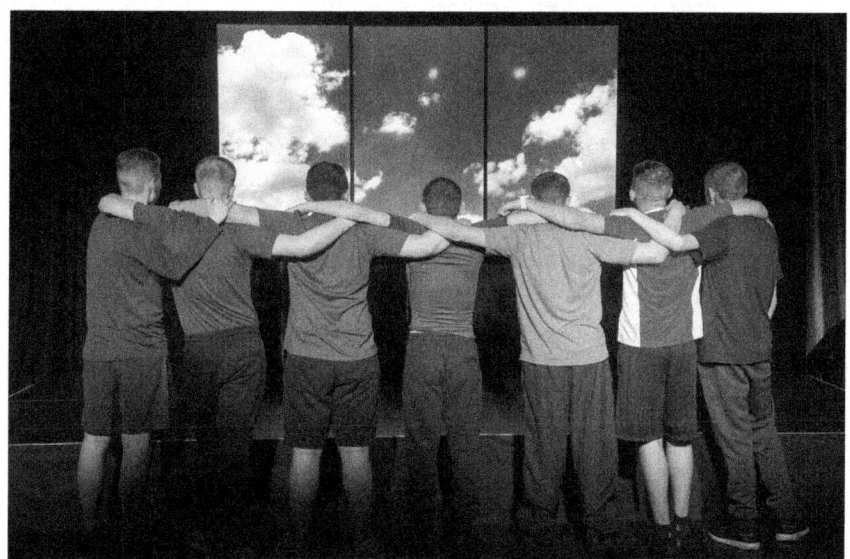

Figure 8.3. Blue Sky with Clouds. From MOTION. Photograph by Tim Morozzo.

He could hardly hold a conversation with people. He was not able to look you in the eye. He was always clowning about to get attention, mouthing off and being controversial. One of the proudest moments for me was at the end of the show. He was in a group with fifteen members of the public around about him, asking him questions about his journey. He had the confidence and the communication skills to talk about what he had actually done over the last ten months. He stood there with confidence, speaking to people he did not know, and he had his head up. I started to see that's what it is all about. It is still one of the proudest moments of my career—seeing somebody being able to do that.

JESS: We are five years on from where we started. Now Polmont Youth Theatre is a part of prison life and they do several shows every year. What I find interesting is that there is a culture of theater making at the prison now. There is a waiting list and the young people are leading with their own ideas and they expect a certain quality. Every time I visit, I am totally surprised—I don't know why—at the level that they are working at. I like to think that this is because the original project started with a very high bar and even though it was challenging at points, the result has been a shift in the culture of the whole prison.

We now have a variety of shows every year made by the young men in the mainstream population and we've extended our program to include women and members of the AFAB [assigned female at birth] community as well as the young people in the protection wing. The shows are always packed with a mix of the public who come to support the work and audience from the prison halls. We have refreshments afterward. The Performing Arts Space has the buzz of a cultural hub where people are meeting and mixing and dialogue is taking place.

That is what I think is most exciting to me now. How ambitious can we be? How far can we push the system? Another goal I have is around who we get in the audience. We need their families; that's the priority. We need people their age and members of their community. But we also need strategic leaders and policy makers from across Scottish Justice. We need those people who are making decisions about these young people's lives—who are handing out sentences—to be in the room and see them be articulate and brilliant. To see them as more than a number or a problem, but as people worth investing in.

For every show we make, we now have a Q and A so that the group can also hold space and we can further humanize them in front of their community. In this way, I think the youth theater can be part of strategic and systemic change.

GEORGE: I also think the Scottish Prison Service [SPS] is changing and evolving. When you look at our new Community Custody Units for women that are created as flats with individual rooms with en suite living rooms and kitchen where prisoners can cook and eat together. There are key cards that they can use themselves and communal social spaces where they can gather and plan events. These buildings are so different from the old Victorian prison buildings with cells in rows that we have been used to. The new ones have shared kitchens, communal gardens, and community spaces where people can gather and events can happen.

As an organization, the SPS is also recognizing theory around adverse childhood experiences [ACEs] and conversations around trauma and recovery. We have replaced the word *custody* with *care* in our strategy and have an asset-based (rather than deficit-based) approach, where we work with the skills an individual already has in order to help that person to build a positive future. I see all these things as changes both operationally and culturally in how we manage things, adopt things, and engage with partners and services going forward. I think the performing arts can be a critical part of this, and based on my experiences from Polmont, I really echo what you are saying. I think every establishment should have a performance space. We need to think about this when we are building prisons.

JESS: Or hopefully not building them?

GEORGE: You know what I mean! Creating new buildings. Updating spaces.

JESS: Essentially, it's about prioritizing spaces where people can gather together that are not just functional spaces for things like eating or exercise. Prisons always seem to offer the gym for arts projects, as it's often the biggest space they have, but in reality, it is never actually available because people always want to work out. It would be amazing if we really understood the huge importance of communal spaces in the

health and growth of these communities that are usually defined by isolation. Could Scotland be the first country to have an Arts and Cultural space in in every prison?
GEORGE: It's definitely something we can work on.
JESS: I'll take that as a start.

9

At a Threshold Around Race

BY ALEXANDER ANDERSON AND KEVIN BOTT

Alex and Kevin met in late 2008 in New York City, when Kevin, then an NYU doctoral student, was developing Ritual4Return (R4R). Drawing on theories and practices from community-based theater, criminology, ritual studies, trauma studies, and more, the project consists of twelve weeks of workshops, culminating in a public homecoming rite of passage that "returning citizens"—the preferred term for people released from incarceration—enact in front of witnesses comprised of family members, loved ones, and other community members. It's intended to begin a healing process that starts with the returning citizen and extends to other people who have been harmed in connection with crime and the criminal-legal system.

Alex, a returning citizen, was one of five men who went through R4R's pilot program and "crossed the threshold," as R4R calls their public ritual, in 2009. The experience changed his life, helping him finally to feel free of the psychological shame and social stigma that comes with being an "ex-con."

Then Kevin moved away from R4R. With the demands of his first job in higher education, 250 miles from New York City, obligations to his young family, and the difficulty of funding a project that didn't fit neatly into either a criminal justice or arts bucket, it took ten years before he was able to run the program again. Back in New York in 2019, Kevin secured funding and made his first call to Alex, to see if he wanted to come on board as the project's first resident social worker.

Alex and Kevin worked together as colleagues and partners for a year before COVID-19 shut everything down. But by that time their partnership and, in some ways, the entire project, was falling apart. There was unspoken tension and frustration between them and a pretty explosive

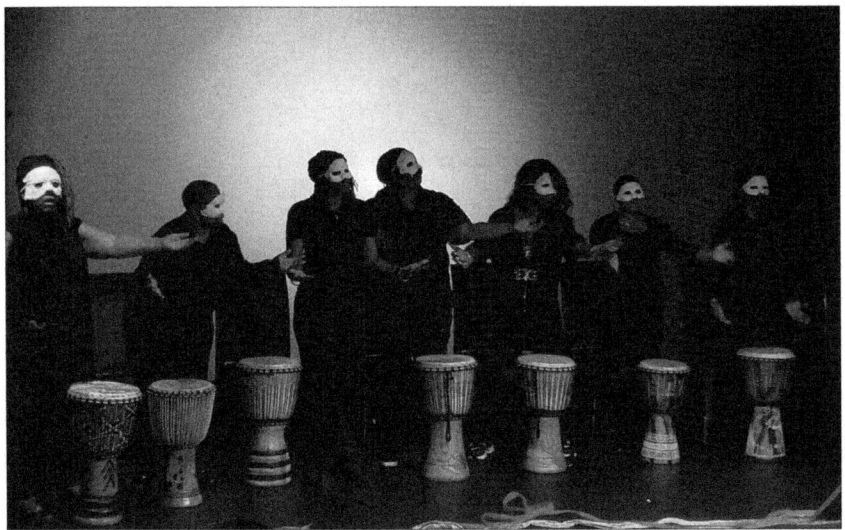

Figure 9.1. R4R rite of passage, fall 2019. Photograph by Jonathan Brill.

argument in June 2020. *They finally agreed that each of them would take R4R separately in the direction he saw fit.*

From summer 2020 to winter 2023, they didn't speak much. And yet both knew the other had something necessary to realizing the full vision of the work. Plus, they missed each other. Alex had continued creating theater with returning citizens in Manhattan. Kevin had been halfheartedly trying to write a book about the work, and had taken a new job in New Jersey. He tried launching the project again, in Newark. Again, he secured funding. And again, his first call was to Alex.

What follows is an edited transcript from several conversations they had in spring 2023, part of an intentional effort to talk through what had happened between them so that they might carry what they'd learned into the new project and incorporate it into their relationship, both personal and professional.

KEVIN: I keep going back to 2020 and the argument we had on the phone. I don't remember every detail, but it's very much linked in my mind to George Floyd's death and the protests that followed. To put it succinctly, I think you were telling me to get off your neck and work through my own issues as a white man.

ALEX: For me, it starts earlier than June, much earlier. I understand the dynamics of what happened between us better now because, since then, I've been in spaces with other white people, and I experienced the same kind of dynamics in terms of what race brings into those spaces.

I'm involved in some programs for people coming out of prison that are supported, and often led, by groups of good-hearted, wanting-to-help white people from affluent backgrounds. I look at it like Richard Wright writes in *Native Son*. In that space, the impact that whiteness has on Black people is sort of to create a relationship that oftentimes revolves around subjugation and domination. And oftentimes with you and me, I had the feeling of our relationship being one of subjugation and domination. I guess it's just white maleness in that space. I think it's something that happens in the American psyche. I can't speak for white people, but I think there's probably something that goes on that creates that kind of relationship.

I look at it that way because of how some Black people subjugate themselves in these spaces. Sometimes when I would step in because you weren't available, I noticed that people were acting differently toward me than toward you. I was interested in why. It starts with coming into a space. The first thing a Black person wonders if white people are in the space is, How do you act? How do you interact? You can step into a space with only Black people and that's a different kind of "How do you act?" question.

KEVIN: How would you characterize the difference? With and without white people in the room? Specifically, when we were doing R4R, what was the difference between when I was there leading the session and when I was absent?

ALEX: One difference, just to be fair to everybody, was that I would say to myself, *Maybe they don't trust me. Maybe they trust Kevin.* But then I would ask myself, *How did they get trust for Kevin and distrust for me?* Because I was always very supportive of others in the space. Always led with empathy, and wanted them to learn like I learned. But the relationship was . . . I hate to use these terms, but it was the difference between "learning from your master" or "learning from your brother." I think that's a part of it—this history of trauma, of slavery, which automatically impacts that relationship. The history of enslavement and domination

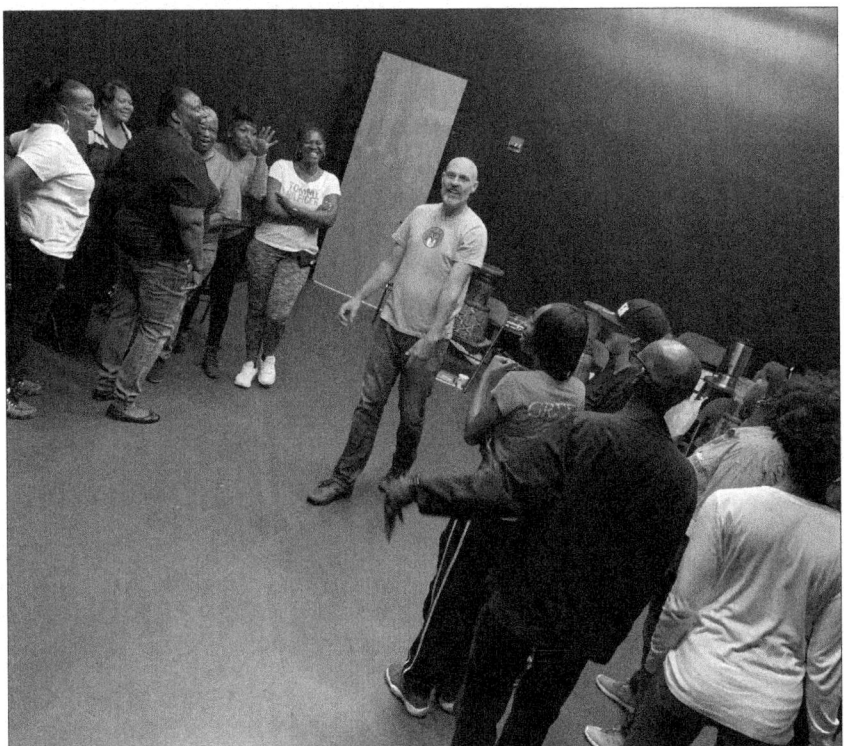

Figure 9.2. Kevin facilitating an R4R workshop. Photograph by Alexander Anderson.

by whites in America against Blacks is a process that's still happening in those spaces. You understand what I'm saying? I don't know if I'm explaining it fully.

KEVIN: You are.

ALEX: I had never really looked into why those things happen. But I think that some of the things that were happening for you was your proximity to Black experience. And what was happening to me was my proximity to white experience.

I recall one session, you came in and you were going through some personal financial stuff. And it created something for people. I'm thinking of Dick [names of workshop participants have been changed], who said, "I don't want to hear that shit from you!"

KEVIN: I remember.

ALEX: Rafael told Dick, "You can't talk like that, Dick. You need to shut up!" It got to the point where Rafael wanted to fight Dick. I found that very interesting. Why? What did Dick do other than feel something? Look, Dick sees you as a white man who's supposed to have it together. And if you don't have it together, that's your business. Because *he's* not together....

The part I couldn't understand was why Rafael and a couple of other people wanted to attack Dick. Even Anita, who is also a very experienced social worker. Later on she told me that Dick shouldn't have done that. And I thought to myself, *Why? Why couldn't he express himself and we have just left it at that?* But it created such conflict, where everyone was telling Dick, "Leave this space. 'Cause you're doing . . . something." To me, that was at the heart of it. What was Dick doing that was so violating that even the Black folks wanted to violate or attack him? Was it because of Kevin, because they loved Kevin so much? Or was it because of the dynamics? Malcolm called it the "house n—r" and the "field n—r," you know?

KEVIN: Well, as painful as it is for me to dwell on that moment, let's dig into it a bit. That might have been the last session before the pandemic lockdown. And I was in free fall, personally. I was in a very bad place. And looking back on it . . . I think I was trying to bridge a gap by kind of saying, *Look, I'm fucked-up, too. Maybe if I admit how fucked-up I am and how bad things are, then I can, I don't know . . .* It wasn't wanting to pretend I was something I wasn't. In fact, the opposite. I think it was wanting to communicate that we're not so different: *I'm a mess, as well.* You know? On one level, I *do* understand that it's not the space for me to come and cry tears about whatever's going on for me. It's just not appropriate. But I'd like to hear more about how you understood Dick's reaction.

ALEX: The reaction isn't intellectual or cognitive. It's on a very deep emotional level. I guess what you did to Dick, when you started talking, I guess Dick's reaction was, *You can't be fucked-up . . . because I'm fucked-up. Because if you're fucked-up, then we're all fucked-up.*

KEVIN: Wow. Okay. I didn't see that until just now, with you explaining it.

ALEX: Yeah.

KEVIN: Yeah, I always thought the reaction was more *Fuck you, privileged white guy; whatever your problems are, they're nothing compared to what anyone in this room is dealing with.*

ALEX: Yeah, I don't think so. To me, that would be the intellectual, cognitive level. But I don't see Dick seeing it on that level. I see him reacting to you.... You were expressing your humanity.

KEVIN: I think that's what I was trying to do.

ALEX: But for some Black people, whites are like *super*human. You know? To hear a white person speak about their humanity and their vulnerability, I guess some Black people, on a certain level, can't perceive that. Like if you're conceiving white as being all right, all *together*, if you're perceiving whiteness as being your teacher, your principal, everyone that's above you, and if everyone that you need to sort of surrender to is white ... It impacts me, as well. I refer again to *Native Son*. I see it all the time. Blacks are one way when they're among themselves and another way when they're among whites. My wife does it all the time—acting differently depending on whether or not whites are in the room. I just sit back and observe it.

To bring it back to me, when you and I came into the room together, I would let you do your thing and I would just sit back. For example, I remember that I was to work with Shanae, Anita, and two other women. Shanae clearly said, "I don't want to work with Alex. I want to work with Kevin." And I wondered why. I was watching her struggle, and watching you working with other people. Then at the end, after we did the performance and everything, she went around saying we caused her harm. She really bad-mouthed us. You know, I can't get space at Fortune Society anymore. I can't get that relationship back because she told people how *I* harmed her. She never mentions you! And I never even worked with her!

KEVIN: I remember. Shanae struggled to write her story, detailing ways she had been sexually and emotionally violated over the years. I encouraged her to edit it, and did some cutting myself, but the result was still very explicit and raw. Though adamant about wanting to tell her story, it was too much exposure to too many strangers, without enough support following the final ritual. It's understandable how Shanae could have felt exploited. The situation is my greatest shame and regret from all of the rituals I've been involved in. And right, Alex—you weren't involved at all.

ALEX: So that, the situation with Dick, my own feelings and what I was going through, was getting me into a space of . . . lessening myself. I was falling back on not wanting to cause people to leave the program. I decided to take the role of being quiet and let Kevin direct and let them get whatever they got from Kevin. But to myself I'm saying, *This is wrong; they shouldn't be treating me like that.* Anita, whom I've been friends and colleagues with for a long time, was a confidante for me. I told her it was wrong and that people shouldn't be treating me that way. I said, "In fact I have more insight into things than Kevin because I come from that space y'all are coming from, so with the help of Kevin, I can help put it in a way that will relate to your own personal experience of being Black in this society. But if you think Kevin can give that to you better, then by all means, go ahead. But don't hate me when it doesn't work out the way you wanted it to, because that's your choice."

I've found that going on in other spaces, too. It wasn't just something you did, like thinking, *I want to get closer to the group. I want to be human.* And at the time, you needed it. I saw it. You needed the group to embrace you and tell you it was going to be all right.

KEVIN: I think maybe I can articulate it a little bit better now. I think speaking up that night was my attempt to flatten the hierarchy. What you're saying is that it screwed everything up. It screwed Dick up. I mean, it's very parental. And if the parent is out of control, what does that mean for the kid? That the kid's not safe. You're describing a very paternalistic dynamic that has existed—that still exists, I guess—between Black people and white people; if the master is saying "I'm messed up," then what does that mean for everybody else? But I think my intention was, if I'm just real about what's going on, then we can stop having this "me on top" dynamic. We can see it more like we're working together. But it completely backfired.

ALEX: Yeah. The solution, to me, is that you have to do more work in that relationship. I do, too. I can't expect you to tell everyone, "You all have to listen to Alex when he's talking and do what he says, too." Like I'm your *help.* Like, in *Django* [Quentin Tarantino's movie *Django*

Unchained], I'm that guy, Charles [a stereotype of a "house n—r," played by Samuel Jackson] when he says, "What's that n—r doing on a horse?"

(Both laugh.)

ALEX: I'm Charles. And I don't like feeling I need Kevin to validate me. We bring different skills into the space. That's what they didn't understand. I was coming in as a social worker and you were coming as a teaching artist. It was the dynamic that we felt could produce a better impact on this population. Or at least provide this population with the relationships that they needed to become better. In my mind, the population didn't see it. They put you up here [gesturing with his hands above his head] and I was Charles. Hired help. How do we deal with that?

How I deal with it today is to go in first, before they even meet Tom [Oppenheim, the white artistic director of the Stella Adler Studio of Acting, where Alex continues to work with returning citizens] or anybody else at Adler. We just work on that relationship. I give them clear evidence of my leadership skills. With this cohort I'm with now, I have the best relationship that I've ever had. They established a relationship with me not based on what they saw between me and a white person. Because in their minds, automatically, it puts you up and me down. Now I know you're not superhuman, but they didn't know you like that. So they come into that space with the psychological impact of being Black in America and automatically conditioned by it. To me, in the theater space, we can break those old molds and act in a different way. I mean *act*. We can act differently toward one another. We can treat one another as human beings.

KEVIN: Back in 2020, when I felt like the project had fallen apart, I didn't think I would have acted any differently in that space had they been white students. Because I was just being a theater director in the way I learned how. Which is essentially, I'm in charge. I'm the final decision maker. That's how I was coming into it. Just the way I knew. . . . So I was often in tension, in this project and other community-based projects I initiated, because the collaborative part of it was in tension with my own artistic vision. You saw that in our project together. The way that I had ideas for what I wanted to happen and it didn't really matter what other people thought. I was going to have my way because I felt *artistically* that was the way to go. Which was also problematic.

ALEX: On the one hand, like you say, you're in charge—that's what a director does. On the other hand, people are stepping into that space, wanting to be in charge, too. I don't want to be coming into that space with Kevin in charge and I'm just there to help, because that feeds into what's already going on in people's minds.

KEVIN: Yes.

ALEX: They already mostly see the white person is in charge. That has to change. We need to bring people into the space and tell them that this is collaborative. You know, I don't lead with an outline anymore. We do some tableau exercises just to get people into the space. Then I tell them they're in charge of putting their piece together. And give them some ownership. That's one of the things you and I will have to deal with, that I didn't see myself *owning* Ritual4Return. When I did try to feel some ownership, I think I got some pushback from you.

KEVIN: Yes.

ALEX: You know? "You don't own this. I own this." I don't know if you remember but after the women's group, I came to you and I said, "Okay, can I be a teaching artist now?"

KEVIN: Alex—

ALEX: And I . . .

KEVIN: Alex, unfortunately, I remember it all.

(Both laugh.)

ALEX: And you said no. It wasn't so much it hurt as it was, *Okay, I'm going to show you what I can do.* Those kinds of things we just have to point out in what we're doing to show whites this dynamic that happens in that space. Even though we all talk about being all about the art and all about theater, I think there's something else deeper, which, when it shows itself, creates conflict and hostility. If we don't catch those things in time, eventually you'll hear it all. That's what you heard in the argument we had—all those things that I was suppressing in order not to damage our relationship. But in the end I had to say what I was going through. Because, if you remember, I went through that situation at Lincoln Hospital that really impacted my mental health.

KEVIN: If I remember correctly, you'd won awards for your empathetic treatment of patients as a licensed clinical social worker, and got consistently glowing performance reviews, yet you were bypassed for promotion in favor of a much younger, less experienced white female.

ALEX: Kevin, I was bypassed for promotion twenty-seven times!

KEVIN: Wow.

ALEX: And each time by people who were less experienced than me. So with Ritual4Return, I felt I was coming into a space where I could be myself and be in control and have all the things everyone wants to have: freedom to express myself, freedom to learn, freedom to help.

Maybe the place to start is in people's responses to your whiteness in that space. And your response, trying to lead with your own humanity—empathy and all—wanting to be a part of it, is another issue. Because whites do that—they want to come in and they say, "Hey, I want to do time, too!"

KEVIN: Kind of romanticizing oppression, and wanting to find a way to identify as one of the oppressed.

ALEX: Right. So for me that's the start: thinking about the way everyone is trying to come into that space as their whole self and how that can get misunderstood.

KEVIN: I also think that my work for these past three years . . . Listen, I always joke with my wife that I canceled myself. But it's actually no joke. I needed to be canceled. The amazing thing to me about our blowup in 2020 is that it was the exact same day that my wife also had some pointed things to say to me. I think back on that day as one where I almost lost my marriage and actually, for a time, did lose my friend and creative partner. But clearly the universe was telling me there were things I needed to hear. I realized I was creating harm and I had been truly unconscious of it. My reflection on it, and I think the work I need to do as I reenter these spaces, is to be aware of the way that whiteness, white maleness, even *white middle-class maleness* operates so that I can mitigate it on my end, and acknowledge it. To even point out, *This is what's happening,* if only to myself: *These are my privileged identities at work in this space.*

Because it haunts me—that moment when you were asking to be an artist in the space. It wasn't so much that I didn't think you could do it—although I think there was that arrogance of "Well, I know how to put a show together; that's my training and expertise." It was more this fixed idea I had of what everyone's role is. My mind . . . Look, you said it, the whiteness—and maybe this is also typical of men—operates in *knowing*. "I know! I have the idea of how things are supposed to go and how things are supposed to be." So unconsciously, this is the way it is. You're the social worker. I'm the artist. That's how this is going to make sense, to funders and the participants. Or maybe just to me! And so yeah. I'm sorry. I'm sorry I did that.

ALEX: No, I think it's good. I think it's great what we're doing. Because these dynamics do happen and we need to explode them together. I'm not white, but I am a man. So when I come into the space with females, I see the same kinds of responses that Black males have with white males.

And Black males are going to act differently in spaces led by white females. If Black women are also in that space, then they are going to show up differently. That's something I was dealing with back then and I'm dealing with now. How to show up for women who have been harmed by men.

KEVIN: That's so important. And it's also important to cultivate women leaders. And trans leaders. The people who make the most sense to lead in their own communities. And then you and I will have to learn to be allies to them.

ALEX: Right . . .

KEVIN: You know, Alex, this group we're going to work with in Newark—I'm really excited for you to come with me. They are a very empowered group in and of themselves. Every week there are at least fifty, mostly men, of course, but more and more women. They get together every week and feel empowered together. And I have nothing to do with it. I'm just coming into their space, which is very different from what it's been, which was me generating . . .

ALEX: It was always *your* space.

KEVIN: Yes. I generated the energy and I pulled the group together and then it was sort of my group. Whereas in this space, *they're* organizing. They've got a whole thing going on, and over these months, I've just been in the room, listening, not saying much. . . . I've explained the project, briefly, a few times. I've been building a relationship with the executive director behind the scenes. But the point is, I mostly don't matter to them. They just see me and this project as a tool for what they're already trying to accomplish. I'm not trying to convince anyone that this is a good project or how good it will be for them. . . . It changes the whole dynamic. It puts me *out of charge*. So I'm curious now when you come into this space and start to build relationships. I think we could have a really different dynamic with this group. There will almost certainly be unconscious stuff going on with regard to race and gender dynamics. But the power dynamic is a lot more balanced than I've ever experienced. And it's because I'm mostly in the background.

ALEX: That's great. And listen, with my group, too, I'm trying to cultivate leadership and step back.

KEVIN: That's the vision.

ALEX: Right. Each one, teach one.

KEVIN: Let's talk about solutions. How do we change the perception of the white guy in charge that can happen when the white guy walks into the space?

ALEX: It is a very powerful dynamic, but I think one of the things that helps is being in the theater space, where you can play out roles, right? So if this role doesn't work, let's try out this other role. And if this role doesn't work, what about this role? People can't take it personally because we're just playing out roles and seeing which fits. What we actually did was an evolution, allowing the roles to change. I changed my role. Now that people see and interact with me in the role, and get comfortable in it . . . it wouldn't be a problem *now* because they've already experienced me in the role and we've calibrated to one another, in relationship. They've seen me as a . . . director.

KEVIN: As a leader.

ALEX: Right. And that wasn't easy. That took getting rid of old ideas. I had to show how I'm a leader. That's the thing about walking into this theater space with Black people—at least this particular population. You could just walk in and say, "Hi, my name is Dr. Kevin Bott." And BAM! They would give you that leadership. *Doctor? Okay!* You know? But me, I have to step into the space. A lot of people don't really get that I'm a social worker. I have to *remind* them, repeatedly. Like, "Don't forget,

I'm a social worker. I have insights about things y'all are going through based on that." I had one guy ask me, "You have a *master's* in social work?" I said, "Yeah, why? What's the problem?" And he said, "No, I just wanted to know." I think that's great. But it often isn't enough for me to come in and say I'm the director of the program. I have to actually show them *why* I'm the director.

I wound up having to shape a lot of their pieces. Because they were struggling. They have a lot of trauma, and they don't have experience dealing with it in healthy ways. A lot of participants start out by telling me all the experience they have in theater. And I say, "Okay, that's great . . . when we get to the part when we're doing theater. But right now we're not doing theater. We're talking about rites of passage, and that's a little different. In this space, we're using theater to help us express something about ourselves to the community. This is about changing ourselves, developing ourselves, and healing." I needed to remind people the ways it's like and not like theater. The point is, I was able to earn that respect and recognition because people could say, "Okay, he's in a space that we're not used to, and we've never been in before." So they gave it to me.

If you walk into the space now, there really wouldn't be any conflict like that. Because I've been able to do some teaching, some mentoring, calling people after rehearsals, uplifting, writing pieces for people, some poetry, and creating some stuff. I showed them some videos of work you and I did together. Stuff I did during COVID. That showed me in a light I needed them to see me in and helped me establish myself in the role I needed to be in for the process to be successful.

And in my experience, a lot of Black men don't trust that. They don't trust leadership, or can't accept leadership like that.

KEVIN: Do you mean from another Black man?
ALEX: Right. You know, that alpha male bullshit gets in the way. "I'm better than you. You're not better than me!" When we do this work again, we need to be changing roles, all the time [makes a motion with one hand then the other in front, back and forth]. Until people get an understanding that we're both the same. It comes back to this theater space and the idea of changing roles.

KEVIN: Yeah, it's such a great point. My experience in traditional theater, as I reflect on it in light of what you're saying, is that we are in the business of playing roles. One: playing. Two: roles. In the traditional theater, the people in charge—the director, producer, stage manager, the heads of the departments of dance, costumes, et cetera—they're very damn serious about their roles. They only change to one perceived to be of a higher status. Very few directors move to stage crew, you know?

My journey these past few years wasn't just about this project or about my unconscious biases. For me it's been asking why I was so unhappy in my *life,* and how that unhappiness was hurting people I care about. A big part of my journey has revolved around my life as an actor, starting when I was eight years old. That's a very important identity for me. Growing up, I really loved being onstage. Acting was everything to me. And one of the things I loved, I think what every theater kid loves, is the camaraderie and just the playing. Being in a chorus number and learning with the group. Laughing and bonding and all of that. Rehearsing a big musical production number as a chorus member is really one of my favorite things.

But beginning when I was about ten years old, I started getting leading roles. And very unconsciously for me, it became what I'm talking about. I became very serious about that *role.* Being the leading man. Being at the center. Taking one of the last bows at the end of the play, you know? What I finally realized during this three-year self-cancellation is how much I lost by playing that role. I lost all the fun, the camaraderie, the community. All my rehearsals were me and one or two other actors and the director. I remember one day being in a small classroom, working on a scene, and actually *hearing* the chorus on the stage, through the walls, having what sounded like a lot of fun rehearsing a big production number. It sucked. Over time, I'd lost my ability to play a role other than the star of the show.

I think I can apply that insight to a lot of nontheater realms in my life. I could use that as a metaphor for my privilege in this society, as a white middle-class man. I was chasing this thing that I was told was important to chase but which was actually very isolating for me and over time drained my happiness. It separated me from the people who were actually having more fun! But I was sold on the idea that the goal is to be in the spotlight, successful, noticed, singled out, rather than part of the chorus. There's so much more freedom—and *fun*—in the chorus! That's the *community*, you know?

ALEX: Well, maybe that's another thing right there. Not calling ourselves directors or what have you. We're just *all artists.* Just to keep it in the framework of art. We're here to collaborate and build and create. We can model how we support others, and each other, so that the participants can do that for one another, too. You know, this is fun and it's play. You come in this space, just be an artist. You have imagination to create in this space. We all do.

KEVIN: I love this idea of playing with roles and how empowering that can be. I've seen how it builds confidence. . . .

ALEX: When you're talking about empowerment or growing in confidence, I really see it as healing. When you first contacted me to work with you, I was in a space of homicidal and suicidal ideation. Thoughts that I wanted to do things because I felt discriminated against and denigrated at my job. So for me this whole process is one of healing, in a real sense. When I was at Lincoln Hospital, my aspirations were to be a director. I was very good at my job. I was working to be all that I could in that space, coming from where I came from. I hoped that I could step up and help other individuals see that if they follow their own path, they can be successful, too. But then I ran into a racial trauma and it just knocked me off my space. I was told I didn't fit in. They told me that all the time. And I was the only Black man in any position of leadership.

Being told I didn't fit—I wanted to burn the whole thing down. Just tear the whole institution down. If I don't fit in, then no one's going to fit in. So coworking with you, Tom, and all y'all has been about healing for me. And to be frank with you, as long as you were in that space, I couldn't get to where I wanted to go. So it started to feel oppressive, to be honest. But at one point you stepped back and said, "Alex, I'm going to let you step forward because I think it's time for you to do that." And I thank you. Now it's just healing. That's what I feel more than anything, like I've accomplished something in terms of my emotional and psychological process. I feel I've achieved it. I've healed. I feel really good about myself.

KEVIN: It's wonderful to hear you talk about it. My healing has been on the other side of the coin. The only way I could begin healing was to exit the stage. I had to cancel the version of myself that worked for so long and then, in ways I care about, stopped working. I had to learn how not to be in the front, to make space for others to be in front. Recognizing that it's not going to fall apart if I'm not there. And might actually be better!

ALEX: Well, it's going to be better when we can all step out of the narrow roles, or the roles that have been put on us. That's the beauty of being in the theater space. We have the chance to create the roles we want for ourselves.

KEVIN: I need to say one more thing. When I think about my healing journey, which was very uncomfortable, I know that it only happened because you and I came into this space together. And built a relationship over many years. So when the shit hit the fan, there were stakes for me. Potentially losing your friendship meant something. Having you reflect back to me something that was painful to see—I took that seriously. In the same way I had to take my wife's feedback seriously. That's what forced me to do the actual work on myself. I stood to lose things I cared about—including the respect and friendship of a person I respected and cared about.

It's rare for white people to have stakes that involve people not like them. And those stakes existed for me because you and I were in a space together, over time. This theater space is amazing because it brings people like me and you together, and if we care about the work, then we have to work through these painful issues. So whereas in regular American life, I think you'd agree that Black and brown people *have to* deal with white people, with white culture, on some level; white people really *don't* have to *ever* deal with nonwhite people and nonwhite culture. It is 100 percent possible for white people to exist in worlds that don't include nonwhite people except as busboys and landscapers and cleaning ladies. And if that's true, how can this country ever heal from the dynamics we've been talking about?

I want to say to white people: Figure out how to be in nonwhite spaces. Or nonhetero or nonmale spaces. People in dominant, privileged positions need to put themselves in spaces with nondominant, nonprivileged people. And build relationships. And listen. And not be

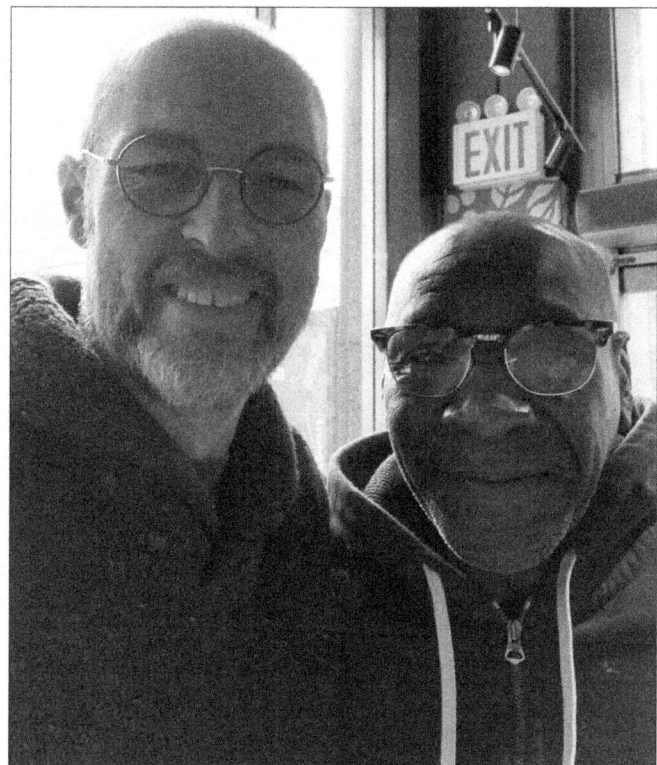

Figure 9.3. Alex and Kevin, the chapter's authors. Selfie by Kevin Bott.

in charge. And be willing to take feedback, painful though it may be. And eventually, you might be lucky enough to find a friend who can help you grow and heal. So I thank you for your friendship, man. And I thank you for being willing to be in this conversation with me over time, even when I know it's been hard to stick with me. I'm a better person for knowing you. Thank you.

ALEX: Well, listen, brother, I'm very happy that we are reconnecting and going forward to do more reentry work together. I hope our conversation will help others deal with the impact of racial trauma and how it shows up in our lives. This is my last word: Doing reentry work is sometimes very difficult and frustrating. I wanted to quit many times. I learned that healing is always a very painful and uncomfortable feeling, especially dealing with our own issues. But our healing comes when we honestly start seeing, hearing, helping, and creating space for ourselves and others to improve and obtain better prospects, especially those who are made to feel like outcasts.

10

The Lives We Lived

BY JOHN BERGMAN AND SAUL HEWISH

John (MA, RDT, BCT) was the founder and artistic director of Geese Theatre Company USA, one of the longest established theaters working in prisons in the world. Geese taught and performed in nearly every state in the United States as well as internationally. Saul, a founding member and a former director of Geese Theatre Company UK, is currently the artistic director of another prison-based company, Rideout (Creative Arts for Rehabilitation), established in the UK in 1999. John left prison work in 2020 and now teaches nationally and internationally, especially using drama therapy with violent men.

Saul and John have known each other for thirty-seven years and have worked together on numerous projects. This conversation is about the personal impact of the work that they did together in the United States from 1994 to 1996. Geese performances had all been done by the company, on subjects ranging from maintaining families despite incarceration to controlling violent and eventually sexual aggression, and were interactive and quite raw. Saul came to the United States as John was moving into the creation of original productions by men and women in prison, beginning to work as a drama therapist with violent and sexually violent men, and expanding into more prisons and juvenile facilities.

John and Saul acknowledge the support of Jena Gaines for her transcription of their words.

The Work

JOHN: We always asked two fundamental questions: "Were/are we pissing in the wind?" We asked that of everything we did and as often as we could. What right did we have to do any work inside, or any teaching?

SAUL: Yeah, and "Who is the audience, who is this work for?" All theater makers should ask that question.

JOHN: The answers turned out to be complicated and got more so as we went on! Our work was designed to get the audience—incarcerated men, women, and kids—to really review what was going on in their heads. And we were working with people who were investigating the psychology of offense. Like Stanton Samenow, who was working at St. Elizabeth's Hospital in Washington, D.C., which had a section for the criminally violent. Instead of trying to interpret the men using Freud, he said, "Listen to these guys, listen to what they're saying, and accept that when they're saying, 'I wanna kill you,' it means 'I wanna kill you!' No Freudian subtext. Or when they say, 'I do whatever I want in the world,' this *is* what they're really saying." This was sort of revolutionary.

We in Geese USA had the most terrible battles about what we were really doing. Were we fascists? Was it that we were somehow not really listening? Were we misunderstanding who these men really were? Were we ignoring what they had come from? And some of that was true.

SAUL: I think that journey into exploring criminal behavior was inevitable because of working with people in prison. We asked why they were in prison, what they did to get themselves there, and what they did to try and stay out of prison that failed. That led us to looking more at the internal landscape in their heads. When I joined Geese UK in 1987, the year it was founded, that shift had already happened. We just came straight into work you had been developing for a number of years using the language you developed of the mask. *Here's the Mask. What's behind the mask?* Masks were part of the strategies we were discovering that alerted us to the tactics the prisoners used to protect themselves or deny others.

JOHN: I wonder, would we have done the work that we did then if it were now?

SAUL: I don't think we could. The times, the politics, the system, the state of the prisons have changed. Since I worked with you in the States, the prison system and the prison population in America has exploded. It's out of control.

JOHN: My answer is slightly different. What you say is a very important part of it. In some odd way, in these lawless places that we were in, and they were lawless, we were able to do the most astonishing things while riding the rails—taking chances, letting things develop as they may.

SAUL: And the odds against change for the men were just so huge.

JOHN: We didn't really know that at the beginning. . . . I'm thinking about one of my favorite pieces, the AIDS play.

SAUL: In the UK. it was called *Are You Positive?* It was a classic piece of TIE [Theatre in Education]. Except that nobody was talking about AIDS in prison at that time.

JOHN: There weren't any practical AIDS pieces in prison back then—I think 1988. Of all the pieces we created, it worked the best because it was the simplest. We played a trick on the guys, which was getting them to love a character who's a fuckup, who's amoral but lovable. Then at some point, we make him sick from unprotected sex and needle use. And the audience fights the sickness with him. And he dies. And then we teach them how to prevent their own deaths. We did so much research for that piece—we all got tested and waited ten days for the results—we talked to everyone. It was still called ARC [AIDS-related complex] in those days. No one really knew anything.

SAUL: But that was a model. Research, discussion, and then creating characters that the audience identifies with, recognizes, and likes. You always said that the character has to do something that the audience would do. You get them on board and then the character does things that they wouldn't do. And that's when you investigate it.

There's another show I still talk about. I think it was the most radical show we did together—the drug show, *Hooked on Empty*. It was so radical because it was so abstract. It was about dealing with craving.

The premise was brilliant. We're going to go in, and we're going to get you stoned without any chemicals. Get them stoned through their imaginations and then teach them strategies to bring themselves down, all in a sixty-minute show. Using everything from hypnosis and sound to word associations. We did the whole play set inside a body. With masks by Sally Brookes that represented what we called the demons of addiction: Suck, Wheedler, Buzz, and Crash. We knew that it worked from the first time it was performed, and there were prison officers with alcohol problems who were going, "That's absolutely bang on."

JOHN: And always the intensely improvised, endlessly dangerous interactions with the audience; the decisions we shared with the guys about

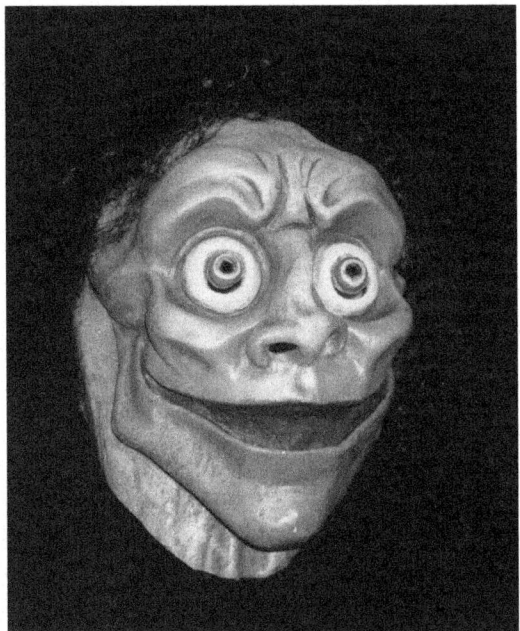

Figure 10.1. Geese Theatre mask known as Buzz. Photograph by Saul Hewish.

how the characters would deal with situations onstage. We never really knew how they would react—especially with the early plays like *Plague Game,* where they argued with one another, or told us we didn't know what we were talking about, or thought we were charities or Christians and put us down.

SAUL: As well as the plays we performed for them, there were a lot of original shows with the guys that you and I created together.

JOHN: So a question, Saul. Were the shows theirs or just somewhat ours?

SAUL: I was thinking about this earlier today, remembering the shows I made with you. In my memory, they always began with your coming up with some ridiculously long title for a show that was basically a brief. Like *Where Am I Supposed to Go with Sixteen Cents?* And another one with a great title: *Hanging in the Tenderloin I Hear Old Voices.*

JOHN: That one also became a mural by the artist Ruth Morgan, which hangs in one of the wings of the prison. This was at CJ7 [County Jail] in San Francisco—brilliant prison, brilliant staff!

SAUL: The games, improvs, work with images, all that was ours. But the content got created inside the prison by the men.

JOHN: Yeah. It was theirs, for sure. When we went into institutions to make a show, we would say, "Look, this is the game; this is what's going to go on in the next ten days." And we'd lay it out. But what really happened was, Day 1, they'd love us. Day 2, they'd work hard. Day 3, they'd hate us: "I don't wanna do this shit. Why am I doing this shit?" Day 4, they got it. Day 5, they started telling us how to direct the show. Day 6, et cetera.

As you got closer to performance, it began to strike some of them. *This is real!* So then you had to really work fast to get them through all of that, with us generally having do set and props, costumes, any of that other shit and trying not to do too much of that stuff. Then, there'd be the whole thing of stage fright, the amount of sheer terror that they had. Many of these guys were often very fearful, and suddenly they had to do something incredibly different, where all their prison experience didn't count. Remember how they didn't understand applause because they didn't know what it meant, because nobody had ever applauded them. And we'd have to go and teach them that as well.

SAUL: Yup!

The Effect

JOHN: Let's talk about effect—how this work *really* affected us—not always directly and not always in ways that we immediately understood. Sometimes it took years.

SAUL: Yeah, I think it's what happens when you're working in the belly of the beast.

JOHN: Like wearing a belt. I became very conscious that I was allowed to come in with a belt. And that a belt was a very significant thing for many of these men. Because—and this we learned in drama therapy sessions with them and in making new shows with them—the belt was a tool of punishment that they had experienced as children. The men often tried denial in a session, saying, "I feel nothing" and "Leave me alone." Just like they had tried to do when they were children being beaten. All you have to do is point to a belt on the floor and say, "What's the belt saying?" And they tell you—and so awfully, painfully fast.

And you hear it. I called it "The Song of the Belt" (from a play by Peter Weiss, *The Investigation*). It was painful to hear.

SAUL: When we tried to talk about these experiences in mental health conferences, they invalidated us! They'd say we were essentially frivolous, as if we wore bells on the ends of our trousers. That we had funny little tricks—referring to warm-up games or role reversals, for example—or that we wore funny masks, so we were close to just being clowns. And because we were clowns, that meant that our techniques were fake, no matter what. Always at these conferences, when you and I would keynote, you could see the look they flashed because we said we were theater persons. We were up against that all the time. It takes a toll. Makes you feel less than. That had an effect on us.

JOHN: Do you remember the sexual assault on the counselor we knew?

SAUL: I remember because you phoned me.

JOHN: I was working in that prison in a little sort of island, surrounded by barbed wire. The horn went and I said to the prison officer, "What's going on?" and he said all the men had to go to their bunks, and I said, "What do we do?" He said, "You have to wait till we figure out what's going on." At some point, we found out that this counselor we knew was being held hostage. It didn't look like the prison had much of a game plan. All staff were being kept in the prison, which just intensified the grimness of it all. All of us knew the counselor. People were in shock, including me. It was one of our own. And still we weren't getting any information, so you either imagined what was happening to her or you tried to block it out.

She'd been in there for hours and hours and there were stories coming out and you didn't know if they were real. I won't say what they were here. You know them. Gradually, all the prisoners became enemies in the officers' heads and in many of the therapists' minds, too.

The chief clinical psychologist—an astonishing, brilliant woman—brought some of us back to thinking like human beings. She said, "Has anybody been around the men?" And everybody looked at her and said, "What?" "Has anybody been around the men? They're gonna be shocked." She went around the men, and the men were just as freaked-out as the free people. Obviously, they knew that counselor. They lived there. Some had been there twenty years. So the notion in all the staff's minds about a hideous rape fantasy was not true. They were frightened. That experience marked me, burrowed down into me.

SAUL: It didn't make me feel more scared. I could imagine how awful it was, though, because I knew the prisoner involved, and I knew the counselor. I was more affected by a guy who slashed his face after a project I did in prison some years later. It was one of those instances when I had a feeling about him—that something wasn't right. I thought it was my fault in some way. The other men in the project told me it wasn't. He was mentally ill and was asking for some additional meds, as was his right. But the staff refused and that was his response. . . . How did you feel that assault on the counselor affected you?

JOHN: I can't tell you precisely. I think for years, given that we took a lot of risks to go to very protected but very dangerous places, that the balance between the danger and mostly being successful and feeling safe tilted a little after the assault. And moments in rehearsal, or drama therapy sessions when the guys bared their teeth, so to speak, and threatened to come after you, added to the feelings about the assault and other scares I had had, and raised the level of my internal anxiety. I mostly tried not to think about it. And we had our strategies for taking our minds off that part of the work.

SAUL: And we ignored the small things that got through.

JOHN: You make me remember San Quentin—a small thing that rattled us for a moment and a larger memory that shows how others were also scarred by prison. We were accompanied in San Quentin by an officer who was on some type of special detail. He was very laconic, but he was how we were gonna stay safe. We had a full company of actors. We were going to do a performance off the loading dock, for the prisoners in their cells, and some workshops. Then we were to go up to the education building, which was just this dilapidated brick building. We did a workshop with the guys and decided that the theme was a cabaret and then we went to eat.

We were eating in the joint. It was hamburgers—not too good, but free. We come back into the prison again and the officer on the gate said, "Do you know that we use western hostage rules?" I said, "No, what are they?" And he grins and says, "Good-bye!" I now know that western hostage rules mean they don't negotiate for hostages and that always chills you just a little bit and sticks in your mind.

So we went back to finish off this workshop. It was really a throwaway workshop, a one-off. I decided that the theme for the cabaret was gonna be burgers. And so the guys went off in groups. One guy became the speaker and said, "Yeah, okay, man. So here's what's going on." And he said something that momentarily chilled me again: "Wherever you look, there're body parts and blood." It was seven o'clock in the evening. We were on the sixth floor of an old brick building, in a prison, and I had a bunch of young company members working with me. And he continued: "Then something happens, man. And all the body parts come together and make . . . Burger Queen!"

And everyone laughed, relieved, and started creating the burger cabaret. We always said that if we were good for anything at all, it was to give these guys a respite from the nightmare that prison really is. But our officer was gone, and I looked for him. He wasn't laughing. He looked at me like he was really angry. I went up to him and said, "If we fucked up, you need to tell us whatever it is."

And he said, "No. I've worked here eight years. The reason why I wasn't walking around with you guys was because I've been on the tiers and they'd thrown bags of piss and shit in my eyes. And I've been in the hospital, and they sent me up with you guys and I didn't particularly want to do this thing at all. Then I watch what you're doing and what makes me mad is *they* never told me that these guys could be like this." I never forgot that prison officers could be reached. When you work closely with the men in prison, the excitement and details of the work make you forget the danger that is always underneath.

SAUL: I did a lot of improvising in a top-security English nick. We did actor exercises and we improvised monologues. It built over a period of weeks. It was no big show, more like a "scratch" session where we were sharing some small pieces. We invited people to come from the rest of the unit. I think for some of those men who'd been in a long, long time, it was a kind of revelation for them. But all I know is in those moments—and we've talked about those moments that occur in prison—something is going on inside them, something that is special. It was part of the reward for the work we did. Sometimes unforgettable. And it affected us and prison workers who saw only the worst. But when we worked, they would see something new.

JOHN: While were talking about being affected—something else specific to the touring performing company in the United States and the UK was how crazy we got /felt/behaved after prison performances.

SAUL: We all lived together and we were often on the road. We spent two or three weeks in the van, and we were all young. Our energy levels were off the planet, so much so that I remember the guys were always saying that they'd think that we were coked up or something because we had all that energy. Especially in a prison, which is so dull and where everyone's moving in slow time. I was not that aware what the prison performances and workshops were doing to me or us until we would get people, sometimes students or other theater makers who'd heard about our work, who would want to come and spend a day with us. We'd always go, "Yeah, of course!" Then I realized that these people were getting quite freaked out. Not by what was in the prison, but by us, because we were so dark. It carried over.

My overwhelming memory of the early days of Geese here in the UK was just an insane amount of argument. There would be all of this sort of shouting. I just thought, *It's like being in a band.* Because I'd been in

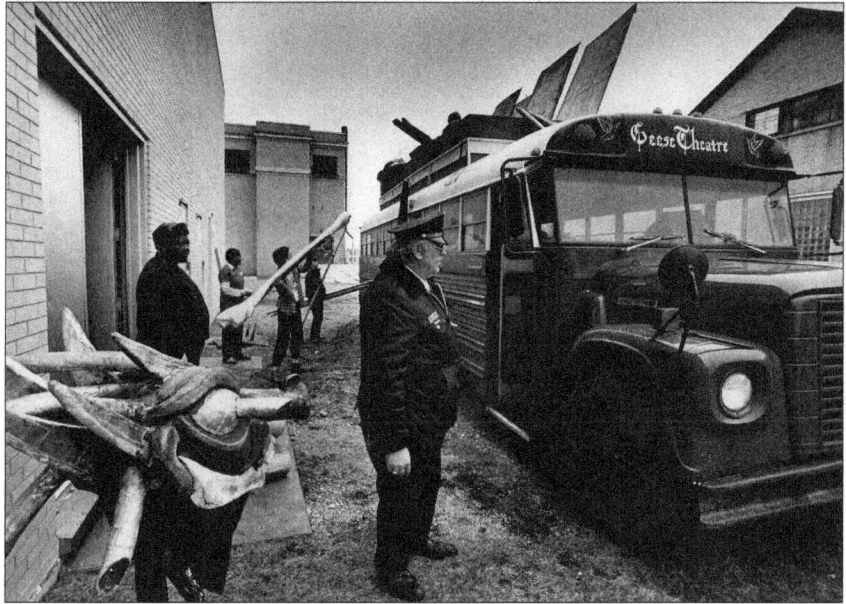

Figure 10.2. The Geese Theatre van at a prison. Photographer unknown.

bands and that's what it was. *Just like* being in a band—a good description of the hyped effect we experienced! I always came out of prison high in some ways—not drugs, just massive amounts of adrenaline.

JOHN: Yes—all that absolutely intense energy. And because our shows followed a type of *via negativa*, we were always in the eye of the storm. These were not "nice" plays. We were there to drive the guys to come up with change! Every performance went right to the fucking edge. I always had this notion that I knew where the edge was. Was I wrong—and certainly the edge drove all of us. And then we would get in our old bus and we were gonna drive, somebody was going to cook, somebody would be a copilot, run the map, food. It might be driving through the night. We maybe had to drive another three hundred miles. To the next prison. And then another prison somewhere in America.

And the conversation, shouting, laughter, stories in the bus were blue—dark, darkest blue, darkness. It was coming out of all of our mouths. Immediate. Dark, some obscene, some almost violent. And like you said, Saulie, high energy, crazy high energy. Darkness from acting and entering the darkness. Because of the prison's darkness. Because of those awful stories? But it was also a scary high. Yeah, everybody . . . everybody in the company. If we were talking honestly about how the work affected us, this was part of it. Of course after performance there were our company-based self-crits about the performance and the work—always: *Did it work? What were we missing? Were we pissing in the wind?* Always an antidote to the ego.

SAUL: But that darkness and high energy were very powerful defense mechanisms for us. Whether we knew it or not, we were figuring shit out. I don't know if it was the same in the States, but in the UK company, we would become these characters that we would create, which were based on certain prisoners we'd met. You would have a character and you'd do him. And it was kind of like it was playing, but it was a dark play.

JOHN: Which raises the issue of when we played characters, or did therapeutic sessions, and we experienced the sense of being "slimed."

SAUL: Some of the characters were more than dark—they did seriously horrendous things to other people. And a very few were very invested in what they did. When you had to act with those people, it was difficult not to be touched by that darkness.

JOHN: We called it "slimed." But we could have called it "Hadrian's Wall." If we are honestly talking about how the work affected us, and not just burbling on about how beautiful everyone was/is, then especially for those of us working around issues of sexual abuse and particularly of children, we all experienced, as we listened to the men, a sort of projected ugliness, a patina that felt like slime. As if we were being covered in it.

Here's a story, one that has a touch of the slime but also a touch of the heroism that we experienced in some of the men we worked with, and maybe a way for people to see into how close to the edge we often were. We were working with a group of men, all of whom had been convicted of sex offenses. We were trying to make little forays into reducing their shame. We were playing a game we called "Dirty Word Opera." Everyone had to come up with a dirty word, which would get used in an improvisation that had nothing to do with the meaning of the word, like hailing a taxi on the moon. For some men, it's really difficult. We came to this prolific offender and his word was *tongue*. It was just one of those moments that seemed to add itself to my inner ugly suitcase.

But at the same time I had a guy who had had sex with an animal. He couldn't understand why I was saying, "You've gotta apologize to it." And I said, "I want you to imagine it's in a chair and what I want you to do is to apologize to it." But there was also a guy there who, whenever any of the other guys were being questioned about anything at all, he thought it was his job to jump into the trenches with him and try to stop it. And the therapist that we were working with kept saying, "Now you just leave John alone. He's got work to do." He wanted to go and beat me up. Finally, the man *really* apologized to the sheep. And everybody, therapists and the men in treatment, experienced relief, excitement, and that thing that happens in theater: a real catharsis. And though one hour before I was trying to slough off another slimed experience, yet an hour later I was flying, excited, delighted, proud of the men whom I had worked with.

SAUL: Then we'd get off the road for a few weeks and fill up with some routine because we had to come down, cool down.

JOHN: Oh yeah. Did we know that we were really just changing the tuning in our heads? Did we know that this was often because of the darkness that we would have to breathe? Don't know—just remember we cleaned the house, then went to town and religiously ate bagels, cream cheese, and smoked salmon.

SAUL: And puttered around the secondhand shops. Bought odd stuff—you were buying old clocks. Then the Chinese meal and home to a movie.

JOHN: I don't think we consciously realized what we were doing. It was routine to calm the inflammation. We saw, heard, experienced so much darkness!

SAUL: It was *not* always dark—especially when we made theater together.

JOHN: Working with the guys as actors could be extraordinary. Almost from the very beginning, at Statesville Penitentiary in 1980, I learned that with the right stimulus, the men could create as quickly and as well as my University of Iowa students. That was a thrill and a knowledge that stayed with me all the years of the work and to this day! I did this exercise with the Statesville men, in a room that was actually for wrestlers. I said to them, "I want you to imagine I'm holding a box up, but I've taken the front wall off. What do you see inside that box?" And there was *no* difference in the speed of creation between the men and my university students, just the incredible difference in what they came up with.

SAUL: Talking about acting and performance and being "in the moment" . . . We'd be sitting in a prison with a bunch of guys and someone would tell a story and it would just floor the room. The telling of the story was so brilliant and so "in the moment." It was the kind of storytelling that actors spend years trying to master. But, of course, the challenge was, could we ever get them to do that again as well?

JOHN: When we would first start with them, they couldn't tell a story. So in the first couple of days or so, we'd do a lot of physical stuff and just stretching. What we were doing, I think, was throwing words and ideas and memories at them because prison flattens everything. Then slowly they would get there.

SAUL: What makes a brilliant actor in a way is that ability to do it as if it has never been told before. Which takes so much work. Which was what was so amazing about the man we worked with at CJ7 in San Francisco.

JOHN: Yeah.

SAUL: Remember, he was maybe sixty-five, African American, white hair. He had been pretty quiet, and it was his turn to tell a story. So he told us about being on a bus, coming into Detroit very early on a winter's day—I remember somehow he said 6:00 A.M. It was cold and he was alone. Then he said the wind picked up and this piece of newspaper on the pavement flipped up and wrapped itself around his leg like it was his only friend in the world. And you got this incredible picture and feeling of loneliness, cold winter loneliness. And we all were floored!

JOHN: Never forgot it.

SAUL: Do you remember the problem, though? Do you remember what happened when we asked him to perform it in the show? He could remember the story. The problem was that when he told the story, he kept turning around. So we'd created a place onstage for memories, a circle where you come to remember, and he would start the story. But as he would start to tell the story, he'd start to shuffle. He was telling the story, but the story kept taking him back to that moment.

JOHN: Funny how slightly differently I remember the problem. I remember that he had been a big user of alcohol and was not long in recovery. And his memory was shot. So he'd start to remember the story and then would get lost. But the story was so important—and we really honored any genuine story that the men created, so we worked and worked with him. And in performance he nailed it. But listening to him the first few times was like when we were interviewed by Studs Terkel and he told a few stories—you knew you were in a very different land.

SAUL: For me one of the biggest lessons about making theater in prison is that we have to trust the art form. Do you remember when we would be making a show with prisoners getting really anxious and kind of going, "Is there a show? I don't think there's a show. It looks like shit. It's gonna be awful. It's a disaster." All of that. Just nerves! Then it would happen and their adrenaline would kick in and everything would happen. Even if the show wouldn't necessarily happen how you expected, something good always happened. We would always say yes to our process. Because in the end, we just have to trust our process. In the end, of course, we had to trust theater.

JOHN: One of my favorite stories is about once the guys understood upstage, downstage, stage right, and stage left. We'd teach them that early on. And sometime around Day 4 or Day 5, if creating a new show with them, someone would come up to me and say that some entrance should have been from stage right and not stage left. They'd all become directors. But it also meant to me that they were seeing like theater folk, processing in a new way. The unvarnished prison imagination was often crude. We shaped it, pushed them. That's the truth of it. And every time they got it was such an emotional kick. For me, a strong, positive prison experience.

SAUL: One of my defining prison experiences was the first time that I worked with life-sentence prisoners. Yeah, all lifers. I'd been asked to make a show with them. I remember being a bit terrified by the notion, not because I thought they were going to hurt me, but, rather, it was, "What do I do with them?" It was just before I came to work with you. I was still in my late twenties and was this skinny white kid with long hair. And I'm thinking, *What the fuck do I know about being a lifer? Nothing!* So that's essentially what I used the show to do—to find out. The men were extremely generous in sharing their experiences and the show had some great moments. I remember at the end, a participant came up to me and said, "That's the best week I've had in prison, ever." My initial response was feeling overwhelmed by the weight of the comment, followed by a concern that I didn't really know how to respond. In the end, I was just honest with him and said, "Well, this is one is the best weeks that I've ever had, as well." Those shared experiences, and their shared life experiences, inside this theater process, are so compelling.

JOHN: We're not the same as the regular artists who go off and make something commercial. We work for the good of the people we interact with. There's that question we always ask: "Who's the audience?"

SAUL: What the fuck does it say about us that we're more interested in the experience of working in a room in the back of shit with a bunch of guys to make something than we are in wanting to be famous actors, wanting to be on television? There's a fundamental thing for me, that doing drama and theater in prison is so core to my identity, and my sense of myself, that if it wasn't to be there, I wouldn't really know who I was. Maybe because I came to this work when I was barely twenty-one years old, and for a period of nine years between, beginning in 1987 and going to work with you in the States in 1996, I didn't talk about anything other than prison, prisoners, and theater. It was certainly formative of my professional identity, but I think it goes deeper than that.

JOHN: I had a friend who called this work "throwaway theater," really put it down. She hated it.

SAUL: Yeah, but the thing is, it's not throwaway theater, or you could say all theater is throwaway. It's temporal. I mean, it's fucking there, and then it's gone, right? But actually, we know that it wasn't throwaway because it was . . . real. Even when the stories were invented, it was all about the men and their struggle right there to get it right, show their kids, show the officers. It was about them trying something new. And we helped them get there.

JOHN: One more memory about the light, not darkness, that we found in some of those places was at a Texas prison, a long drive from the Northeast. Five hundred guys and an evening performance. The man who brought us in told us to ask the inmate Motown group to sing before the performance started. They were dressed in these fancy waistcoats and they could really harmonize. So they opened our set. And as we got to the end of the show, which was really dark, people too tired for anger, drunk, gone in some way, I went over to the Motown group and said, "Would you sing out the end of the show? It's just downbeat. I leave it

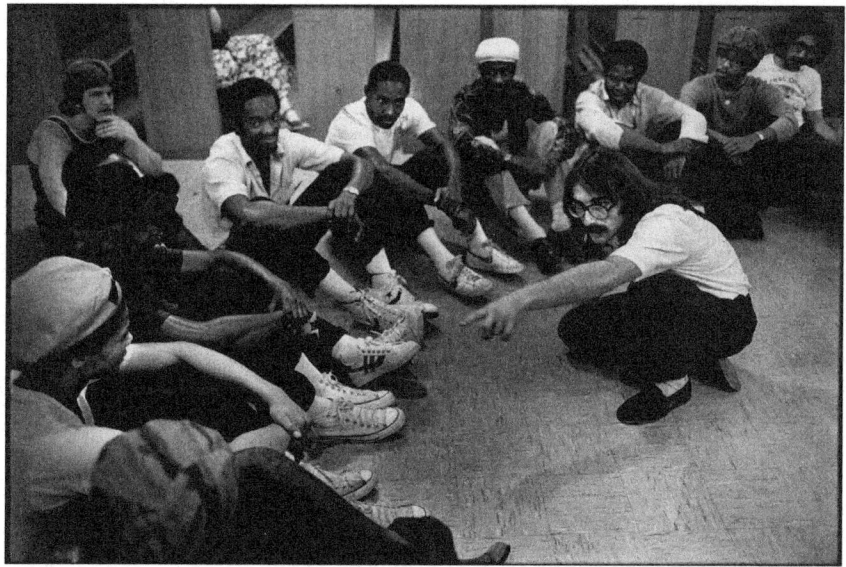

Figure 10.3. John Bergman facilitating a prison workshop in the early days. Photographer unknown.

up to you." And they watched, and came in at the last moments in the show and sang this beautiful song. Silence. Eight P.M. in a prison in Texas, five hundred men and us holding on to the beauty that had just happened for as long as anyone could. No darkness—perhaps even some hope, if just for a moment. And the feeling of the translucency of all the arts and all our places in that light. Stayed with me for always.

11

Unshackling the Body, Mind, and Spirit: Reflections on Liberation and Creative Exchange between San Quentin and Auckland Prisons

BY RAND HAZOU AND REGINOLD DANIELS

This essay was cowritten by scholar-facilitator Rand Hazou and facilitator–former inmate Reginold Daniels about their cross-national collaboration. Very different in tone from the story-driven accounts that precede it, the essay bears witness to the many ways we express our experiences. It is adapted from an article that appeared in Humanities 11, no. 1 (2022) *and can be read in full at https://doi.org/10.3390/h11010007. We are grateful for permission to adapt and include it.*

Introduction: Performing Liberation

In September 2019, incarcerated participants at Auckland Prison, Pāremoremo, attended a short creative workshop that was offered over two afternoons. During the first session, Reginold Daniels, a formerly incarcerated Black educator and arts facilitator from the United States, led the mainly Indigenous Māori participants through an exercise. The men were asked to stand in a circle and chant the word *dream* repetitively. During the chanting, Daniels recited a poem entitled "Dream," which he had written and performed in a theater production exploring the experience of incarceration. The chanting and recitation had a profound effect. A space opened up that was personal, emotional, and moving. Then the participants were given a series of questions about liberation composed by Antwan "Banks" Williams, who was incarcerated at San Quentin prison.

At the workshop session the next day, the incarcerated participants shared their responses to the questions. They reported that they had been inspired to stay up late the night before to write poems, songs, and stories. Months later, in reflecting on the efficacy of the workshops in helping to activate the creativity of the prisoners, we kept returning to that moment on the first day, when Daniels shared his poem, to the communal chanting of the men. This essay attempts to make sense of that moment and explore its significance as an act of liberation.

Daniels's workshops were part of Performing Liberation, which aimed to empower communities with direct experience of incarceration to create and share creative work as part of a transnational dialogue. A central politics informing this project was the need to center the experiences of incarcerated communities themselves so that they are empowered to lead creative explorations without reliance on outside artists or educators. The project aimed to facilitate creative dialogue and exchange between prisoners at Auckland Prison and at San Quentin Prison, in San Francisco. While these two communities are geographically, historically, and culturally distant, they are nevertheless connected by global mass incarceration and a carceral logic that disproportionately impacts racial minorities. In the United States, Black Americans make up 40 percent of the incarcerated population, despite representing only 13 percent of U.S residents. In New Zealand, Māori constitutes more than half the prison population (Department of Corrections NZ 2020), despite being only 15 percent of the overall population (World Population Review 2021). The overrepresentation of Māori in corrections has been linked to the ongoing legacy of colonialism (Jackson 2017; McIntosh and Workman 2017).

A central provocation for the project was the question "What does liberation feel like?" The project sought to test the human limits of understandings and creative explorations of liberation despite the constraints of confinement and distance. The idea emerged after Dr. Rand Hazou met with members of the Artistic Ensemble at San Quentin Prison in July 2019. The Artistic Ensemble is a troupe of sixteen diverse men in prison working with five outside members creatively collaborating through language, sound, and movement to explore social inequalities. Hazou brought some image theater exercises as well as a desire to explore how the experience of incarceration might colonize the self so that the segregation, isolation, and confinement that carcerality imposes can become internalized and normalized. This provoked a discussion about general notions of liberation and how it might involve resisting or refusing the normalization of behaviors and responses imposed by carcerality. As a result, a member of the Ensemble, Antwan "Banks" Williams, supplied a list of questions and creative prompts on the theme of liberation, which he asked Dr. Hazou to share with prisoners at Auckland Prison. These included:

- Tell me what is liberation.
- Does it look like you or me?
- Tell me if it is worth what you did.
- Tell me if liberation goes by another name.
- Does it change, stay the same, live forever, or die in vain?
- Tell me, please tell me.
- I want to know if your shackles and chains are visual.
- Tell me, are they literal, biblical?
- Tell me if liberation starts within.
- If so, tell me you've freed your mind.
- Tell me time is a figment; tell me your cell's dimensions.
- Tell me liberation can come from forgiveness.
- Tell me liberation is near.
- Tell me liberation is here.
- Tell me liberation can't disappear.
- Do you find liberation in the faces of people you love?
- Does liberation look like movements of silence?
- If so, how often are you quiet?

This chapter explores the sharing of these questions and prompts and the space for creative exploration that opened up during the workshop at Auckland Prison. We recall two key moments in the workshop to explain its efficacy in stimulating the creativity of the participants: the *pōwhiri*, or Indigenous Māori cultural welcome that the men performed, and Daniels's exercise involving the group chanting and the recitation of a poem. We interrogate the creative space that these two moments produced in relation to the concept and practice of liberation and conclude with some reflections on our own blind spots in attempting to facilitate the workshops and the larger collaborative project.

Rather than reporting the experiences of the workshop participants, we focus on our own personal perspectives as the workshop facilitators, educators, and creative producers located outside the prison complex concerned with creating opportunities for those inside to participate and learn through the arts. We wish to avoid professing to speak for and voice the experience of those inside and therefore circumvent engaging in cultural colonization that either extracts the experiences of the prison participants for our own advancement or imposes our interpretation as outside facilitators on the incarcerated participants. We explore this creative stimulation in relation to the notion of liberation, as a concept that interrogates various forms of oppression and a practice concerned with unshackling the body, mind, and spirit.

Our Approach to Writing This Chapter

This chapter is coauthored using autoethnography and practice as research methods. As researchers/practitioners, we were engaged participants of the Performing Liberation workshops at Auckland Prison. Both of us possess knowledge of working in carceral spaces as creative facilitators. One of the authors also possesses personal experience of incarceration, having spent time inside. In situating ourselves this way, we acknowledge that claims of subjective bias do not arise from the level of immersion in a cultural setting, but, rather, from a researcher's or scholar's ambiguous placement in a field of inquiry (Coffey 1999).

The motivating factor in writing this chapter was to try to understand our experience of the workshops facilitated at Auckland Prison. Ultimately, our writing is informed by autoethnographic research that draws on experience, emotion, and subjectivity for its material. As John Freeman states, autoethnographers "write their experience into narratives and are themselves key participants in the research, and often also its subject;" thus, "the idea of research as a neutral process is abandoned in favor of a self-reflective form that explores the researcher's perspective on the subject in question" (Freeman 2015, 2). We describe these key moments and analyze them in relation to the notion of liberation and bell hooks's (hooks 1994) conception of an ethic of love.

Theater in prison is most often defined in terms of participatory programs carried out by professionals who enter into criminal justice settings to carry out theater workshops and projects with prisoners

(Balfour et al. 2019). Recent scholarship extends the discussion of prison theater to consider carcerality as a pervasive neoliberal strategy and the role theater and performance can play in highlighting the rights of those experiencing state-sponsored control, confinement, and exclusion (Woodland and Hazou 2021). In this chapter, we extend the discussion of theater in prison to other forms of performance and creativity that emerge from and speak to the specific cultures of the incarcerated communities with which the Performing Liberation project engaged. In both the United States and New Zealand and particularly among Black and Indigenous Māori communities, oral performance traditions such as storytelling, speaking, poetry, song, and rap as well as dance and movement are art forms that hold cultural currency.

The Performing Liberation project built on creative endeavors that spoke directly to the cultural realities of the communities involved. This focus on oral traditions and the privileging of vernacular expression was also an important consideration in our approach to coauthoring. In pursuing the question of the larger collaborative project, "What does liberation feel like?" we found that we needed to find answers in our method of coauthorship, as well.

Wanting to do justice to oral traditions and Black and brown vernaculars was a central concern in our coauthoring and writing methods. Early in our collaborations, Daniels expressed some concerns with the format and conventions of academic scholarship, which he felt continue to disadvantage Black intellectuals. While Reggie is an eloquent educator, facilitator, and scholar, he has often struggled in finding ways to articulate his ideas using written academic conventions. As Myra Khan points out, within the academic field, priority is often given to physical and tangible materials such as books, documents, photographs, while historical knowledge in the form of oral traditions are often overlooked (Khan 2021).

Daniels is acutely aware that historically the traditional methods of knowledge transmissions for people of color are based on oral traditions. For Daniels, oral traditions and Black vernacular is familiar and has a kind of radical legitimacy and currency among incarcerated communities. In attempting to reflect on the experience of facilitating a creative workshop for prison participants and articulate their significance for an academic readership, there is something about oral knowledge transmission that clashes with the privileging of the written word and certain grammatical conventions in the academy.

The coauthoring of this chapter took the form of a series of discussions we organized online through Zoom. During these meetings we attempted to re-create and document key moments from the workshop. We would meet, discuss an issue or a question, and Hazou would type up responses and share these in a Word document. At our next meeting we would revise what had been written, reading out loud the writing and making sure that Daniels felt comfortable with the words. An effort was made to record Daniels's words and reflections accurately and not alter his speech patterns or vernacular too much in transposing his words to paper.

Like our creative collaborations, the writing and research also incorporated a dialogical approach, which attempted to privilege Daniels's lived experience, feelings, and vernacular. In reflecting on our method of coauthoring, Daniels explained, "It felt very familiar for me. To be able to speak from the heart and then have that transposed into words and then be able to see the words and go, 'Ah, yes, that sounds right.' It allowed me to access some emotional spaces that I might not have been able to if I was preoccupied with writing and thinking about it in my mind" (Daniels 2023). Academic conventions have a way of distancing you from the emotion you are trying to convey, but the way we worked had a way of narrowing that distance and bringing Daniels closer to the feeling that he was trying to say and convey.

Key Moments in the Workshop

Since 2017, Hazou had been involved in creative engagements at Auckland Prison. He invited Dr. Daniels and Dr. Amie Dowling from the University of San Francisco to New Zealand to participate in the international Performing Arts and Justice Symposium, to discuss and share knowledge about the role of the arts and culture in decolonizing corrections. Daniels and Dowling facilitated a workshop at Auckland Prison to help establish connections with the incarcerated community in San Francisco. It was organized by Hazou, working with Auckland Prison staff, and drew on his previous relationships with senior managers and prisoners. The twelve prison participants were from diverse cultural backgrounds, experiences, and ages. Five identified as Māori, four were of Pacific Island origin, and the remaining were Pākehā, or New Zealanders of European heritage.

The resulting workshops were short—conducted over two afternoons and conceived as a starting point that might develop into longer and more sustained creative collaborations in the future. Yet, while brief, the workshops created a personal, emotional, and powerful moment that seemed to open up a creative space that helped catalyze the participants' creativity.

Our approach to facilitating the workshops was guided by acknowledgment of Māori protocols that "privileges Māori knowledge and ways of being" (Smith 2008, 120). The workshops were informed by a *pōwhiri*, a traditional cultural welcoming ceremony performed by the Maori prisoners for the visiting U.S. artists. This ritual welcome set the affective and intellectual register for the workshops, which the facilitators responded to in genuine, emotive, and meaningful ways.

The *pōwhiri* is a unique customary welcome practiced by Māori, which shares some similarities with other Indigenous welcome protocols, such as the Australian Aboriginal "welcome to country." The etymology of the word *pōwhiri* are the two words *pō*, meaning "unknown," and *whiri*, meaning "plaiting." A *pōwhiri*, therefore, is about the weaving of unknowns (Rameka et al. 2021, 5). The purpose of a *pōwhiri* is to provide a process of engagement between two parties and involves one group welcoming another into its place of belonging. The ritual is composed of a series of specific sequences of enacted events. Typically, a *pōwhiri* would be performed on a *marae*, or the courtyard of a Māori meeting house, but the location and the sequence involved can be adapted to suit the situation.

At Auckland Prison, the guests were welcomed into the space with a *karanga* (ritual chant of welcome) performed by a transgender prisoner who held knowledge of language and *tikanga* (cultural protocols). The *karanga* is a call that "reaches not only the physical ears of those who stand waiting, but also the ancestors who have passed to the spirit world" (McCallum 2011, 95). Following the call and a *whaikōrero* (formal speech) by the hosts, the visitors and the prison participants sat facing one another for the duration of the ceremony, which involved further speeches and songs before the ritual concluded in a *hongi*, or the pressing of noses together, signifying the sharing of breath. This entire ceremony is considered *tapu* (sacred), as the guests and hosts engage on both a physical and spiritual level. According to McCallum, for participants of the *pōwhiri*, "there is an efficacious shift in their state of being, which is emotional, ontological, and psychological" (McCallum 2011, 93). The final aspect of the ritual involves sharing of refreshments, usually a biscuit and a cup of tea.

Dowling led the first workshop, which involved a physical warm-up and some introductory movement work. Following this, Daniels shared some of his personal story as a formerly incarcerated Black man. He explained that his ancestors were taken to the United States as slaves and that he found through a DNA test that he was 74 percent Nigerian. He explained that he was interested in visiting his ancestral African homeland and reconnecting with his ancestral customs and culture.

Next, Daniels asked the participants to get into a circle and shared his experiences as an actor in the production *Man. Alive.* (Dowling et al. 2009). After more than ten years of incarceration, Daniels was invited to participate in this theater production, codirected by Amie Dowling, Paul S. Flores, and Natalie Greene, and first staged at the Studio Theater of the University of San Francisco (Daniels 2021b). The play featured stories and experiences of incarceration and involved highly choreographed sequences of repetitive actions that represented the regimented routines of prison. The original production opened with Daniels reciting a poem he wrote (Brigham and Conner 2018) referencing the famous speech by the Reverend Dr. Martin Luther King, Jr., and expressing hope and a vision for a new reality for people impacted by white supremacy, slavery, and incarceration:

>I dream
>My eyes are closed
>But it's not that kind of dream where I am relaxed and sleep
>I am awake and focused
>Focused on my seeds of hope
>Watering them
>and I am dreaming and I am nurturing my ideas . . .
>
>I concentrate harder because the demons

come to frame my thoughts and ideas
because I am practically a middle-aged black man
   ex-offender
   ex-drug dealer
   dickslanger
   mind entangler

And while I was lying on my back looking up at the sky
   surrounded by a bunch of able-bodied men
      trapped in a nightmare of
      ain'ts can'ts do's and don'ts
   mindless labor that does not land me on the
               runway of my dreams.
      I fell deep into a trance
when the man with the keys to my freedom told me to dream
      and have it ready for him today

      So here is my dream . . .
   The world is a safe place for me and my seeds
I nor my seeds are no longer treated like the invisible man
But there is a team of experts waiting for my next dream
      So they can start putting my thoughts
         immediately into action
Me and my seed walk in the garden and share our dreams
      And we don't have to worry about
      becoming the next black president
      because we have finally figured out that
         we are all world leaders

         Happiness is more than just
         a hit, a toke, a fix, or a snort
         It's my station in life and now
         my goals have a train, a railway
      And I am no longer just lying on my back
         Incarcerated, shackled in my mind
               I am free to move forward
      To take flight
               And never look down . . .

With the participants still arranged in a large circle, Daniels asked them to chant "Dream, dream, dream" over and over as he shared his poem. As the group slowly began to chant, Daniels began reciting his poem. The chanting would occasionally subside throughout the recitation as Daniels's delivery grew in tempo and volume, only to be taken up again in brief pauses between the stanzas.

The recitation of the poem with the chanting was a palpably emotional and important moment that seemed to create a sense of unity among the workshop attendees. Daniels was moved to tears. The participants were also visibly affected. It was a profound moment that was further confirmed by the sincere thanks expressed by the participants to Daniels for sharing his words.

The participants were then given Banks's list of questions and prompts on liberation. They were printed on paper, handed out to the participants, and read out loud by Hazou. In response to the sharing of his personal story and the recitation of his poem, the participants appeared galvanized and inspired to respond to these questions. The next day, participants shared what they had created, staying up late the night before to write stories, draw, and compose poems and songs. One of the participants shared this response, which he composed as a rap:

> Let me tell you my meaning
>   of Liberation in a Rap
> It's a message of a warrior
>   who won't hold back
> Beneath the pain and all the
>   suffering your hope shines through
> Embracing Liberation is a way
>   of knowing your truth
> Release the spirit from within
>   to free the body and mind
> Acknowledge life is beneficial
>   if your living it right
> Taking the negative and positive
>   creating a plan
> Illuminating what is possible
>   and making a stand

Overthrowing your insecurities
    is always a fight
Never giving up is a way
    that I be living my life.

Anticipating for the time when
    all I want is a sign
Without the memories of everyone
    I'm leaving behind
Always knowing that it be possible
    to change what we think
Knowledge is given in a pen
    so all you need is the ink
Eventually you realize that
    Liberation's a key
Now with the message that I'm
    giving you go and follow your dreams

Analysis: Liberation and Creative Expression

In *Prison Theatre and the Global Crisis of Incarceration* (2020), Ashley Lucas argues that while theater in prison might lift performers and audiences momentarily out of the prison setting and offer a different and shared experience, this does not free people from incarceration. Lucas argues that theater in prison "can promote freethinking and empathy, but it is not, in fact, liberation" (Lucas 2020, 39). While we agree that the material conditions of carcerality are oppressive and require persistent efforts in order to challenge and transform them, we nevertheless take issue with this position as it defines liberation solely in terms of social mobility and uncritically associates being outside prison with freedom. Being free from prison does not necessarily mean freedom from exposure to ongoing surveillance, confinement, and control by the carceral system. We suggest that a more critical engagement with the theory and practice of liberation is required, which deepens an understanding of the affordances of creative engagements for incarcerated communities. Moreover, our own conception of liberation is informed by the seemingly contradictory realization that some might experience more emotional and spiritual freedom inside prison than on the outside.

This is confirmed by Daniels, who spent more than ten years incarcerated. The prison regime can be a place in which incarcerated individuals can forge strong familial ties and find a sense of connection that they did not have on the outside. For Daniels, liberation is connected to an appreciation for humanity, love, and spirit that can free us from thoughts that bind us. This can result in an emotional vulnerability that one might not experience in the world beyond the prison. Daniels explains that he sometimes yearned for the feeling of connection with his brothers on the inside—an understanding and brotherhood that he could not find on the outside.

We understand liberation as a useful tool to critique various forms of oppression and exclusion. An aim of social justice and articulated in various civil rights movements, social liberation is connected to the process of striving to achieve equal status and rights. At an individual level, liberation can also articulate the notion of personal freedom of expression, thought, or behavior. Here we articulate liberation as a process of casting off the shackles of the mind, body, and spirit. Liberation can thus be expressed in multiple ways and can be physical, mental, emotional, and spiritual.

Unshackling the Body

In the context of a prison, where technologies of surveillance and control are mobilized to produce "obedient" bodies, the *pōwhiri* and the creative workshops offered opportunities for the participants to transcend these restrictions and free up the body temporarily. Moreover, incarceration lives in the body in the sense that the institutional power of the prison works to habituate bodily behaviors and expressions. Hazou has documented how physical performance can facilitate a sense of "re-embodiment" for men who were living within a system and space that routinely polices bodies (Hazou 2021). The *pōwhiri*, the short movement exercises that followed, and the chanting and recitation helped to create a space to unshackle the body in the sense of temporarily transcending rigid and habituated physical behaviors and movements that are imposed within carceral spaces.

The *pōwhiri* set the physical, affective, and intellectual registers for the creative workshops. In particular, the use of the *hongi*, in which guests and hosts press noses together, provided opportunities to break from the physical and relational distance that is often constituted by and enforced within prison settings. Reflecting on the impact of the *pōwhiri* and the sharing of breath, Daniels explained later, "It brought tears from my eyes. The hongi—the pressing of the noses and the sharing of breath. This was powerful because in the U.S. prison system we are prohibited from touching" (Daniels 2021a).

At San Quentin, for example, it is not just touching that is prohibited but any perceived transgression of interpersonal boundaries. The California Department of Corrections and Rehabilitation policy prohibits "undue familiarity." Within U.S. correctional institutions, the incarcerated are warned against overfamiliarity, correctional officers are cautioned to avoid it, and outside volunteers and contractors are advised not to inadvertently commit it.

For Hatton, overfamiliarity as a concept and its prohibition are "at the center of the dehumanizing culture of incarceration" (Hatton 2021, 519). The *pōwhiri* at Auckland Prison helped set up a different kind of engagement between participants in the workshops that emphasized relationality and physical propinquity that challenged some of the dehumanizing restrictions that carcerality often places on the body and that can result in the loss of individuality and physical agency.

Unshackling the Mind

When asked why he began his workshop with a very personal and emotional sharing of his story, Daniels (2021a) cited the emotional impact of the *pōwhiri* and explained:

> I shared my former experiences with crime and my cycles of addiction. I shared how I was seen as the black sheep by my family. I wanted to make them know that I understood what it was like to be written off. I wanted to share so that we could be on an equal footing. People inside are often expected to bare their souls in front of observers. I was leading by example in terms of demonstrating vulnerability.

Daniels insists that his approach was to ensure that the participants did not feel judged for their mistakes and defined solely in terms of their criminality. This reductive and deficit approach underpins the corrections system. Daniels wanted to ensure that the participants would be seen as whole human beings at least for the duration of the workshops. For us, this approach is informed by an understanding that oppression has done its darkest work when it has become internalized. In attempting to facilitate creativity in carceral spaces, the work of liberatory practice is to resist the internalization of oppression created and reinforced by the carceral system, which so often dehumanizes the people that it confines.

Internalized oppression works when the dominant discourse becomes powerful to the extent that people internalize negative ideas about their group (Aguilar 2014, 14). Griffin defined internalized oppression as involving a subordinate group adopting a dominant group's ideology, resulting in the "acceptance that their subordinate status is deserved, natural, and inevitable" (Griffin 1997, 76). The focus for liberation should involve not only resisting mass incarceration and finding alternatives to punitive approaches to crime but also resisting the internalization of carcerality and the normalization of these processes. Reflecting on the impact of the recitation and the chanting, Daniels explained: "The chanting became a ritual evocation of hope. It humanized the space and gave participants an opportunity to show up in an authentic way and not have to be restricted by their crimes or the mistakes of their past. But that they could show up as human beings and be real and recognized without judgment" (Daniels 2021a).

While we acknowledge that the material reality of confinement and incarceration is important, far more important to tackle are the consequences of incarceration that lead not only to the dehumanization of incarcerated individuals but also to the internalization of this carceral logic.

The recitation of the "Dream" poem was a repudiation of the internalization of carcerality and self-doubt. The first part of the poem features a man lying on his back surrounded by able-bodied men and trapped in self-defeatist internal logic. The second half of the poem presents the narrator no longer lying on his back but instead giving himself permission to dream without excuses. The mental cycle of self-defeat is broken, thereby providing hope for the poet and the audience to move freely toward liberation. These sentiments seem to be echoed in the song written by one of the workshop participants at Auckland Prison, who explains liberation as "a message of a warrior who won't hold back." For this poet, liberation is acknowledging the hope beneath the pain and the suffering: "Embracing liberation is a way of knowing your truth." Both poems express sentiments about the unshackling of the mind that involve recognition and empowerment, in which self-doubt is no longer the dominant or controlling voice.

Daniels suggests that artistic engagement and expression within carceral settings is a productive way to challenge the self-doubt and the internalization of carcerality produced by prisons. The prison works to impress on you the idea that you deserve to be punished, that you don't deserve to be in society, and that you have no real value. For Daniels, "artistic engagement can say that there is a part of us that is creative that always has value, even if we are incarcerated, even if we have made mistakes. Mental freedom here is about the creative self" (Daniels 2021a).

Unshackling the Spirit

A way to understand the impact of Daniels's poem and the communal chanting is through bell hooks's notion of love as a spiritual practice and an act of liberation. For hooks, "the moment we choose to love we begin to move toward freedom, to act in ways that liberate ourselves and others" (hooks 1994, 298). She points to a problem arising from our "blind spots" when we confront oppression and domination, observing that many of us are ultimately motivated by "self-interest" when fighting domination. Rather than being motivated by a desire to end politics of domination or further collective transformation, often our confrontations with oppression express a desire "simply for an end to what we feel is hurting us" (hooks 1994, 290).

As Michael Monahan explains in his insightful reading of hooks, we tend to focus on one aspect of domination, the one that most directly impacts us, and either "ignore altogether, or offer only lip-service to the ways in which different kinds of domination are linked systematically to each other" (Monahan 2011,104). For hooks, the ability to acknowledge blind spots can emerge only if we alter our motivation away from the alleviation of our own suffering and instead expand our capacity to care about the oppression and exploitation of others. For hooks, a "love ethic makes this expansion possible" (hooks1994, 290). Hooks cites M. Scott Peck's working definition of love as "the will to extend one's self for the purpose of nurturing one's own or another's spiritual growth" (hooks 1994, 293).

For hooks, love is as a dynamic process, not a static state of being. It is a spiritual practice that one manifests and must be nurtured to thrive and grow. Monahan explains that we must take up the challenge of coming to know those we love "both as they are now, and as they have it in them to become" (Monahan 2011, 107). For Monahan, this involves an affirmation of nurturing and the facilitation of growth toward the possibility of a future flourishing.

Reflecting back on the workshops, the cultural opening of the *pōwhiri* provided a space of nurturing and becoming that was further enhanced by the sharing of Daniels's personal story, the recitation of the poem, and the communal chanting. One way we might understand the workshops at Auckland Prison is through hooks's conceptions of love as a spiritual practice and an act of liberation. The workshops utilized creative expression within a carceral space to shift the attention of the participants from a narrow focus on their own interests and the alleviation of their own suffering to a concern for the care of others. This was a central inspiration informing the Performing Liberation project, which sought to provide opportunities for two communities to engage in creative dialogues together to acknowledge and potentially address systemic issues of oppression that underscore global mass incarceration, which disproportionality impacts Indigenous peoples and communities of color. Through artistic engagement and dialogue with each other, the project sought to facilitate an awareness of the systemic issues of oppression that these different communities face.

Conclusions

The workshops at Auckland Prison provided opportunities for participants to share creative work that engaged with concepts of oppression, liberation, and love in ways that are not necessarily grasped intellectually through words, but, rather, explored experientially through poetry, dance, ritual, and song. The workshops highlighted experiential and affective dimensions of liberation as practices that nurture the intellect, heart, and spirit. We have attempted to analyze this workshop through hooks's notion of an ethic of love as an act of liberation. Central to hooks's conception of love as a practice of freedom is self-awareness and the importance of acknowledging our blind spots. Thus, we take this opportunity of hindsight to reflect on our own blind spots entering into this project.

For Hazou, the workshops were part of a larger project attempting to create agency and empowerment for two communities directly impacted by incarceration by facilitating sustained creative dialogue. Unfortunately, despite the initial creative responses from the workshop participants at Auckland Prison, the ongoing dialogue did not eventuate. While the questions on liberation and Daniels's workshop produced compelling responses from the participants at Auckland, when these were shared with the incarcerated community at San Quentin, they did not provoke a follow-up response. The creative engagement did not result in the sustained and ongoing creative dialogue between these two incarcerated communities that was envisioned.

In reflecting on why, we acknowledge that Banks got released from San Quentin and as such had more pressing and immediate concerns beyond incarceration, such as the need to care for his family and secure employment. In hindsight, one blind spot was that while artists or facilitators on the outside might have time and financial security to set up connections or opportunities for incarcerated communities to engage in arts practice and collaboration, it is difficult to expect someone who is incarcerated or recently released to lead these initiatives. The practicalities of sending and following up on emails or getting permissions to visit prison may be too challenging to contend with. While connection is one of the main tools that we can use to break through the confinement and isolation imposed by carcerality, when we as outside artists create these opportunities, we need to be aware that those impacted most directly by incarceration might not have the will or the way to connect.

For Daniels, the workshops were an opportunity to explore a blind spot in relation to the cultural specificities of engaging with Māori culture. Daniels's invitation to deliver the workshops at Auckland Prison acknowledged his expertise as an educator and cultural facilitator, which was informed by his experience as a previously incarcerated Black man. While this acknowledgment recognized certain commonalities among marginalized communities impacted by global incarceration, Daniels also had to contend with the specificity of the Māori cultural context at Auckland Prison. Daniels had encountered and befriended a Māori prisoner during his time in jail in the United States and had become aware of his own judgments regarding the practice of tribal facial tattoos, or *tā moko* (see Nikora et al. 2007). In the United States, tattoos on the face are often regarded as part of antisocial behavior. In approaching the workshops at Auckland Prison, Daniels was aware of his previous judgments when encountering aspects of Māori culture and had to approach his interactions with participants with humility. In hindsight, this blind spot was about the need to register and acknowledge the specificity of cultural engagement within the assumed "universal" experience of carcerality.

According to hooks, awareness is central to the process of love as the practice of freedom. She writes, "Whenever those of us who are members of exploited and oppressed groups dare to critically interrogate our locations, the identities and allegiances that inform how we live our lives, we begin the process of decolonization" (hooks 1994, 295). The workshops at Auckland Prison provided a platform of creative engagement to allow an ethic of love to emerge that facilitated experiential engagements with notions of liberation. What might be required are opportunities for additional self-awareness so that communities impacted by mass incarceration can interrogate further the locations, identities, and allegiances that inform the ongoing struggles against oppression and mass incarceration.

12

Roundtable

BY AUSETTUA AMORAMENKUM, ALEXANDER ANDERSON, JOHN BERGMAN, KEVIN BOTT, JAN COHEN-CRUZ, SAUL HEWISH, KATHY RANDELS, JESS THORPE, AND GLORIA "MAMA GLO" WILLIAMS

After drafting the whole book, I invited the contributors to read one another's essays and then join me in one of two Zoom calls to discuss what stood out for them and to ruminate on prison theater workshops together. This chapter is edited from those conversations, in which nine of the writers were able to participate, and organized around the themes that came up.

The Workshop and Participant Relationships

KEVIN: I loved reading about the depth of the relationships, the transformative power, how everyone got there, all the complications that emerge when we are raised in a culture to distrust and do harm to one another. It's a piece of this work I'm always thinking about, particularly the dynamics of white people from outside the community coming into spaces with predominantly people of color.

MAMA GLO: The essays gave me a different insight into how we are so connected, whether you were incarcerated or not. In the Drama Club, I was able to get rid of a lot of the anger, bitterness, and shame from my past, building characters and putting them out there. It was a safe place. One of the ladies said we were the sacrificial lambs putting our pain out there, hoping that we could prevent other people from going through what we'd been through.

JAN: Finn describes getting rid of his false selves as "committing suicide on the stage." It was only possible because he trusted not just me but also the temporary community that was our workshop. It was equally a place to try out unexpressed parts of ourselves we wanted to be. I see both of these dynamics—purging some parts of ourselves, manifesting others—in many of the workshops you all write about. And the importance of the other participants witnessing it.

KEVIN: Enacting the parts of the self that one seeks to grow into connects with Jill Dolan's idea about theater as utopia: By manifesting the imagined world onstage we're simultaneously manifesting it in the real world. Alex [codirector with Kevin of R4R] talks about putting on different hats, trying different roles, and the opportunity it affords. Then it becomes true; he becomes that person in real life. When I first met him, Alex seemed very uncertain of himself in the world. First he went through the R4R program [as a formerly incarcerated man], then, because he was a social worker, I asked him to join me in that capacity. But then he started experimenting as an artist and intervening in people's stories, making suggestions, and by the end of it, he *felt* like an artist. Now he sits in meetings at the Ford Foundation, and with other funders, talks about this work, and describes himself as an artist.

SAUL: I really like what Rand and Reggie wrote about unshackling the body through theater workshops. John and I used to observe, particularly with prisoners who'd been in a long time, how they'd become physically like the prison—like the building. Guys who'd spend hours doing weights so their bodies would be huge but in terms of their abilities to move their bodies—like we would say, "Lift your arms in the air," and I remember a guy who couldn't lift his shoulders because bodybuilding had made his neck so thick. The longer you're incarcerated, the more you're stuck in prison because you've become part of the machinery. I've worked with choreographers in prison and it's amazing how asking people to move in ways they never have before impacts what happens in their brains. It's really critical.

AUSETTUA: I teach dance to two different groups of people—incarcerated women and college students. And it ain't much different. The students feel like they're in prison with their parents, which is why they go to college. And then they don't want to graduate and go into the real world. Many of the people who danced in the prison weren't trained, but they were dancers at heart. I gave them movements that they had never done before. My base is African dance; it's polyrhythmic. We brought drums in—theater, dance, and music metaphysically transform a space. It's not a figment of our imagination. People are literally changed.

The Purpose of Prison and of the Workshops

JAN: I like the question of change in the workshops. We did not go into Trenton with the intention of changing anyone. It was a space to reflect, but not for me to push for particular conclusions. Take Kuwasi, who was a Black Panther and clear about being a violent revolutionary. He came to that decision in response to the world as he saw it; it would have been presumptuous of me to try to convince him otherwise. Kareem also saw the virulent racism, but postprison, he chose a nonviolent route, with service to community as the highest good. Certainly Finn and I went on to work more collectively than the paths we were on would have taken us.

SAUL: What Ausettua wrote, starting with *umbutu,* really chimed with me in relationship to social justice and the importance of hope. Hope in prison is something I'm seeing less and less of at the moment in the UK. It's sort of a counter to this obsession we seem to have with punishing people and putting them in prison for longer and longer and longer. The fact is, if people have no hope, there is no reason why they would ever do anything different from the things they did in the past, and there isn't any opportunity for anything different in the future.

MAMA GLO: In 1971, I was involved in the taking of the life of a Caucasian man. I didn't go to trial for the actual crime, but because I was a Black woman and violent harm had been done to a white man. The person who pulled the trigger said, "I did it." But it didn't matter to the system who actually pulled the trigger, but who'd been killed. I spent fifty-one years in prison for being there, even though someone else pulled the trigger. After the person who actually did the shooting passed away in prison, I still remained there another twenty-some years.

I was sentenced under the "10/6" practice, which means if you keep your nose clean, the AG [attorney general] will decide if you'll be released after ten years and six months. Elaine Hunt was secretary of the Louisiana DOC [Department of Corrections] at that time. Rumor has it that the man who was killed was related to her in some way. So it became a personal thing. As long as somebody paid, they didn't care. Somebody had to be punished. The male involved who worked for the governor—he only did sixteen years. So there's all

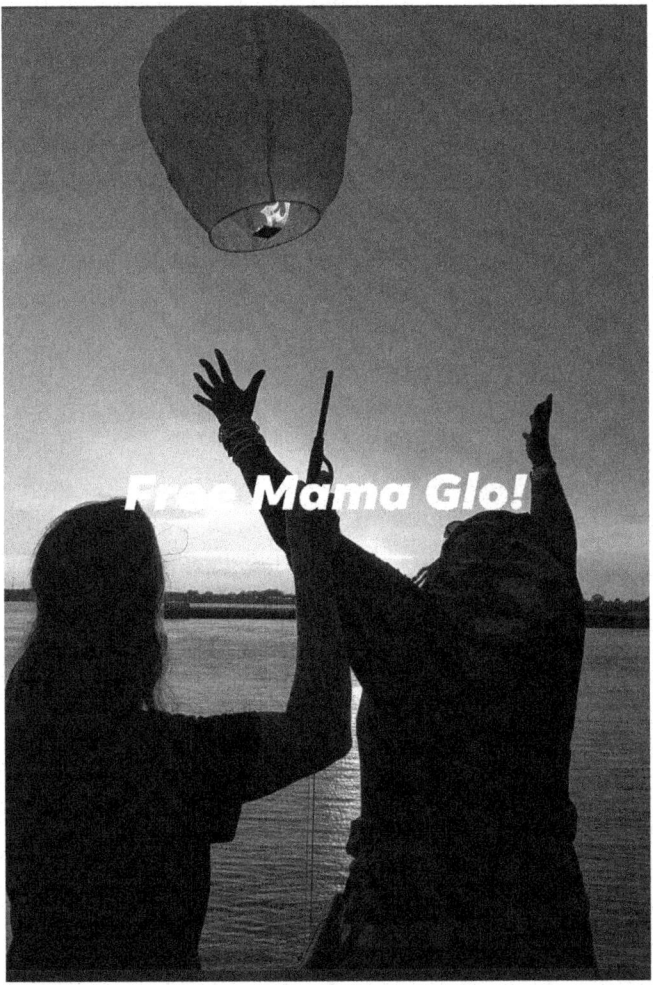

Figure 12.1. Ausettua AmorAmenkum and Kathy Randels at the "Glow up for Mama Glo Rally," May 28, 2020. Photograph by Alison McCrary.

kinds of discrimination in the system. It doesn't have to be color, white and Black; it's the whole darn system needs to be revamped. It's who you know who gets the breaks. Same thing when you go up for pardon—who has the influence in society, who writes the letter on your behalf? It took a whole village to free me and they had to fight to get it done because I had so many obstacles in my way.

KATHY: We witnessed another Pardon Board hearing in Louisiana last week. Three women from the Drama Club came up. They do a bunch of people the same day. And the racism, sexism, paternalism on the board—they treat the people who come up before them like eight-year-old children. Like Mama said about writing the right letter, who you know on the Pardon Board—each Pardon Board member takes one case on as his own and brings it before everyone. It is clear when the person has decided to lift up the incarcerated person they are standing for. And clear when one of the judges (and they aren't supposed to be judges!) has decided, "I'm not letting this person get out. I'm going to make them look as bad as possible."

On some level, we all talk about "the system" in our chapters—and we're dealing with the United States, New Zealand, England, and Scotland—we all started under the thumb of England! How do we all see our work as an alternative to the system? John and Saul ask if this work is "pissing in the wind"—hell no, none of this is pissing in the wind. I think we are all involved in changing the criminal-legal systems in our various states: bringing equity, healing, beauty, love. Indeed, some of us are involved in abolition of those systems!

KEVIN: I think the purpose of the U.S. carceral system is to crush human spirits. . . . I worked for a theater organization that goes into prisons that have the word *rehabilitation* in their name. I always struggled with it because the suggestion was that we were rehabilitating the incarcerated participants of our workshops and performances. It was ignoring or lying by omission not to suggest there were many bigger system things that needed rehabilitation. Just those words, *punishment and rehabilitation,* and what this work does inside—it's a question I wrestle with.

KATHY: Related is the notion of criminality. Where does the notion of criminality come from and how has it gone hand in hand with these systems of othering and separation, rather than seeing people who do harm and commit violence as having been victims of violence in the first place? For who knows how long, we've just said, "You are a monster and we will treat you like a monster." Some incarcerated people say, "Fine, you wanna make me a monster, I'll *show* you a monster!" And some, like Mama Glo, go on a long journey inside and find the depths of their own humanity, despite how we treat them. I appreciate the depth they go into in the New Zealand piece about racism and colonialism and the role the carceral system plays in maintaining systemic racism. Powerful.

JAN: In the Introduction, I quote Angela Davis asking why are we focusing on punishing or rehabilitating individuals when core social systems that should be supporting everyone are broken and that's what we should be fixing.

JOHN: When we attempt piecemeal change in a prison system, we're completely forgetting the other parts that got them in there. There's the social justice part and then there's the police part. Police have no idea how to interview the victims or the perps to get the "whole story." A member of our company, Patrick Tidmarsh, went on to train police how to be human when they interview folk. So if you get the victim's whole story, and the perpetrator's whole story, and the prosecutors, who instead of trying to win the case are focused on the whole story, including everything that goes into it, you get a completely different justice system than the one we've got right now, which simply favors people with money and the notion of winning.

Postrelease Support and Resources

MAMA GLO: The biggest fight for formerly incarcerated offenders is once you get out. They're selling you lies on the inside, telling you, "You can get help here; you can get help there." It's so not true. That's one of the biggest concerns; once you are out of the system and back in the world without training or job skills, you go back to what you know. So I say rehabilitation comes from within. You gotta really want it and make the sacrifice to get it in order to change yourself. To put your focus on something other than what brought you to prison. And by sucking up everything the system has to offer you that would help you better yourself. You gonna use it in your life once you're free to stay free.

SAUL: Reggie and Rand wrote about a guy getting released from San Quentin and though he'd been really involved in the exchange with the prison in New Zealand, he had more pressing things, like the need to care for his family and find employment. When I'm teaching my students, I caution—there's a lot in the literature about theater and transformation, which on the one hand can be very real but at the same time, if there aren't things in place for people as they come out of prison, it doesn't matter how good our theater program was. Some people are released homeless. They will be back in prison very quickly. For some of them, prison provides a place that's safer than living on the streets. We should be mindful of that. I think what we do is important; we enable possibilities and imagination: Could I live my life differently? We can't do that all on our own.

JOHN: We can't attempt to change prisons without changing any of the other parts of society as well. They are making a major effort to do things differently in New Zealand now, especially with Māori folk. We are not trying anything different in the United States; it remains exactly the same and therefore is completely tilted, racist, gender-biased, a nightmare.

KATHY: Well, I have to say there are people all over the United States who are actively trying to change the system, reimagine it, or even tear it down. In New Orleans and Louisiana generally, that system change is being led by formerly incarcerated people, which is very exciting and as it should be. In recent years, New Orleans elected Jason Williams as district attorney and Susan Hutson as sheriff. They both ran on platforms of reform, saying we need to treat people who get caught in the system as humans. And they've begun to embrace restorative justice and other alternatives to incarceration. They are both having trouble in their offices because system change is a huge shift on every level, in every position, in every human involved in enforcement. Progressive New Orleanians elected them and are holding them accountable—this is largely because we are ground zero for mass incarceration in the world, and we are finally saying enough is enough!

We've had a conservative Democratic governor, John Bel Edwards, in Louisiana the past eight years. He's made several reforms to our criminal legal system while in office, and has pardoned many people. I pray he pardons everyone on his desk before he leaves office, because we've got a former police officer/attorney general that is the front-runner for this upcoming fall election. But I want the world to know that system change is happening and being led by system-impacted people in Louisiana.

JESS: One of the benefits for me of living in a small country is that we only have fifteen prisons and I work in six or seven of them regularly, so I see the same people and can track their progress. As I said in the chapter we wrote, it's my dream to have a cultural program in all of them. I don't think it's so far away; we are already talking about it. It's exactly what you're saying—the most important thing is creating opportunities when people come out. I stay in touch with a lot of people I meet in the prison, like I'm doing a podcast with one person who's now out, and I go to a lot of meetings. I recently went with a woman who'd just been released from prison to meet with a church that she felt wasn't listening to her. I have nothing to do with the church. I just went to listen and try to be an advocate for her because we have a relationship. It started in the prison, but it can extend to the outside.

We have a youth theater that we run in a Scottish prison. Recently we invited lots of other youth theaters from the areas that the young people in prison live in to actually offer them places in their youth theaters when they get out. We are constantly trying to map the prison's geography with Scotland's, to find opportunities back in the community. I also work in a theater in Dundee, and so I can invite people to come and work with us there when they leave prison.

I want to create inroads into Scottish society and get away from the "othering" we do to people in prison. Only doing theater programs in prison isn't going to change anything; it can just seem like prisoners have more opportunities than the rest of the community and it doesn't respond to the bigger picture. There's got to be "What next?" When people leave, I give them my email address and I say, "Come and have a coffee and let's see what we can get you involved with." It's not for everyone. I've met people on the outside I knew from prison who have avoided me in the street; they just don't want to reconnect to that part of their lives. But other people are like, "Oh my goodness, amazing!" The relationship doesn't have to end here. I want to help them with their futures.

SAUL: How does security deal with that?

JESS: In the beginning, it was, "We don't do that," and now we *do* do that. I don't know quite how that happened, apart from the fact that we got a special work email address that people can contact and then I follow up. Right now I am connected with around eight or ten people I met first in prison—one who is now teaching in a project with us. That is the potential of a small country like Scotland. So what's the potential here? How can we change Scotland? It sounds quite ambitious, but why not?

JOHN: In the States, you stay inside because of what's called "three hots and a cot"—three meals a day and a place to sleep. We did an interactive show called *Lifting the Weight,* about pulling the curtain off the whole issue of getting out. It was set against a mythical character called Death Bird, who was your death is some way, be it psychologically, physically, drugs, whatever. We had a cage, a critter was in it, and every time the guys onstage got it right, you built a wall against it. And every time they didn't, it would eventually get loose and get you.

For some guys, as we know, theater works, because they can see. It was very interesting to me when I began doing drama therapy in prison. Often when I started working with guys, they couldn't see. I don't mean they were literally blind; I mean they couldn't see what was going on. That was part of the problem that got them inside. A simple exercise that all of us know—pass the imaginary object and change it into something else. We'd say crumble it up, whatever, but they'd get stuck! Or they'd make a two-dimensional representation of it on the ground. You'd say it could be anything—the word *anything* would floor them. I'm back on Saulie's reference to unshackling—and one of the things we do is unshackle vision.

It was important to us, and I think to many of the guys, to see what their lives might look like outside. When someone gives them these "getting out" classes, they're half sleep. Because they're boring, because people don't really know, because they talk about them doing an interview. My guys used to role-play job interviews. After about five minutes they just wanted to run.

KATHY: That's beautiful. . . . The performance we're making right now with the LCIW Drama Club is called *The Key to the Gate*. Mama Glo came up with the title, from a woman who is still incarcerated at LCIW. She once said to Mama Glo, "When are you going to realize that *you* hold the key to the gate?" Because we've been able to have deeper conversations now that Mama Glo is out and also because I've been involved in system-change efforts on the outside, I am bringing that back in to the women who are inside now.

I want them to spend their time working on their way out and planning for what they want to do with their lives once they are out. On the practical artistic level, I want them to have monologues/performances ready to share on the outside, so they can work with the Graduates when they come out. It is much harder to rehearse with them "in the free world" because we are scattered all over the state and across state lines. Also, reentry is so filled with playing catch-up on every level—family, relationships, finances, home stability, medical issues, driver's licenses, etc.—that carving out space to come together to rehearse is much more challenging.

Relationship with Prison Staff

KEVIN: Does this theater work inside have a rehabilitative effect on the system's administrators? Does it extend out beyond the participants and change anything about the prison system? I don't work inside anymore, so I'm eager to hear your all's thoughts about that.

MAMA GLO: By being in the system as long as I was, I can say that particularly the performances we did brought a lot of understanding between staff and "offenders." Because you come into the system, they read what's on the record and hear all the gossip on the compound. But when we do our performances, you get to see the real me—my pain, what I been through, and possibly what put me on the road to destruction. You get to see another side of me that you don't know besides that number that I wear. As an individual standing before you, which might echo what you are or have gone through.

KEVIN: Mama Glo, did you find that people treated you differently after hearing your story and seeing you perform?

MAMA GLO: Yes, they did. When I lost my mother and I was still incarcerated, I did a tribute to her. A lot of people in the institution wanted a copy of what I had written in that tribute so they could do it at their churches.

KATHY: Jess and George's chapter is a great example, that watching performances actually helped George see the inmates as human beings. He began to value the power of art because Jess came into the facility.

JESS: At the same time, it's really tricky making good relations with prison staff and learning how to work together; it's always, How ambitious can we be? How much can we question? Sometimes it backfires. You end up making the system look like it's working. People go, "We've got all of these arts programs in the prison," and they use it as an advertisement of all the things that are good about the system. But we know that it's not working, absolutely not, not even close to working. "What's working" isn't even the conversation. It's Victorian.

I'm think about my country specifically. Aside from a few progressive institutions, we are basically still putting people in small cages for twenty-three hours a day. It's ridiculous. There are so many ways it's not working, depending on how you want to look at it; another is, it costs so much money. I believe in individuals like George, but I don't believe in the system. But I have to be able to work in the system to make space for the people and the work I do believe in. I find that a tension.

SAUL: Yes, I agree. The prison uses your work as a PR opportunity. Over here in England, the inspectors come around and the prison will get points for having art projects and people doing "innovative" activities. It's a tension. It's great they're allowing that to happen, but like Jess says, why not have theater in all the prisons? As long as we follow the American model of building prisons for two thousand–plus people, things aren't going to change. There doesn't seem to be any indication from any of the political parties to do anything different.

I've seen governors or wardens embrace what we do and allow it to become part of the regime. It can really create something special within a prison. But it's always so vulnerable because that person could leave. Whenever we found the good people in the system who would enable what we wanted to do and work with us to create more, when they left we would just follow them like little dogs to the next prison because that would allow us to continue to do the work.

KATHY: Mmm, yes. This is very familiar. But staying in the corrupt system, even when your allies leave, is the only way we'll ever fully change it. It is essential in system change to realize that *people* uphold these corrupt systems; we have to encourage the humanity of those folks to bring about positive change. And when you find good ones, keep them, learn from them, and put their philosophy into place on a larger, systemic level.

In the early years, it felt like every time we spoke too much about freedom, there would be a clampdown from the administration. The women created BLACK LIVES MATTER banners for a performance, but the administration wouldn't allow them to display the banners. We were all angry; but/and we gave the banners to Take 'Em Down NOLA, the grassroots movement responsible for removing four Confederate statues from our city, an action that sparked a national movement.

It was a glorious moment, in 2018, when we finally were able to bring in our twentieth anniversary Drama Club celebration, which had been planned since 2016. That's when we were closed out of LCIW for two years because of a flood that displaced the women. Warden Boutte shared that he had recently visited a prison in Sweden and learned that there is another way to handle harm that occurs between humans. He even said that we should stop using the word *inmate* and start saying "incarcerated people" to maintain and affirm their humanity, and this to a room full of incarcerated women and security. That was a win right there!

SAUL: It's a constant struggle to fight against the inhumanity of prison, the dehumanizing element, because that seems to be what prison does really well—strip people from their sense of being human beings. For me, that's become really important in the work I do now. It grew from the work I did with John all those years ago. Because it was about reminding people in prison that they're human. Maybe that's where love fits in. Something occurs, emotions get released, purging, not always catharsis, and also play is really important. It's why what we do is so important—for the prisons, the staff that works with us, and also for continuing to chip away, fight back against the prison machine.

JOHN: Saul and I were incredibly lucky to work at a place where humanity occurred—County Jail 7 in San Bruno—San Francisco, essentially. The guy who ran the jail had been in prison for something pretty intense and he was remarkable. One of the things he'd do to make sure his staff was being decent was get in the line with new prisoners as they were coming in. So he'd see how the jailers were jailing. And if they weren't getting it right, they'd be gone. He was for real about the training we were giving. And that place was amazing. They had a sculpture program with a three-quarter-ton block of marble and guys with hammers and chisels, which is not common in a prison. So it can work.

AUSETTUA: When we started working in the prison over twenty years ago, the staff was not receptive. They made it difficult. We couldn't bring the props in, they complained about us wanting rehearsal time, and they would keep people from our Drama Club in lockdown. But when we did the performances, which were always original works that the women came up with, subject matter that resonated with them—I tell you, the staff would be in there crying, saying, "I never knew this." This is why I'm convinced we need to do something for staff. I know we already have beaucoup stuff on our plates; we can't possibly work with the inmates and the staff, too. But just recently Kathy and I were saying that we gotta start focusing on them and get them to the level we get these women. Because we know the laborers are few and the work is plenty. And if we keep only working with the inmates, it's going to be lopsided.

KATHY: I have learned a lot from formerly incarcerated activists like Fox Rich and Dolfinette Martin—that we don't have to accept the prisons rules. It is a fine line of diplomacy every time we walk in there; but/and, until I started working with criminal-legal system reform activists, I didn't try to challenge the system at all. I tried just to be sneaky and bring my love into the institution. Now I am working hard to find creative ways to challenge and question the system while still holding the right to be able to enter it and serve the women.

Love

KATHY: Love runs through all the pieces, starting with Jan and Finn writing so honestly about how much y'all fell in love; how openly the two of you wrote each other sparked that openness in all of us. I think on some level we all talk about it, but none of us quite gets to it. Like when we make theater, we fall in love with one another. Theater can be a space of love; it can also be a space of intense dislike and conflict. Like John and Saul talked about being slimed, but they also talked about whatever the opposite of "slimed" is.

JESS: They spoke of the light that comes into the body from doing this work.

KATHY: And the notion of ritual, like Kevin and Alex, the name of your program, Ritual4Return. On some level, everyone talked about ritual. Theater is a space in which we can ritually express our love for one another on a larger scale. The sacrificial lamb idea gets to the heart of that—telling my slimy story can actually help clean the slime off of myself. My doing that ritually in front of others gives the example that it's even possible to do. It's interesting, there are so many different expressions of love in our texts. And Kevin and Alex, your love letter to each other is pretty intense. Y'all go to places that not many men, especially white and Black men in our country, can do right now.

MAMA GLO: Yes, beautiful.

JOHN: Anything that any of us do inside—that's what Saul calls human, I think, also humane—is an act of love. Inside the joint, it just doesn't exist. When we were in Rikers years ago, that awful place, they said to us, "Just follow the blood trails; you'll find them." There were literally drops of blood.

JESS: Love stood out the most for me, as well. I was really moved by how brave some of the conversations are. And Rand and Reggie framing their chapter with bell hooks on love. When I first began working in men's maximum-security prisons, in my twenties, I was also reading bell hooks and trying to work out the place of love in this work. I felt very clear that there was a role for love and of care in creative work. I felt a connection with the men I was working with in prisons and the work we were making, and like John and Saul talk about, it was getting under my skin.

There was a particular time, a congratulatory moment after a particular play, when I talked about love. Not just me—one participant gave a speech to the audience and as part of it he talked about how we had really bonded as a group and had connected through making theater and that I was a leader they had liked and who had shown them love and consideration.

As a result of this speech, a prison officer raised concerns about me. There was a question of appropriate behavior, a question of whether I, as a young woman, was perhaps doing some kind of witchcraft with the theater classes and leading everybody on some kind of romantic dance. Why else would they talk about connection? Because I was a young female, there was an assumption that the love expressed by the group must be romantic and must be inappropriate. It was a total sideswipe and a confidence crisis for me. It was a story that followed me around for ages, to the point where I once heard "Is it true you had a relationship with a guy in prison?" Of course it wasn't true.

It made me sad for ages, and nervous of framing the work I did as love. It gave me a sort of hard edge in relationship to how I introduced what I was doing, because I felt that in order to be taken seriously I needed *not* to talk about love in any way. So I feel now as a woman in my forties, doing it for seventeen years, I'm fierce in a different way, unapologetic about the work I am doing, and clear about the importance of connection and care. I feel I've earned it, but I also feel angry on behalf of myself at that age, that I couldn't just talk about love as a radical and critical pedagogical tool. It was infantilizing. And I was reading bell hooks. So that's a slightly different perspective on the love thread.

KATHY: And while for you, Jess, love in prison has not been romantic, for Jan it was, in the '70s. It's so interesting how times have changed and what is and isn't acceptable. That's one of the things I love so much about Jan and Finn's exchange. I was a child in the '70s—being raised in a white Southern Baptist preacher's home in New Orleans! I've heard that the '70s were an amazing time for all of our movements. Freedom was contagious and palpable. Reading Jan and Finn's piece, and hearing Jess's struggles in another country, look how far we've come; and look how much we've regressed. We now have a movement in the United States called Pleasure Activism—because our society has made pleasure a negative aspect of life, one to be eradicated! So we have to fight for pleasure. To me, it comes back to humanity. Why have we decided that people who are in prison can't love and be loved? Sex has always been a punishable offense inside LCIW. Why? You'd have a lot healthier people if they were allowed to make love to one another!

JAN: Thanks, Kathy. And although my love with Finn began romantically, over the years it has morphed into something else. It brings to mind Martin Luther King, Jr.'s idea of the "beloved community," which he says is not *eros,* or romantic love, nor *philia,* a reciprocal love between friends, but *agape*—an overflowing love that seeks nothing in return, understood as goodwill for all. I think the kind of work we all did or are doing in prisons demands a great reaching out to everyone we encounter there, which seems akin to King's idea of love as *agape.* And also what Finn emailed me recently—that even back at Trenton, what was most important between us was being able to truly see each other.

AUSETTUA: I started going to prisons when I was in my twenties, as well. I was not formerly incarcerated; I went in through dance. Although the acts that I was performing were love to the tenth power, I never thought of it as that. I never walked in it as that. Listening to you speak, Jess, was very interesting. I believe it was love, but I never framed it that way.

The first years I was working with men, and the staff was always afraid something was going to kick off. You can't touch them; you can't hug them. . . . In women's prisons, it's the same way. You can't hug them, show any kind of emotion or compassion. Well, Kathy and I just ignored that. Because you can't come into this, work with people for over twenty years, and not have some level of compassion. And if they want to treat them as subhuman, they're not gonna make me do the same thing. It was pretty easy just to ignore them.

And to this day, the women and men who have gotten out and were lifers, who got pardoned, when I run across them, what they say to me is, "The love you showed me . . ." Wow. That concept of what love should be and is, and allowing yourself to be a vehicle—to manifest it through the work. I'm an optimist. We gotta keep coming with this love—it's the greatest force in the world. So thank you, Jess. And I'm sorry they made you feel bad when you were twenty, girl, because hate is going to be hate. . . .

JESS: I think it was a mistrust or a kind of fear and I don't know if maybe that's a British thing, but maybe not, what with what you are saying.

AUSETTUA: No, it's not just British. Like when Kathy and I were trying to arrange Wellness Days for the women and bring in alternative holistic teachings for them, we had wardens tell us, "You all must have nothing to do with your time." In other words, why would we even consider doing this? Because the people they hire—not all of them, but the great majority—do not feel that the inmates are worthy, that they are subhuman. So it's not just a British thing. I'm from Louisiana, the number-one incarcerated state in the world.

JOHN: I think we were very lucky in the first couple of big joints that we went to where the officers we had to interact with—there was a wonderful one, Vera Cunningham— were relatively very good. When we first went in, *we* were messing up. Then we went down to a prison and it was really clear that the officers just hated us, and had no problem overtly saying so. They were perfectly happy to spread that sort of nonsense throughout the entire system. And I decided enough was enough and sent a letter to the commissioner of prisons. We confronted it. And damn me if he didn't write back and say, "You need to come in to the prisons again. We have no problem with you doing that and all the rest of it."

It took a long while before I realized what that was teaching me, which was that these are organic islands in which we're there for a tiny little time, and when we go, everything else is occurring. Sometimes we are an important influence, but a lot of times we really aren't. We'd like to believe that we are because we love what we do and the people we do it with love what we do and the work is a passion all its own. But the reality often is that unless we have a relationship like you, Jess, have with George, which is very special, oftentimes we didn't have that.

We had it in one place, where they actually said, "We need this." They converted all the therapeutic strategies that they were using in that jail into theater-based therapeutic strategies, which was quite fabulous. A remarkable place and we learned a lot. Some years later, I did three-day trainings with all the prison staff in the state of Victoria, Australia, and it lasted eighteen months.

How effective were we? I have no idea, because we couldn't figure out how to go and measure it, because the types of measures we needed were day to day, minute to minute, hour to hour. Were they giving them grief, stopping the men from proper visits, putting guys in isolation—all that stuff that they were capable of doing, without us being able to stop it unless we had more of a voice than at that time we had? And oftentimes our voices were so marginalized. That was really a problem.

Eventually we said, "How is there anything we can do to influence it?" I've gone far from the thing about love. I'm a boy—we don't talk about love publicly. But the reality was, we went on to create places that were far more peaceful, and gentle, set against a backdrop of men and women doing time or working in these institutions, whose emotions were blunted by day to day being in this infernal battle that was going on, sometimes made better and sometimes made worse.

We all know people who went into prisons very romantically and saw the staff who were there as enemies. And sometimes they were; they'd do any damn thing they could to impede us from doing any real work based on gender or race or anything. Whatever the hell they wanted. But they would send officers in with us who they knew didn't fit in, and we'd say that's why they were sent to be with us. And we'd start relationships which were so important because for an outsider, all a prison is, is relationships.

This thing you said, Jess, about losing your reputation—I've lost my reputation so many times in prisons. They'd say to Saul, "You're all right, but Mr. Bergman . . ."—because Saul is an incredibly decent man people just love and I am not and people get so pissed off at the sight of me. . . . The issue about it being about relationships and losing your rep. It's very hard to let that shit just fly by. You can think to yourself, *There's no truth in any of it.* The moment we touch real emotions, hell breaks out. Nobody wants to go close to that. The closer you get to that, the more uncomfortable everyone is going to be.

KEVIN: To me, obviously, prison is dehumanizing. I don't know what love means outside of one's humanity. I know from the guys in my workshops that classes they are able to take are great, groups are important, but what I see in these essays are spaces where people piece by piece are invited to express their humanity and do find true love with one another. My partner, Alex, and I truly do love each other. I don't think we'd have gone through this whole process of writing together if our relationship wasn't important enough. To get through the dehumanizing ways that we were taught by this society to see each other, going in both directions. We found that love for each other in our theater work. We were able to see each other's humanity. And I think that echoes throughout these essays. Reading them, what comes up is humanization.

MAMA GLO: Very good. And the system that I spent fifty-one years in was built to dehumanize people, make you have a whole lot of anger. But because of some of the volunteers that were allowed to come into the system—they wouldn't let us go into that place. They were very supportive; they brought you things to think about, building a character to express yourself, and no one ever knew that you were talking about yourself. That within itself kept me sane fifty-one years. Drama and other people coming in, sharing with us. And I was a fighter; I never allowed them to incarcerate my mind. You can physically incarcerate me, but I have control of my mind, and if I'd been there 'til I took my last breath, that would have never happened.

KATHY: The Drama Club wrote a song: "Love, Love, Love, Love, It's My Medicine." That was during COVID, wasn't it?

MAMA: Yes, it was. A lot of people in the workshop were losing people. Drama Club was where we could throw our pain and our ugly things in the middle of the floor and didn't have to worry about it becoming a topic of gossip. What came up in Drama Club, stayed in Drama Club. For many of us, it became our favorite place. We protected Drama Club; if you didn't do the right thing, you had to get out of Drama Club.

ALEX: I like that we are talking about love. Because I consider myself a lover of humanity. So I do this work from a lover's perspective, like you, Jess, that has nothing to do with kissing, hugging, holding, or squeezing. But to get people to understand that!

As a lover of humanity I'm often getting my heart broken. My lover often abandons me, cheats on me, lies to me. Then there's times when my lover is gracious, beautiful, and attentive.

Love is where I come in at in the piece that Kevin and I wrote here—people I was working with didn't know that I wasn't getting paid and that I looked at it as a work of love. How I give back for the things that got me incarcerated, the things that I've done in my community, the pain I caused my mother, being in the streets and running in gangs, how I hurt and disappointed her. Family members having to live with that—you're the sister or brother of that crazy guy who's doing that crazy stuff.

I'm the youngest of my mother's six children and I have three older brothers who were Black Panthers or Malcolm X followers. They always gave me that speech about not being *offenders* but being *defenders* of the Black community. So I always knew it, but there were two forces in my neighborhood, and I sided with the streets.

Once I got incarcerated and got that moment of clarity, separated from drugs, money, gangs—it all started coming back to me. Meeting some of the political prisoners when I was incarcerated that I'd heard about. They're the ones who actually taught me about being a revolutionary. And I said, "Yeah, give me that gun," and they said, "No, a revolutionary is a lover of humanity. You don't get a gun! You got what you need—compassionate, love—to do this work."

So my love, coming back to my community after doing time in prison, was to do this work to help others, the individuals who came from my community and were caught up in this mass incarceration. It was not to help "humanity." And while I was incarcerated, I kept seeing them coming in and out of prison like some kind of merry-go-round and I really wanted to do something about that.

I went on my own and got my degrees in college and all that. But even then, it was always in me; I didn't even need this. I was working with social workers who didn't know what to do. We were working with the homeless population in New York, which was really bad at the time. And no educated person wanted to go into the camps. I just went in. I even said to myself, *We don't need degrees. We need lovers of humanity.* To support you, Jess—we always get our hearts broken and hurt when we are lovers of humanity. Some of humanity are great lovers, but not all of it.

In some instances when I came into a space with people who just got out, I wanted to share with them what I knew about the power of using theater to change narratives. And I got my heart broke. I got "We don't want to hear from you. We want to hear from the white guy" [Alex's partner, Kevin]. So that's where I was coming from in writing the chapter—doing this work from a love perspective, to engage with people, have relationships with people, out of love of humanity and to heal humanity. I'm glad we are talking about love.

ACKNOWLEDGMENTS

In addition to the contributors, I am grateful to the following people for being in conversation with me or otherwise supporting this book: Bill Cleveland, Dionisio Cruz, Debi Freeman, Jennie Gilrain, Susie Ingalls, Amy R. Johnston, Lorie Novak, Rad Pereira, Simon Ruding, Mady Schutzman, Sarah Unrath, Doris Vila, Lucy Winner, and Jody Wood.

And I acknowledge Finn and I see him, with a full heart.

REFERENCES

Aguilar, Danielle Nicole. 2014. "Oppression, Domination, Prison: The Mass Incarceration of Latino and African American Men." *The Vermont Connection* 35: 13–20. https://scholarworks.uvm.edu/tvc/vol35/iss1/2.

Balfour, Michael, Brydie-Leigh Bartleet, Linda Davey, John Rynne, and Huib Schippers. 2019. *Performing Arts in Prisons: Captive Audiences*. Bristol: Intellect Books.

Brigham, Erin, and Kimberly Rae Conner. 2018. *Today I Gave Myself Permission to Dream: Race and Incarceration in America*. San Francisco: University of San Francisco Press.

Coffey, Amanda. 1999. *The Ethnographic Self: Fieldwork and the Representation of Identity*. London: Sage Publications.

Cullors, Patrisse. 2021. *An Abolitionist's Handbook: 12 Steps to Changing Yourself and the World*. New York: St. Martin's Press.

Daniels, Reginold. 2021a. Personal communication. University of San Francisco, San Francisco, CA, August 8.

———. 2021b. "Still Alive: Reflections on Carcerality, Arts and Culturally Responsive Teaching." *Research in Drama Education: The Journal of Applied Theatre and Performance* 26: 406–18.

———. 2023. Personal communication. University of San Francisco, San Francisco, CA, July 8.

Davis, Angela Y. 2000. "Masked Racism: Reflections on the Prison Industrial Complex in the USA." *Lola Press* 1, no. 12: 51.

———. 2003. *Are Prisons Obsolete?* New York: Seven Stories Press.

Department of Corrections NZ. 2020. Prison Facts and Statistics—March 2020. https://www.corrections.govt.nz/resources/research_and_statistics/quarterly_prison_statistics/prison_stats_march_2020.

Dowling, Amie, Paul S. Flores, and Natalie Greene. 2009. *Man. Alive. Stories from the Edge of Incarceration to the Flight of Imagination*. San Francisco: Theatre production. The University of San Francisco Studio.

Finn K. 2023. Personal correspondence with the author.

Freeman, John. 2015. *Remaking Memory: Autoethnography, Memoir and the Ethics of Self*. Faringdon, England: Libri Publishing.

Gornick, Vivian. 1978. Excerpt from *The Romance of American Communism*. Quoted in *The New York Times Book Review*, January 15, 3.

Griffin, Pat. 1997. "Introductory Module for the Single Issue Courses." In *Teaching for Diversity and Social Justice: A Sourcebook,* edited by Maurine Adams, Lee Anne Bell, and Pat Griffin, 61–81. New York: Routledge.

Groot Nibbelink, Liesbeth. 2012. "Radical Intimacy: Ontroerend Goed Meets the Emancipated Spectator." *Contemporary Theatre Review* 22, no. 3: 412–20. doi: 10.1080/10486801.2012.690739.

Hatton, Oona. 2021. "'If You are Going to Treat Someone Like a Human': White Supremacy and Performance Programmes in Northern California's Correctional Facilities." *Research in Drama Education: The Journal of Applied Theatre and Performance* 26: 511–27.

Hazou, Rand. 2021. "Theatre, Incarceration and Citizenship." In *Tūtira Mai: Making Change in Aotearoa New Zealand,* edited by David Belgrave and Giles Dodson, 137–51. Auckland: Massey University Press.

Hazou, Rand, Sarah Woodland, and Pedro Ilgenfritz. 2021. "Performing Te Whare Tapa Whā: Building on Cultural Rights to Decolonize Prison Theatre Practice." *Research in Drama Education: The Journal of Applied Theatre and Performance* 26: 494–510.

hooks, bell. 1994. "Love as the Practice of Freedom." In *Outlaw Culture: Resisting Representations,* 289–98. New York: Routledge.

Jackson, Moana. 2017. "Prison Should Never Be the Only Answer." https://e-tangata.co.nz/comment-andanalysis/moana-jackson-prison-should-never-be-the-only-answer/.

Kaba, Mariame. 2021. *We Do This 'Til We Free Us: Abolitionist Organizing and Transforming Justice.* Chicago: Haymarket Books.

Kafka, Franz. 1937. *The Trial,* translated by Edwin and Willa Muir. London: Victor Gollancz.

Khan, Myra. 2021. "The Role of Oral Traditions Within Marginalized Societies and Their Validity Within Archives." Community-Driven Archives (CDA) Initiative. Arizona State University Library. https://lib.asu.edu/news/role-oral-traditions-within-marginalized-societies-and-their-validity-within-archives-myra.

Lucas, Ashley E. 2020. *Prison Theatre and the Global Crisis of Incarceration.* London: Bloomsbury Publishing.

Machon, Josephine. 2013. *Immersive Theatres: Intimacy and Immediacy in Contemporary Performance.* Basingstoke, England: Palgrave Macmillan.

McCallum, Rua. 2011. "Māori performance: Marae Liminal Space and Transformation." *Australasian Drama Studies* 59: 88–103.

McIntosh, Tracey, and Kim Workman. 2017. "Māori and Prison." In *Australian and New Zealand Handbook of Criminology, Crime and Justice,* edited by Antje Deckert and Rick Sarre, 725–35. Melbourne: Palgrave Macmillan.

Monahan, Michael J. 2011. "Emancipatory Affect: bell hooks on Love and Liberation." *The CLR James Journal* 17: 102–11.

Nikora, Linda Waimarie, Mohi Rua, and Ngahuia Te Awekotuku. 2007. "Renewal and Resistance: Moko in Contemporary New Zealand." *Journal of Community & Applied Social Psychology* 17: 477–89.

Prager, Karen J. 1995. *The Psychology of Intimacy.* New York: Guilford Press.

Rameka, Lesley, Ruth Ham, and Linda Mitchell. 2021. "Pōwhiri: The Ritual of Encounter." *Contemporary Issues in Early Childhood* 24, no. 2: 1–14.

Smith, Linda Tuhiwai. 2008. "On Tricky Ground: Researching the Native in the Age of Uncertainty." In *The Landscape of Qualitative Research*, edited by Norman K. Denzin and Yvonna S. Lincoln, 133–43. Los Angeles and London: Sage Publications.

Tofteland, Curt L. 2011. "The Keeper of the Keys." In *Performing New Lives: Prison Theater,* edited by Jonathan Shailor, 213–30. London: Jessica Kingsley Publishers.

Woodland, Sarah, and Rand Hazou. 2021. "Carcerality, Theatre, Rights." *Research in Drama Education: The Journal of Applied Theatre and Performance* 26: 385–405.

World Population Review. 2021. Incarceration Rates by Country 2021. https://worldpopulationreview.com/country-rankings/incarceration-rates-by-country.

INDEX

A
abolition, 4–6, 175
African culture, 95, 97, 99, 172–73
AIDS, 139
The Alamo, as metaphor, 33–34
Alexander, Michelle, 92
Allen, Michelle, 98
AmorAmenkum, Ausettua, 81–84, 87, 91–92, 95–102, 172–74, 183, 186–87, 205
Anderson, Alexander, 119–36, 172, 184, 189–91, 205
Anderson, Selina, 98
Angola Drama Club, 95, 96–97
applied theater, 4
Are You Positive?, 139
Artistic Ensemble at San Quentin Prison, 154, 155
Arts-in-Corrections program, 6
Arts Justice Safety Coalition, 5
Auckland Prison, 153–56, 158–59, 165, 167–70

B
Balagoon, Kuwasi, 12, 25, 26, 27, 43, 64, 173
Barnardo's, 103
Behind the Wall, 85
belly of the beast, 5, 10, 141
Bergman, John, 137–52, 172, 175–77, 179, 182–84, 187–88, 205–206
Biggs, Lisa, 5
Black Lives Matter, 182

Black Panthers, 25–27, 42, 173, 190
blind spots, 167–68, 169
Bloodworth, Jacqueline, 85
Bott, Kevin, 119–36, 171, 172, 175, 180, 184, 188–91, 206
Boutte, Warden, 182
Bread and Puppet Theater, 15–16
Brecht, Bertolt, xiii, 10, 28
Brookes, Sally, 139
Brotha T, 92
Buber, Martin, 1, 2
Burroughs, William S., 51
Butch Cassidy and the Sundance Kid, 27

C
California's Arts-in-Corrections program, 6
Carter, Jimmy, 63
Catherine of Sienna, Saint, 76
Chaplin, Charlie, 68
Cleaver, Eldridge, 24
Cleveland, William, 5
Clinton Prison, 34, 35
Cohen-Cruz, Jan. *See also* Trenton State Prison drama workshop
    about, 209
    backstory of, 14–18, 21–22
    involvement of, in Trenton State Prison drama workshop, 10–13
    physical appearance of, 10, 11–12
    sexuality and, 44–45, 48, 66
    after Trenton State Prison drama workshop, 71–78

collaboration, 1, 3–4, 126–27, 133, 154, 169
collective living, 34–37, 40–41, 71
Collier, Jackie, 86
comedy, 68
communitas, 4
community, 3–4, 40–41, 51, 186
The Complete Works of Edgar Allan Poe, 24
contact visits, 38, 64, 70
Coogan, David, 5
Corman, Roger, 21
County Jail 7 (CJ7), 140, 148, 183
COVID-19 pandemic, 119, 131, 189
criminality, concept of, 175–76
Cullors, Patrisse, 5
Cunningham, Vera, 187

D
Dah Teatar, 90, 91, 92
Daniels, Reginold, 153–70, 172, 177, 184, 206
Davis, Angela, 4, 6, 176
decolonization, 158, 170
Defillo, Taece, 98
The Dialectic of Sex, 31
dialectics, 68
Django Unchained, 125–26
Dolan, Jill, 172
Dostoevsky, Fyodor, 50
Dowling, Amie, 158, 160
drama clubs. *See* theater workshops and drama clubs
Duke, David, 96
Dylan, Bob, 64, 72

E
Edwards, John Bel, 178
Emerson, Carry, 98

F
family, 18, 39, 50, 65
FBI, 25
Ferguson, George, 103–18, 206
fieldwork, 6
Finn, Huckleberry, 2
Finn K. (pseudonym). *See also* Trenton State Prison drama workshop
  about, 207
  backstory of, 18–22, 38–40
  family of, 59–60, 65, 70
  fear and, 9, 23–24
  involvement of, in drama workshop, 9–10, 23–24
  physical appearance of, 12
  after release from Trenton State Prison, 74–78
  sexuality and, 45–48, 51–52
Firestone, Shulamith, 31
Fleetwood, Nicole, 5
Flores, Paul S., 160
Floyd, George, 120
Ford Foundation, 100, 172
Francis, Saint, 76
freedom, 66, 72
Freeman, John, 156
Freud, Sigmund, 10, 47, 138
Futureproof program, 106

G
Gaines, Consuela, 98
Gaines, Jena, 137
Geese Theatre, 137–41, 145
Gibson, Lorraine, 82
Gifts of Our Ancestors, 82, 92
Ginsberg, Allen, 51
Gore, Tashi, 104
Gornick, Vivian, 58
The Graduates, 99–100, 101

Greene, Natalie, 160
Grotowski, Jerzy, 15, 16, 36

H

Hanging in the Tenderloin I Hear Old Voices, 140
Hanson, Kitty, 63
Hatton, Oona, 165
Hazou, Rand, 153–70, 172, 177, 184, 207
healing, 69, 133–36
Hearst, Patty, 62–63
Hegel, Georg Wilhelm Friedrich, 68
Hellman, Lillian, 44
Hewish, Saul, 137–52, 172, 173, 175, 177, 179, 181–84, 188, 207
HMP & YOI (His Majesty's Prison & Young Offenders Institution) Polmont theater project, 103–10, 114–17
Hoffman, Abbie, 76
hongi, 165
Hooked on Empty, 139
hooks, bell, 156, 167–70, 184, 185
Horney, Karen, 9
Howell, Mary, 95, 97
Hunt, Elaine, 173–74
Hutson, Susan, 177

I

Iliad, 33
Illinois Clemency Project for Battered Women, 90
improvisation, 12–13, 50, 53, 139–40, 144, 147
incarceration
  abolition movement and, 4–6, 175
  change and, 177–78
  dehumanizing culture of, 165–66, 182, 188–89
  postrelease support and resources, 176–80
  purpose of, 173–76
  rehabilitation and, 68, 111–12, 175–76, 180
  slavery and, 92
internalized oppression, 166
In the Penal Colony, 50
intimacy, xii–xiii, xv, 69
The Investigation, 142
Israel, Zohar, 87, 92
I-Thou relationships, 1, 2

J

Jackson, Samuel, 126
Jackson, Spoon, 5
Jane, Harold, 60, 64–65
Jonah, 17, 21, 26, 33
Jonah Project, 17–18, 24, 33. *See also* Trenton State Prison drama workshop
Jones, Rhodessa, 5
Jordan, Warden, 82, 86
Justice Arts Coalition, 5

K

Kaba, Mariame, 5
Kafka, Franz, 48–51, 53, 54
Kahey, Sherall, 81–82, 90, 93, 98
karanga, 159
The Key to the Gate, 180
Khan, Myra, 157
Kierkegaard, Søren, 63
King, Martin Luther, Jr., 1, 77, 160, 186
Ku Klux Klan, 96
Kumbuka African Drum and Dance Collective, 92, 95, 97

L

leadership, 130–31
liberation, 9–10, 153–57, 162–70
LIFE, 86

The Life Quilt, 100
Lifting the Weight, 179
Lincoln Hospital, 127, 133
Little Red Book, 24
Louisiana Correctional Institute for Women (LCIW) Drama Club, 81–102, 180, 182, 183, 189
love, 1, 66–67, 156, 167–70, 183–91
Lucas, Ashley, 5, 163

M
Machon, Josephine, xiii
Malcolm X, 190
Man. Alive., 160
The Man with the X-Ray Eyes, 21
Mandela, Nelson, 95
Māori culture, 153–55, 157, 159, 169–70, 177
Mao Zedong, 24
Martin, Dolfinette, 183
Marx, Karl, 24, 47
masks, 24, 49, 84, 138, 139, 140, 142
Mathis, Ivy, 98
McCallan, Minnie, 86
Medea Project, 6
Monahan, Michael, 167, 168
Moore, Demetricy, 98
Morgan, Ruth, 140
MOTION, 105–10, 113, 115

N
Nathan's Famous, 15
National Theatre of Scotland, 106
Native Son, 121, 124
The New Jim Crow, 92
Newman, Paul, 27
Newton, Huey, 24
New York City Street Theater, 16–17
Nibbelink, Liesbeth Groot, xii
North Carolina School of the Arts, 14
nuclear family, 18, 39, 50

O
Odyssey, 33
Oliver, Rhonda, 98
O'Neal, John, 89
O'Neill, Rachel, 109
Oppenheim, Tom, 126
oppression, internalized, 166
oral traditions, 157–58

P
Pattillo, Laura, 91
PDMNOLA (Participatory Defense Movement New Orleans, Louisiana), 87, 93
Peck, M. Scott, 168
pentimento, 44
People's Institute for Survival and Beyond, 91
Performing Liberation project, 153–57, 168
Peterson, Liza Jessie, 5
Plague Game, 140
Plath, Sylvia, 50
Plato's dialogues, 30
Pleasure Activism, 185–86
Politz, Mary Katherine, 91
Positive Outreach Leaders, 91
postrelease support and resources, 176–80
pōwhiri, 155, 159–60, 164–65, 168
Prager, Karen, xii
Primal Theatre, 74
Prison Creative Arts Project (PCAP), 5–6
Prison Theatre and the Global Crisis of Incarceration, 5, 163
Proust, Marcel, 50

R
radical autonomy, 40, 51
Rage Within/Without, 89, 91

Rahway Prison, 34, 43
Randels, Kathy, 81, 82, 84, 87–95, 98, 101–2, 174–78, 180–87, 189, 207–208
Reddix, Roscoe, Jr., 91
Redford, Robert, 27
rehabilitation, 68, 111–12, 175–76, 180
Reich, Wilhelm, 10
returning citizens, 100, 119–20, 126
Rhodes, Mona, 81–82
Rich, Fox, 86, 87, 93, 183
Rideout (Creative Arts for Rehabilitation), 137
"right experience, wrong conclusion," 61–62
Rikers Island, 5, 184
ritual, 119, 124–25, 159–60, 184
Ritual4Return (R4R), 119–22, 127, 128, 172, 184
roles, playing, 130–33
The Rolling Stones, 23
The Romance of American Communism, 58
Rubin, Alec, 74
Ruding, Simon, xi–xiii, 208

S
St. Gabriel's Nativity, 82, 92
St. Joan of the Stockyards, 28
Samenow, Stanton, 138
San Quentin Prison, 143, 153–54, 165, 169, 177
Scott-Heron, Gil, 27
Scottish Prison Service, 111–12, 117–18
sexuality, 36, 44–48, 51–52, 58, 66
Shakespeare in Prisons Network, xi, 6
slavery, 92, 121–22, 160
Snead, Majeeda, 95, 97
Starr, Sandra, 82, 83, 86, 98
Statesville Penitentiary, 148
Stella Adler Studio of Acting, 126
Strasberg, Lee, 74

street theater, 10–11, 15–18, 31, 33–35, 37, 74, 76
Studio Theater of the University of San Francisco, 160
Symbionese Liberation Army (SLA), 62–63

T
Take 'Em Down NOLA, 182
Tannenbaum, Judith, 5
Tarantino, Quentin, 125
Terkel, Studs, 149
theater workshops and drama clubs. *See also individual programs*
  abolition and, 4–6
  benefits of, 3, 81, 84–85, 101–2, 106, 112–14
  change and, 173
  collaborative nature of, 3
  liberation and, 163–64, 168–69
  prison staff and, 180–83
  purpose of, 173–76
  reasons for participating in, 90–91
  relationships and, 171–73
  risk assessment and, 106–8
  skills necessary for facilitators of, 3–4
  trusting the process, 149
  visibility and, 2–3
Theatre in Prison and Probation (TiPP), xi, 6
therapy, 52, 110, 141–43, 146–47, 179, 187
Thorpe, Jess, 103–18, 178–79, 181, 184–90, 208
Tidmarsh, Patrick, 176
tikanga, 159
Tofteland, Curt, xi
trauma, 92, 111, 112, 117, 121, 131, 133, 135
Trenton State Prison
  appearance of, 11
  divide-and-conquer strategy at, 29–30, 69

Trenton State Prison (*Cont.*)
   location of, 11
   new progressive guard at, 29–30
   nicknames for, 9
   power dynamics at, 30–31
Trenton State Prison drama workshop
   beginnings of, 9–13
   demise of, 69–71
   frequency of, xv
   newcomers in, 67–68
   opposing ideas of, 68
   participants in, 12, 23–28
   performances of, 42–57
The Trial, 48–57, 67
trickster, 26
Turner, Mary, 93, 98
Tyler, Gary, 95–97, 100

U
ubuntu, 97, 173
UC Santa Cruz, 6
utopia, theater as, 172

V
vanilla fever, 61–62
Visualizing Abolition, 6

W
warm-ups, 12, 142, 160
Weiss, Peter, 142
whaikōrero, 159
Where Am I Supposed to Go with Sixteen Cents?, 140
whiteness, 120–24, 126–29
Williams, Antwan "Banks," 153, 155, 162, 169
Williams, Gloria "Mama Glo," 81–87, 92–93, 95, 98, 100–102, 171, 173–77, 180–81, 184, 189, 208
Williams, Jackie, 84
Williams, Jason, 177
window visits, 29, 59, 65
women's movement, 62
workshops. *See* theater workshops and drama clubs
Wright, Richard, 121

ABOUT THE CONTRIBUTORS

AUSETTUA AMORAMENKUM, a native New Orleanian, graduated from Dillard University. She is professor of African and hip-hop dance at Tulane University, Big Queen of the Washitaw Nation Black Masking Indians, director of Kumbuka African Drum & Dance Collective, vegan chef of Soul Sisters, acting president of New Orleans Black Mardi Gras Indian Cooperative, and codirector of the Louisiana Correctional Institution for Women Drama Club and the Graduates, a performance group of formerly incarcerated women. Ausettua was a Junebug Productions/John O'Neal Fellow and contributed to the book *Hot Feet and Social Change.*

ALEXANDER ANDERSON is founder and director of the Reentry Theater of Harlem, and serves as lead social worker and arts consultant on various Ritual4Return projects. Alex was a member of the first cohort of R4R graduates in 2009. He served fifteen years behind bars in New York State and earned his BA degree from Syracuse University in the Auburn Correctional Facility. Upon release, Alex obtained his MSW from Hunter College. Alexander was awarded the Patient Safety Champion Award at Lincoln Hospital in the Bronx for supporting patients seeking cessation from alcohol and drugs in the emergency room. He lives in the Bronx with his wife.

JOHN BERGMAN (MA, RDT, BCT), UK-born drama therapist/theater director/associate professor, has over forty-one years' experience working with prisoners, prison officers, and men, women, and young people in international criminal justice settings. He was the founder and director of Geese Theatre Company USA (1980–2018), which created original educational/therapeutic theater. He has presented internationally at over seven hundred professional conferences and is the recipient of the NADTA 2005 Research Award. He wrote

Challenging Experience: An Experiential Approach to the Treatment of Serious Offenders and coedited *Current Perspectives & Applications in Neurobiology: Working with Young Persons Who Are Victims and Perpetrators of Sexual Abuse.*

KEVIN BOTT is founder and artistic director of Ritual4Return. He earned his master's degree and his doctorate, both in Educational Theater, from the Steinhardt School at New York University. In 2006, Kevin began facilitating theater workshops in several New York State prisons as a volunteer for the nonprofit Rehabilitation Through the Arts (RTA), and in 2007 he became RTA's first director of education. His community-based theater projects include *The D.R.E.A.M. Freedom Revival* in Syracuse, New York, and *Every Time You See Me . . .* , a Staten Island–based meditation on race, class, power, and privilege in the wake of Eric Garner's death. Kevin is the director of Rutgers Arts Online, the online division of Mason Gross School of the Arts at Rutgers University. He lives with his wife and three children in Lambertville, New Jersey.

REGINOLD DANIELS, University of San Francisco, was the recipient of the Black History Month Local Heroes Award and the In the Trenches "Change Agent" Award. He's been a guest speaker on CNN's *In Session* and a creative collaborator on the play *Man. Alive.* at the Studio/Theater in San Francisco. He facilitated theater workshops for prison activists at the Saxonian Prison Theatre in Dresden, Germany, and at Prague's 4th Global Conference on Experiencing Prison. He was featured in the film *Well Contested Sites,* exploring the effects of incarceration on individuals.

GEORGE FERGUSON is a governor (the equivalent of a warden in the United States) in the Scottish prison system, with twenty-eight years' experience in both operational and strategic roles. He was previously head of Operational Planning, where he led projects that included population management, operational staffing, and home-detention curfew. In 2018, while in the role of head of Offender Outcomes at HMP & YOI Polmont, he worked in partnership with Glass Performance and existing partners, supporting them to set up the Polmont Youth Theatre.

FINN K. comes from a dysfunctional family in which crime is no crime but getting caught is. He killed a man when he was twenty years old at the behest of the only person who ever bailed him out of one of the multiple juvenile detention centers where he served time. He found an avocation in a prison drama workshop. Since his release, Finn has performed, worked on communalism in the Church, and written two novels and a collection of essays, as well as various articles on homelessness, incarceration, and film. He is grateful to have a daughter and two grandchildren.

RAND HAZOU, Massey University, Aotearoa New Zealand, is a Palestinian theater practitioner and scholar. His work explores the intersections between arts and social justice. His research focuses on how creativity intersects with human rights, citizenship, justice, and well-being. His current research projects explore arts and citizenship, applied theater, and participatory arts and well-being. In Aotearoa, he has led teaching and creative projects engaging with prison, aged care, and street communities. He recently coconvened the Precarity Creative Arts and Wellbeing Symposium, which brought together scholars and arts practitioners to explore the role of the arts in enhancing well-being among precariat communities.

SAUL HEWISH was a founder, member, and former director of the Geese Theatre Company UK, established in 1987 as a franchise of John Bergman's Geese Theatre Company in the United States. With Geese, Saul worked initially as an actor before moving into workshop facilitation and directing. In 1999, he cofounded Rideout (Creative Arts for Rehabilitation) and since then has developed numerous prison arts projects across the UK and Europe. Alongside his work with Rideout, Saul is a teaching fellow in theater practice, working with both undergraduate and postgraduate students at the University of Warwick.

KATHY RANDELS, born and raised in Bulbancha [the original, indigenous name of New Orleans], founded (1995) and still leads ArtSpot Productions. Her original performances have toured nationally and internationally. She cofounded and codirects the Louisiana Correctional Institute for Women Drama Club and the Graduates, a performing ensemble of formerly incarcerated women. Current projects include ARCH (Arts, Racial Justice, Culture, and Healing) at Orleans Justice Center and *The Road to Damascus,* a performance about the Church's role in creating a damagingly inequitable criminal-legal system. See also www.artspotproductions.org and www.graduatesrising.org.

SIMON RUDING is the artistic director and CEO of the Manchester, England–based participatory arts organization, Theatre in Prisons and Probation. He has over thirty years' experience in developing and delivering arts-based programs in criminal and social justice settings and has worked extensively in prison, probation, youth justice, and social-care services throughout the British Isles and beyond, delivering projects in Scandinavia, South Africa, and the United States. Previously he was the director of the Geese Theatre Company, UK. He is Honorary Research Associate of the University of Manchester and has a PhD in Applied Theatre.

JESS THORPE is a British theater maker, author, and lecturer in the Arts in Justice at the Royal Conservatoire of Scotland. She is currently associate director at Dundee Rep and Scottish Dance Theatre and co-artistic director of Glass Performance, an award-winning company that creates performances inspired by people and place. Jess's research is around the power and possibility of creativity in prisons. In 2018, she was part of setting up the first youth theater in a Scottish prison, Polmont Youth Theatre. She was part of the BBC Expert Women program and was selected as a *Big Issue Magazine* Changemaker.

GLORIA "MAMA GLO" WILLIAMS is a mother, grandmother, and great-grandmother. She served fifty-one years, the longest sentence of any woman in the state at the Louisiana Correctional Institute for Women. While incarcerated, she was part of the Drama Club, Toastmasters, Domestic Violence Survivors, Victim's Awareness, and Vessels of Wisdom, among others. She also counseled numerous women, who ultimately named her "Mama Glo." A public speaker, she is currently working on multiple creative projects about her incredible life story.

ABOUT THE EDITOR

JAN COHEN-CRUZ wrote *Local Acts: Community-Based Theater in the United States, Engaging Performance,* and *Remapping Performance*; edited *Radical Street Performance;* coedited, with Mady Schutzman, *Playing Boal* and *A Boal Companion;* and cowrote *Meeting the Moment: Socially Engaged Performance, 1965–2020, by Those Who Lived It,* with Rad Pereira. She was director of field research for A Blade of Grass, an organization that supports socially engaged artists, and cofounded its magazine. From 2007 to 2012, she directed Imagining America: Artists and Scholars in Public Life, a national consortium of colleges and universities committed to civic engagement, and cofounded its journal, *Public.* Cohen-Cruz earned her PhD at NYU Performance Studies and was a longtime professor in the NYU Drama Department, initiating a minor in applied theater. In 2012, she received the Association for Theatre in Higher Education's Award for Leadership in Community-Based Theatre and Civic Engagement. Jan was evaluator for the U.S. State Department/Bronx Museum cultural diplomacy initiative smARTpower and for seven of New York City's Public Artists in Residence (PAIR) projects. With Pam Korza, she researched and wrote a field guide for artist/municipal agency partnerships. Jan and her husband, Dionisio, spend part of their time in Pennsylvania with their son and his food truck, and part in Brooklyn with their daughter, son-in-law, and two grandchildren. She is currently an art guide with the Brooklyn Museum and is facilitating writing workshops with people in a range of circumstances.